Planning the Megacity:
Jakarta in the Twentieth Century

Planning, History and Environment Series

Editor:
Professor Dennis Hardy, Emeritus Professor of Urban Planning

Editorial Board:
Professor Gregory Andrusz, London, UK
Professor Arturo Almandoz, Universidad Simón Bolivar, Caracas, Venezuela
Professor Nezar AlSayyad, University of California, Berkeley, USA
Professor Robert Bruegmann, University of Illinois at Chicago, USA
Professor Meredith Clausen, University of Washington, Seattle, USA
Professor Jeffrey W. Cody, Getty Conservation Institute, Los Angeles, USA
Professor Robert Freestone, University of New South Wales, Sydney, Australia
Professor Sir Peter Hall, University College London, UK
Professor Peter Larkham, University of Central England, Birmingham, UK
Professor Anthony Sutcliffe, Nottingham, UK

Technical Editor
Ann Rudkin, Alexandrine Press, Marcham, Oxon, UK

Published titles

Planning the Megacity:
Jakarta in the Twentieth Century

Christopher Silver

Routledge
Taylor & Francis Group

LONDON AND NEW YORK

First published in 2008
by Routledge, 2 Park Square, Milton Park, Abingdon, Oxfordshire OX14 4RN

Simultaneously published in the USA and Canada
by Routledge
270 Madison Avenue, New York, NY 10016

Routledge is an imprint of the Taylor & Francis Group, an informa business

Typeset in Palatino and Humanist by PNR Design, Didcot
Printed and bound in Great Britain by TJ International, Padstow, Cornwall

This book was commissioned and edited by Alexandrine Press, Marcham, Oxfordshire

British Library Cataloguing in Publication Data

A catalogue record of this book is available from the British Library

Library of Congress Cataloging in Publication Data

Silver, Christopher, 1951–
    Planning the megacity : Jakarta in the twentieth century / Christopher Silver.
        p. cm. — (Planning, history, and environment series)
    Includes bibliographical references and index.
    ISBN 978–0–415–70164–8 (hb : alk. paper) — ISBN 978–0–203–70001–3 (ebk)
        1. Metropolitan areas—Indonesia—Jakarta—Planning. 2. Jakarta (Indonesia)—
History. I. Title.

    HT334.16S55 2007
    307.1'2160959822—dc22

2007026871

ISBN: (hbk) 978–0–415–70164–8
ISBN: (ebk) 978–0–203–70001–3

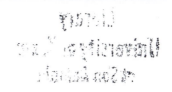

Contents

Acknowledgements   vii

Introduction   1

Chapter 1   Understanding Urbanization and the Megacity in Southeast Asia   18

Chapter 2   Fashioning the Colonial Capital City, 1900–1940   36

Chapter 3   Plans for the Modern Metropolis, 1950–1970s   82

Chapter 4   Planning For Housing, Neighbourhoods and Urban Revitalization   126

Chapter 5   Expansion, Revitalization and the Restructuring of Metropolitan Jakarta: the 1970s to the early 1990s   154

Chapter 6   Urban Village to World City: Re-planning Jakarta in the 1990s   186

Chapter 7   Planning in the New Democratic Megacity   213

Bibliography   241

Index   255

Acknowledgements

The idea for this study grew out of several opportunities to spend extended periods living and working in Jakarta, and my interest as an historian and urban planner to understand better this fascinating and ever changing place. It is essential to acknowledge up front the importance of the two Fulbright Senior Lectureships that brought me to Indonesia. The first one from October 1989 to July 1990 involved an appointment teaching in the American Studies Program at the University of Indonesia (UI). This served as my initial orientation both to the city and to the nation. The American Studies Program Director, Pia Alishjahbana, her talented faculty and bright students drawn from all parts of the country, helped me in so many ways to understand Indonesia from the perspective of Indonesians. Through 'Ibu Pia', I gained not only access to other scholars working on Indonesian development issues, but a true friend to the entire Silver family.

The second Fulbright, for a briefer period (from May to July 1992), was in the Department of Regional and City Planning at the Institute of Technology, Bandung (ITB). Working with the country's pre-eminent urban scholars, I lectured about US urban development and planning and in the process learned about the planning and urban development processes in Indonesia and Jakarta. Many faculty in the planning programme at ITB helped me along the path from novice to the point a few years ago where I became bold enough to write a book on planning and urban development in Indonesia.

Dr Bambang Bintoro Soedjito, my initial supporter, invited me to Bandung early in 1990 (during my Fulbright at UI) to present some lectures on American urban planning, and was most likely one of the individuals responsible for advancing my follow-up Fulbright in 1992 at ITB. He became my boss (for a while) when I later served as an Urban Development Advisor in the Indonesian National Development Planning Board (BAPPENAS). Through our numerous discussions he helped me in so many ways to understand the key issues in Indonesian urban planning. Another boss from my time at BAPPENAS, and also a distinguished member of the planning faculty at ITB, is Dr Budhy ('Ibu Yati') Soegijoko. As evidenced in the bibliography to this book, her scholarly contributions to my understanding of urban development issues in Jakarta are substantial.

Dr Djoko Suparti made available to me his rich collection of historical documents related to planning in Jakarta, his own scholarship on new town development, and his experiences working with Jakarta's planners. Dr Tommy

Firman's friendship and immense body of scholarship on urbanization and planning in Indonesia and Jakarta helped to keep this book project in focus. He and I collaborated on a community-based development project in Jatinangor (under the sponsorship of the US Agency for International Development). So many other ITB planning faculty shared with me their research and their comments on my work, but Haryo Winarso, Teti Argo and Boy Kombiatan deserve special mention. Senior faculty member Dr. Myra Gunawan, with whom I worked on tourism planning projects for many years, also helped me to better understand the nuances of urban life in Indonesia.

My USAID project work with Tommy Firman involved an energetic young planning staff member at ITB, Tubagus Furqon Sofhani. Furqon's first name, Tubagus, means literally 'terrific', and he was a continuous and terrific support to me, first in his role as a colleague on a community-based planning project that helped to contribute to the changing paradigm of planning in Indonesian urban places, and then as a PhD student at the University of Illinois, Urbana-Champaign. At Illinois he did all those things that PhD students do to support the research of their advisors while refining their own research agendas. Furqon helped me to translate several significant planning and policy works that were beyond my Bahasa Indonesia capabilities. Another PhD student, who came to Illinois from a staff position at BAPPENAS, and then returned with his doctorate to head up a poverty alleviation programme, was Pungky Sumadi. Pungky was instrumental in arranging the series of interviews in January 2005 (right after the tsunami struck Aceh with such deadly consequences) which enabled me to gain unique perspectives on planning and governance in Jakarta. Through his assistance, I held conversations with most of Jakarta's planning directors and administrators since the late 1960s. This included a remarkable two hour conversation with Jakarta's famous past governor, Ali Sadikin, and an informative session with former Vice Governor and Director of the Planning Agency, Tb. M Rais. He also arranged a meeting with the current Vice Governor, Fauzi Bowo. Equally enlightening discussions were held with two former Jakarta planning directors, Ery Chajaridipura and Kandar Tisnawinata, and also with Maurits Pasaibu, former director urban and regional planning in the Ministry of Public Works, with Wastu Pragantha Zhang, a former special assistant to Governor Sadikin, and with one of the current planning staff members, Vera Revina Sari.

Especially helpful because of his long association with Jakarta's planning and development was Adjit Damais, former Director of the Jakarta City Museum and in 2005 a special assistant to Vice Governor Bowo. I also want to acknowledge the generosity of the esteemed scholar, Peter J.M. Nas of Leiden University, who has produced so much of the important work on planning and urbanization in Indonesia. He took time to discuss my project when I visited Leiden and generously shared unpublished research on *kampungs* in Indonesian society.

Further assistance from the Fulbright program, a Fulbright Senior Specialist grant for four weeks in 2004, enabled me to complete some key sections of this study, including accessing Pak Djoko's planning documents. I received a grant from the University of Illinois, Urbana-Champaign under the William and Flora Hewlett Program which enabled me to spend a part of my sabbatical in early 2004 based in Jakarta writing and researching.

There were many library sources that I relied upon for this study. The immense book and periodical collections at the University of Illinois, Urbana-Champaign library made it possible to access directly sources I discovered in less accessible places. Three separate trips to the library at the Institute of Southeast Asian Studies at the National University of Singapore gave me access to various periodical and unpublished conference papers that would have been unavailable elsewhere. This library contains one of the most complete collections of Indonesian publications, including many original typescript articles and government publications that helped to shed light on the urbanization and planning processes in Jakarta. The library staff there were extremely helpful. I also made use of the planning library at ITB which contained documents on planning in Jakarta that were not readily available elsewhere. The library at the Royal Tropical Institute in Amsterdam afforded me another unique collection of documents on Indonesia and Jakarta, along with a tremendous collection of photographs and maps from the colonial and early national periods. The staff there helped me greatly over the course of three visits.

My good friends Les Dinsbach and Maria not only provided the comfort of their home for my many research visits to Jakarta (especially over the past 5 years) but Les helped to translate some key materials from Dutch to English. Another planning graduate student at the University of Illinois, Mansi Sachdev, assisted me in creating maps and figures for this book. Glenda Fisher and Brenda Deaville, both at Illinois, helped in other technical matters related to getting the illustrations into publishable form. Barbara Cleveland at the University of Florida picked up where Glenda and Brenda left off, and enabled me to finish what had become a complicated process of orchestrating the text and the illustrations.

This book derives from an intense family experience over a considerable period in our lives. In the Fall of 1989, Isabel, my wife and our two young children, Wesley 5 and Jennifer 4, boarded a plane in New York to head off to the unknown and exotic city of Jakarta. There were many challenges right from the start, including emergency surgery for Wesley's acute appendicitis after just one week in a country where foreign visitors were advised to travel to Singapore for anything more than having teeth cleaned. Wesley not only survived, but thrived, and we learned from that, and so many other experiences, that ignorance of the fine qualities of Indonesian society and its many competencies created the stereotyping which makes those ignorant of the country and its people seem the fools. All four of us returned for three months in 1992. A 5 year grant under the US AID sponsored University Development Liaison Program supported a collaboration with Hasanuddin University in Makassar and enabled Isabel and me to lead various study tours of US faculty and students to Indonesia, and in turn to support visits by Indonesians at Virginia Commonwealth University, after 1992. This typically involved the entire family entertaining and developing lasting friendships with many Indonesians.

On one grant related trip to Indonesia in late 1994, I was queried by USAID-Jakarta about a possible 3 year resident consultant position based at BAPPENAS. The Silver family jumped at the opportunity for such an extended stay in our second home in Southeast Asia. It was over this 3 year stint in Jakarta that I witnessed first hand the transformation of Jakarta and gained a better understanding of the many challenges of planning and administering such a dynamic place. We left on the eve of the political and economic crisis of 1998, but I continued to travel regularly to Indonesia in conjunction with various research grants after that. Without the support of the family, it would not have been possible to experience Jakarta as intimately as I did. Each of us in our own way was transformed by the experiences of encountering this unique and wonderful place. In appreciation of how much that Indonesian experience shaped all of us, this book is dedicated to my wife Isabel and our worldly children, Wesley and Jennifer.

Gainesville, Florida
July 2007

Introduction: Experiencing Jakarta

Few cities in history have experienced the pace of growth and change of Jakarta in the twentieth century. In 1900, the colonial capital of the Netherland Indies, then known as Batavia, was a compact city of approximately 150,000 inhabitants. Over the twentieth century, but especially after 1950, it was transformed into a sprawling metropolis, a 'megacity', of more than 9 million in an urbanized region which by 2000 was home to nearly 18 million. How this metamorphosis occurred, and what it meant for the lives of the city's residents, are key questions addressed in the following pages.[1]

To understand how Jakarta became a megacity requires examination of the role of both the state and private interests in planning its dramatic transformation. The planning processes of government and the private development community that figured so prominently in the emerging form and character of Southeast Asia's largest urban complex were also bound up with the larger project of consolidating and fashioning the new Indonesian nation.[2]

It would have been impossible to predict Jakarta's transformation based on its earlier development patterns. The city's development before 1900 was driven by events during the eighteenth and nineteenth centuries when planning intervention was largely limited to efforts to embellish the colonial city to suit the wishes of a minority of its citizens, namely the Europeans, and Asians who dominated the city's commercial activities. Further, the direction and location of the eleven rivers that run from the mountains to the low-lying areas where the Dutch had established their colonial administrative centre in the seventeenth century created natural barriers which determined both the direction and boundaries of the city's growth. Even as population growth in colonial Batavia accelerated after 1900, there was relatively little divergence in the basic pattern of urban growth. The city remained compact, squeezed onto the highest ground between the frequently flooding rivers. Only after independence from the Dutch in 1950 did the city cast off the shackles of geography, and spread out in all directions. This rapid growth phase coincided with the period when planning institutions assumed a prominent place in the apparatus of local and national government as Jakarta began to assume the form and appearance of a much more substantial metropolis.

When I first arrived in Jakarta in October 1989 to begin a one-year teaching assignment at the University of Indonesia, there was little evidence of the constraints that had previously limited the city's growth. My first impression was of a sprawling and dynamic place.

As I made my way for the first time from Jakarta's recently opened Soekarno-Hatta international airport through roads teeming with vendors, pedestrians, and any number of unusual small vehicles vying with the cars and trucks for a share of that contested space, I sensed that this was a very different kind of large city. But like many first time visitors to such a new and different place, I was prone to misinformed impressions. Jakarta, with its jumbling and chaotic urban activities, seemed devoid of the basic elements of planning typically found in the West. Many other Westerners, and even many Indonesians, shared that same view.

For the next 17 years, including more than four as a Jakarta resident, it became my goal to re-examine my initial impressions of the city and to figure out what made Jakarta so different. In the process, my single most important discovery was that I had been totally wrong about how the city was being shaped and managed. The Jakarta I first encountered in 1989 was in many respects the outcome of carefully calculated planning interventions; a city where planning was an integral part of the apparatus of government management. While Jakarta's planning legacy reached back to the colonial era, planning in the city was also guided by new ideas and approaches intended to fashion it into a modern megacity. Thus this book sets out to examine the rich but neglected planning history of Jakarta, to reveal how planning helped to reshape the compact colonial city into the modern megacity and how that planning has been a vital, but far too little understood, component of the larger saga of nation building in Indonesia in the twentieth century.

Jakarta in 1989

To appreciate such a unique place, I will introduce Jakarta as I experienced it in 1989, together with a background on the city's history, geography and administration.

Located on the north coast of the island of Java (which was and is Indonesia's most populous island), Jakarta began modestly in the fourteenth century as Sunda Kelapa, the capital of the West Java kingdom of Pajajaran. The name Sunda Kelapa was still in use in 1989, but referred only to the traditional harbour in north Jakarta where wooden boats docked with the precious hardwoods and other agricultural products from Sumatra, Kalimantan and Sulawesi.

In 1527, the Islamic Sultan of Demak seized Sunda Kelapa, renaming it Jaya Karta ('great city') and held it against challenges from the Portuguese and other Southeast Asian trading groups until 1619, by which time it was already a thriving commercial centre. It was then that Jan Pieterzoon Coen seized the port on behalf of the United Dutch East India Company and renamed it Batavia. Thus began a colonial occupation which lasted until the Japanese conquered the Netherland Indies in 1942.[3] As late as 1989, the colonial legacy could still be discerned

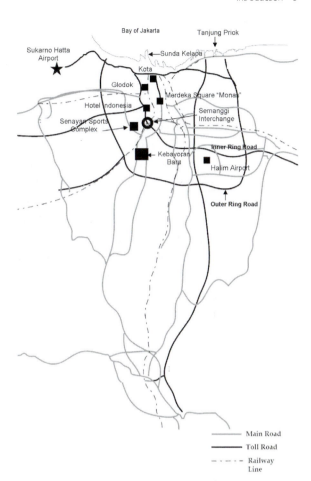

Bay of Jakarta

Tanjung Priok

Sukarno Hatta
Airport

Sunda Kelapa

Kota

Glodok

Merdeka Square "Monas"

Hotel Indonesia

Semanggi
Interchange

Senayan Sports
Complex

Inner Ring Road

Kebayoran
Baru

Halim Airport

Outer Ring Road

———— Main Road

━━━━ Toll Road

– – – – Railway
Line

Figure I.1. Map of journey
in Jakarta, 1989.

Figure I.2. Wooden boats at Jakarta's traditional harbour, Sunda Kelapa, that continue to carry lumber and other produce between the islands. (*Photo*: author)

in Jakarta's inner city and remained a continuing influence on its planning processes.

Jakarta in 1989 was not only a city with deep historical roots but as Indonesia's capital was administered as a Special Territory on par with other provinces. Headed by a governor appointed directly by the president, DKI Jakarta (*Daerah Khussus Indonesia*, Special Territory Indonesia) encompasses just 650 square kilometres, making it the nation's smallest territory. The capital city district is made up of five cities (North Jakarta, Central Jakarta, East Jakarta, West Jakarta and South Jakarta), each headed by a mayor. According to 1989 estimates the population of 9.1 million produced a density of 13,365 persons per square kilometre, making it Indonesia's most developed province. Underdeveloped land in West, East and South Jakarta, coupled with a plan to add new land through reclamation in North Jakarta, ensured that the overall population density would continue to increase as these areas were developed. Because of the complexities in changing administrative boundaries, and the lack of open space within Jakarta, most urban growth, including the new Soekarno-Hatta International Airport, was within the adjacent West Java province. That province of 44,176 square kilometres stretched to both the southern and western coasts of the island. Its provincial capital, Bandung, is over 150 kilometres south of Jakarta, a separation which resulted in little coordination in the planning and management of these contiguous governmental units. As urbanization spilled over the DKI Jakarta borders into West Java, new 'suburban cities' within the Jakarta megacity complex grew in size to rival the stature of the provincial capital in Bandung. This peripheral urbanization also prompted efforts to identify ways for better coordination of infrastructure provision and services between DKI Jakarta and West Java.

The incredible density of population and of the built environment was the most striking impression of Jakarta as I travelled from the airport to the city centre. Situated just outside the north-west edge of the city alongside fish farms that buffer it from the Java Sea, Soekarno-Hatta International Airport had been open for several years when I arrived in 1989. It was the third airport constructed in Jakarta since the 1920s; the first, Kemayoran Airport, was in the heart of the 'old' city of Batavia and had closed. Kemayoran was superseded by Halim Airport, on the south-eastern edge of the city. After Soekarno-Hatta opened, Halim remained a terminal for select domestic flights, and more importantly was used by President Suharto's aircraft and occasionally by visiting dignitaries. Halim possessed enduring connections to Suharto's promotion from army general to Indonesian president and to the ascendancy of his New Order regime. It was there that an alleged, and ultimately unsuccessful, 'communist' coup was staged in 1965 and where the bodies of assassinated army officers had been deposited in a well by their assailants. Suharto was picked by his military colleagues to manage the chaos in 1965 and shortly thereafter consolidated his power into a political organization which backed his claim to the presidency. By the late 1980s, Suharto was already into his fifth term as Indonesia's president, with his Golkar party firmly in control of the government. Supported by Indonesia's powerful and politically engaged military, there were no viable rivals to Suharto's New Order government in 1989.

In 1989 my 10 kilometre journey from the airport to the city centre took more than an hour and a half. By the mid-1990s, a limited access toll road linked the airport to the city centre. This represented the culmination of a highway development project initiated in the early 1960s by President Sukarno. Its purpose was to connect the harbour at Tanjung Priok in the far north-eastern corner of Jakarta to the Senayan sports complex built in South Jakarta to host the 1962 Asian Games. The section of the highway between the Senayan sports complex and the international airport, coupled with another new segment running along the north coast area, provided Jakarta with its first completed ring road in the mid-1990s. Meanwhile a second ring was already under construction and a third outer ring was at the planning stage. (See figure I.1).

But in 1989, the only part of the limited access highway system completed was a short stretch from the airport terminal to an adjacent industrial area. After five minutes of high-speed travel (and two tolls), my journey into the city became a crawling, stop and go adventure, as the minivan wormed its way through the tangle of local roads certainly not designed for the traffic generated by the airport. My route ran beside a canal that extended northward into the Java Sea (which I later learned was part of the flood control system for West Jakarta). Here I passed what is best described as an interlocking assemblage of makeshift structures held up by poles and perched precariously above the inky black waters of the canal. With walls of bamboo held together by assorted scraps of wood, roofs configured out of a combination of plastic, tar paper and metal sheets, and occasionally some ceramic tiles, all held down by large stones or chunks of discarded concrete, these residential structures appeared ready to topple into the waterway at the slightest provocation. Throughout Jakarta, in equally precarious places, similar clusters of makeshift housing accommodated a substantial population; I saw many examples of these in the days that followed.

Within a few years, however, the cluster of housing beside the canal was gone. It had been cleared to provide space for the supports for the elevated inner ring highway. The disappearance of this makeshift housing might seem an environmental improvement, yet for Jakarta's sizable indigent population, the removal of these homes was a major problem since there was scant (if any) alternative accommodation and displaced families typically received little or no compensation for their loss. Catering for the needs of the poor, while simultaneously modernizing the metropolis, proved to be one of the most vexing problems that

Jakarta's planners faced. It was a challenge that had been at the centre of public and private discourse on urban improvements throughout the twentieth century, with direct links to urban policies from the latter years of Dutch rule.

It was not just the makeshift housing along the waterways and rail tracks that was being removed. Redevelopment was citywide in the late 1980s and throughout the 1990s. Those most affected were the indigenous residential communities created by the large numbers of rural migrants coming to the city, generally called *kampungs*. A *kampung* was the urban version of the rural village (or *desa*), typically made up of a dense cluster of single (or sometimes two) storey residential structures packed together in a contiguous area, interlaced by a network of footpaths, and lacking any sanitary infrastructure. In 1980s Jakarta these comprised permanent structures of concrete, or brick faced by concrete, of varying size and finish depending upon the resources of the owner. Typically they were located on under-utilized land close to primary employment areas where their low-skilled residents might find work.

New *kampungs* were still appearing in 1989 but their development had shifted from the inner to the outer city, as large areas in the centre that had accommodated *kampungs* for decades were being cleared for new high end development. The widespread displacement of *kampung* residents was one of the most contentious issues in the late 1980s and 1990s, particularly the question of how much compensation those displaced should be paid.

What was most striking during the ride from the airport to the city was the contrast between the bamboo houses on the urban fringe and the modern office towers that appeared as I approached the centre of the city. My journey had taken us from a modern airport, through third world markets and neighbourhoods to Jakarta's modern, booming downtown. The extensive first world that Jakarta was constructing became evident when I reached the Semanggi interchange where the toll road intersected the city's major north-south corridor, Jalan Sudirman (*jalan* means 'street'). Soaring above the south-western quadrant of the interchange were the hotel and condominium towers of the Jakarta Hilton Hotel complex and on my left a group of glass fronted towers dominated by one of Indonesia's leading banks, Bank Rakyat Indonesia (Indonesian Peoples' Bank). Heading north on Jalan Sudirman towards the historic city centre, I passed another three bank buildings, an office complex known as Wisma Metropolitan, and several new luxury hotels.

The buildings on Jalan Sudirman in 1989 were just the opening act of the New Order economic miracle. Over the next decade, the spaces between the 1980s towers filled with more high-rise glass and steel structures, new roads were cut through to access the areas, and the remaining *kampungs* behind Jalan Sudirman's rising commercial skyline were cleared. This created an entirely new commercial centre, known by Jakartans as the Golden Triangle.

The Semanggi interchange, built in the early 1960s, was the first highway cloverleaf in Indonesia. In April 1998, nearly a decade after I first arrived, it took centre stage in a national political drama when students protesting against the policies of the Suharto regime blocked traffic along the nearby expressway. The army was called in to stop their march to the national assembly to petition the legislators to embrace their call for greater political freedom. Four students were killed in the confrontation which became known as the 'Semanggi massacre', and helped to precipitate the unexpected resignation of Preident Suharto.

But in 1989, the battle being waged at this junction was between a solid mass of cars, vans, buses, and trucks, a gridlock that routinely transformed the three lanes of traffic in either direction into five by eliminating all but a few centimetres between the bumpers and sides of the vehicles squeezing on and off the access ramps. It was all too obvious that Jakarta's road network was wholly inadequate for the volume of traffic it was required to handle. How to solve Jakarta's transport problems was the consuming concern of the city's leadership throughout the 1980s and 1990s, but with no easy solution. In 1989 there were several ideas floating among the planners and policy-makers, but only one strategy seemed to be implemented, namely building more highways and, in effect, creating more congestion.

The merging of Jalan Sudirman and Jalan Thamrin created one of the most congested streets. Various attempts were made to alleviate the problem, one of which succeeded only in slowing appreciably Jakarta's buses – the city's sole means of public transport! But, the real problem was not traffic management but inadequate planning. This was the major corridor linking the rapid growth areas of South Jakarta to the centre and, in 1989, was Jakarta's primary business district. As more commercial developments were added along the corridor, more traffic was generated so negating any quick fix traffic management strategies.

At the north end of this corridor lies Merdeka ('Freedom') Square with the National Monument (or Monas). The Monas, an obelisk topped by a golden flame, was the last major public works project in Sukarno's scheme to beautify Jakarta, but was completed after he was ousted from power in 1966. It is positioned in the centre of the trapezoidal parade ground, laid out by the Dutch in the early nineteenth century, around which were the edifices of Jakarta's European community, including government buildings, clubs, hotels and sumptuous residences. The original plan for this space (known as Konigsplein before independence), its reconfiguration from a military parade ground into a formal civic centre, and subsequent redesign as a symbol of Indonesia's independence movement, constitutes an important thread in Jakarta's planning history, bridging the colonial and independence eras (see Chapters 2 and 3).

In 1989, however, it was not just a site of an important monument but an intensely public arena serving a mix of uses. Some of these complemented its function as the locus of political power in Indonesia while others reflected the unfulfilled expectations of a broader civic involvement in political life that could not be expressed directly under the New Order government. Ringing the grounds of the Monas were four boulevards, along which were some of the most prominent institutional buildings in the city. On the north side of the square is the Freedom Palace (Istana Merdeka); built as a country house at the of the eighteenth century, it became the in-town residence of the Governor General in the early nineteenth century and is now the official residence of Indonesia's president. The Bina Graha, constructed after independence on the site of the former Hotel der Nederlanden, and the main office complex of the powerful Ministry of Home Affairs (to which all local planners were accountable under the Suharto government) also lie on the north side of the square. On the south side are the offices of the Vice-President (also in a restored Dutch country villa), several offices towers, and the US Embassy compound. A hodge-podge of government offices occupied new and restored structures on the west side of the square, including the National Museum, purpose-built in 1868, while on the east side was one of Jakarta's main train stations, Stasiun Gambir, as well as several ministry office buildings.[4]

At 5 am on the morning after my arrival I set off for the Monas with my two children in tow. Although a Sunday, Merdeka Square was already teeming with humanity. The Monas was majestic and the buildings surrounding the square unique in their composition, but my attention was drawn to the hundreds of people, dressed in coordinated athletic wear (presumably identifying their employers,

Figure I.3. Merdeka 'Freedom' Square, with national monument ('Monas') at its centre and the national mosque and other key government buildings surrounding it. (*Photo*: author)

political party, social group, or corporate sponsor), doing group exercises to the sound of blaring music and equally blaring instructions from the exercise leader.

Our attention was also drawn to the collection of restaurants and shops lining one of the diagonal streets leading through the square to the monument, totally out of context with the grandiose surroundings, but all open for business at this early hour. Along another of the diagonals was a small children's amusement park, and a collection of simply designed stalls identified by an overhead sign that read, 'Jakarta Fair Grounds'. Throughout the square, and adding to its colourful character, were food and souvenir vendors, groups of children playing soccer, beggars, and an assortment of street life. It seemed that this was where people felt free to enjoy themselves in huge numbers in the heart of the metropolis, and to do so literally on the front lawn of a political regime that was commonly regarded as authoritarian. In short, the participants in that spontaneous Sunday morning festival were using the space just as its originators had intended it to be used. Merdeka Square has been subject to changes to its form and function throughout the twentieth century; ironically, in its most recent manifestation in the newly emerging 'democratic' Indonesia, it has become far less accessible to the people than it was under more repressive past regimes.

Just to the north of Merdeka Square is the area known as Glodok, where large numbers of Chinese businesses and residences traditionally located. Originally developed during the colonial era to segregate the Chinese community outside the city, Glodok had become buried deep within the old part of Jakarta known as Kota ('City'). As Dutch businesses left Jakarta after independence, the Chinese community expanded northwards into abandoned sites in the Kota area. As a result, much of Jakarta north of Merdeka and extending to the old harbour at Sunda Kelapa was dominated by the Chinese community. The importance of the Chinese in the city's development from its inception as Batavia belies the constraints that both the Dutch and Indonesian governments imposed on their activities throughout much of the city's history.

It was easy to identify Kota from the many, often dilapidated, residential and commercial buildings remaining from the Dutch colonial era, including the former City Hall on Fatahillah Square which is now the Jakarta City Museum. In contrast, except for a little architectural detailing here and there, it was virtually impossible to identify the location of the Chinese community. Further, because in 1989 it was illegal to display Chinese characters anywhere in Indonesia, there were no commercial signs in Chinese. The 'no Chinese characters' regulation had been in effect since the mid-1960s when the Chinese community as a whole was branded with the stigma of communism because a few had been implicated in the alleged plot of the Indonesian Communist Party to overthrow the government. The aftermath of the failed coup brought attacks on the Chinese community throughout Indonesia, the removal of Sukarno as president because of his ties to the now outlawed Communist Party, and the beginning of the New Order government of Suharto. By 1989, after 23 years of the Suharto regime, life in Jakarta's Chinese community had settled into a sort of normalcy despite being treated as a group apart.

However in 1997 the Chinese community again became a scapegoat in the wake of the financial crisis that led in 1998 to the fall of the Suharto government. The ensuing violence was directed against them, with Kota, Glodok and several other small Chinese areas bearing the brunt of the rioters' attacks. Whole sections of Glodok were burned, Chinese businesses were destroyed or defaced, Chinese men and women were assaulted, and those who remained to defend their properties used barricades and hired security personnel for protection. The attacks resulted in the conversion of previously accessible inner-city neighbourhoods into gated enclaves, reinforcing the social and cultural divide that separated the Chinese community from the mainstream. This reconstruction of the Glodok area was part of a larger reconfiguration of inner-city Jakarta into a cosmopolitan complex of differentiated areas where class, ethnicity and race still mattered but where the form of these places represented a break from the traditional *kampung* pattern. A growing neighbourhood preservation movement sought to mitigate some of the harsher impacts of this transformation and to retain links to the historic fabric of the city, but the modernization of Glodok and adjacent areas erased much of its traditional character.

A kilometre south of Merdeka Square is the neighbourhood of Menteng. Built in the early twentieth century for the European community at what was then the outermost edge of Batavia, Menteng helped to launch the modern planning movement in the city, and involved prominent Dutch planners and architects practicing in the Netherland Indies. They bequeathed to the city what was one of its most elegant and sought after addresses. Later, I worked in Menteng for 3 years at the National Development Planning Board (or BAPPENAS), which occupied the original residence of the Burgermeister of Batavia. Close by was Taman Surupati (Suropati Park) with its sculpture garden, the residence of the US Ambassador, and the official residences and consulates of other foreign governments.

Several blocks to the north of Taman Suropati was the personal residence of President Suharto. In 1989, he was at the peak of his power, having ushered in the economic miracle that promised to raise Indonesia from the ranks of under-developed nations. His centralized government brooked no political opposition, but went to great lengths to improve the level and quality of basic services to a broad segment of Indonesian society. His 'New Order' government 'is best understood as the resurrection of the state and its triumph vis-à-vis society and nation', claimed political scientist Benedict Anderson. Not unlike his deposed predecessor,

Suharto made modernizing Jakarka a key component of his national development strategy, employing a combination of public investment and government support for the business class to enable it to do what the state could not.[5]

Although home to many of Jakarta's business leaders and Suharto's political cronies, by the late 1980s parts of Menteng appeared somewhat tattered. However, soaring land and property prices then and in the 1990s led to upgrading existing structures to preserve the investment or destruction of the original to make way for modern dwellings or even commercial development. While still the best address in Jakarta, the pressures of high land values, increased vehicular traffic and commercial incursions, threatened the charm of the place.

Much more affordable and equally attractive was another of the city's planned communities, the satellite city of Kebayoran Baru in South Jakarta. Conceived late in the Dutch colonial period, Kebayoran Baru's planning and development was interrupted by World War II, the Japanese occupation, and the subsequent struggle between the Indonesians and Dutch. It became the first ambitious public works project of the national government after independence and sought to alleviate Jakarta's critical housing shortage, particularly for the army of government workers that was spawned by the Sukarno government. In 1989 I found a small house on Jalan Panglima Polim IV, approximately three blocks from one of South Jakarta's major market areas, known by neighbourhood residents simply as Blok M (Block M).

Kebayoran Baru was intensely residential, but supported by local schools and served by several nearby market areas, not just Blok M but also Blok A on the western fringe. On a commercial strip along Panglima Polim Raya (*raya* is a street larger than a *jalan*) there were banks and stores selling anything from hardware to furniture and clothing, while a new neighbourhood shopping centre one block from our house boasted a variety of Western style businesses including Kentucky Fried Chicken, a small grocery, several restaurants, beauty salons, and a cinema with four screens showing Western films. Street vendors, each with a distinctive call – the tapping of a bell or block of wood, or some horned instrument – served the neighbourhood, selling food for domestic workers, fresh vegetables, household goods and a variety of elixirs including magical potions called *jamu*. Nearby, residents could hire a *bajaj*, the three-wheeled vehicle that was the primary means of transport within the neighbourhood. Buses and taxis for travel to other parts of Jakarta were to be found at the transport terminal at Blok M. Some families had cars and many had motorcycles but the majority of the population either walked or relied on public transport.

But there were aspects of the typical middle-income Jakarta neighbourhood that I experienced on Panglima Polim IV that were less charming. Pollution from rubbish burning in the small cement receptacles in front of the houses added to the already polluted air of the city, but burning seemed necessary since those who did not were infested with rats. And petty crime, or at least the perception of it, meant that each house was a fortress, surrounded by a high wall on top of which was broken glass embedded in the concrete and topped with barbed or razor wire to deter even the most persistent burglar. Households hired someone to guard at night (*jaga*), and paid a fee to the neighbourhood official to supplement the household system of protection. Throughout the night, the neighbourhood watch signified its presence by banging periodically with a stick on the hollow aluminium lamp posts in front of houses.

Travelling from Kebayoran Baru to other destinations in the city gave another dimension to experiencing Jakarta. The journey to the University of Indonesia's American Cultural Center on the Rawamangun campus in East Jakarta included the finished portion of inner ring toll road connecting South Jakarta to the port at Tanjung Priok. The elevated roadway provided an ever-changing panorama of Jakarta's neighbourhoods, of new construction intermixed with the old, poor living side by side with the wealthy, and seemingly everywhere building sites.

My other regular trip from Kebayoran Baru was to the US Embassy commissary on Jalan Merdeka Selatan. I experienced then, but even more when later I worked at BAPPENAS, the extent of Jakarta's transport crisis; a crisis created by the proliferation of motor vehicles and compounded by the absence of a mass transit system. Sukarno's disdain for the ancient trams that still plied the streets in the 1950s was understandable, but the decision to scrap the system entirely when the population was growing at breakneck speed, and to rely exclusively on motorized vehicles (cars and buses) proved to be recipe for disaster.

Another aspect of experiencing Jakarta for the first time in 1989 was trying to understand Indonesia's politics and decision-making systems and the effectiveness of the country's leaders in realizing national ambitions. In 1989, it was widely touted, and there were official statistics to back the assertions, that significant strides had been made in addressing the three great challenges of a large developing country, namely poverty, illiteracy and poor health. The aggressive education and public health initiatives of the Suharto New Order government proved effective in reaching sectors of the population that previously had been left out of the system. Evidence from Jakarta's communities conformed to the national pattern of progress in the areas of education and improving the health of the poor. On poverty alleviation, the evidence was not as convincing, but the apparent success of some government initiatives, such as the Kampung Improvement Program and the *Impres Desa Tertinngal* (literally Very Poor Village Improvements) programme supported the image of a nation moving towards a higher standard of living, especially in its cities.

Other areas of national policy which affected Jakarta's development were the provision of basic infrastructure, including highway development, improved power generation, the provision of clean water and better sanitation services, support for affordable new housing construction, and for industrial expansion to ensure greater employment options in the 'formal' sector. As the nation's capital, national development policies clearly favoured Jakarta in the competition for limited resources. However, to sustain its national political base, the Suharto New Order government made a point of bestowing largess throughout all twenty-seven provinces.

In Jakarta, government support for infrastructure investment together with the high local revenues generated by the scale of commercial and industrial investment, ensured a higher standard of services in the capital. However, the city's rapid development proved both a blessing and a curse to the city's planners. The biggest challenge was that changes in the urban environment occurred faster than the plans could be conceived or even revised to guide them.

The situation for Jakarta's planners was complicated further because of uncertain lines of authority. Many of the projects and initiatives within Jakarta were planned outside the structure of local planning, whether by a national ministry, a private firm or group, through the initiative of an international donor, or perhaps on the whim of the president or some associate or family member. Plans prepared by consultants hired outside the local planning structure often were at odds with local plans. And, given the uncertain lines of authority, it was never entirely clear which plan constituted the definitive proposal.

However, if there was a common thread that bound together the multiple actors involved in planning Jakarta, it was the shared commitment to a vision of the city becoming an important place on the international stage – in short, a world city. This, of course, was not unlike the expectations that the Dutch had for the Southeast Asian colonial city of Batavia, Sukarno's vision for the capital of the new nation of Indonesia, or Suharto's quest for a First World city. In recent years a new vision for what might be called a 'participatory democratic metropolis' has been added to those expectations. Whether this succeeds may become clearer if we understand better how Jakarta, the megacity, was created.

Organization of the Study

In order to understand the dynamic of urban growth in Jakarta over the past century, the city's transformation needs to be placed within the context of urbanization in the Southeast Asian region as a whole. Chapter 1 addresses the unique and ubiquitous aspects of urban development in the region since 1900. It is a region where the overall rate of urbanization remains far below other parts of the world and where the interface between rural and urban has resulted in distinctive urban forms. The chapter examines two questions that pervade the scholarship on urbanization in Southeast Asia, one being first asked (and partially answered) by Terence McGee: Is there such a creation as the 'Southeast Asian city'?[6] A related question has been posed in more recent scholarship, which speaks to another key concern of this study of Jakarta: Is megacity development in the region a process of conforming with, or diverging from, international trends in urban development? An obvious difference between cities in Southeast Asia and North America is the seemingly inexhaustible supply of rural migrants in Asia that have been drawn to some large cities because of their overwhelming role in national economic development. How Southeast Asian cities have responded to the challenges that this migration poses is also examined in Chapter 1.

The foundation of modern Jakarta has roots deep within the Dutch colonial era. Chapter 2 looks at the tremendous range of influences on the city's planning and development when Batavia was growing from a city of approximately 150,000 to more than a half million on the eve of World War II. It was not just population growth that distinguished this crucial period in the city's development. Expansion of its boundaries, the preparation of city plans through a Dutch government planning agency charged with managing its growth, the influence of Dutch architects and planners on the creation of distinctive communities and a broad range of improved housing, were just some of the contributions to a better planned, and more liveable city. It was during the 1920s and 1930s that reformers were actively seeking solutions to the problems of health, employment and housing confronting indigenous communities. Out of this came a model *kampung* programme that later became the city's primary strategy to improve poor neighbourhoods. The late colonial period also witnessed the increasing decentralization of service delivery and decision-making to the city level, and in some cases to the community level. The promises of decentralization bringing greater attention to bear on the challenges of urbanization were offset by a tendency on the part of local interests to minimize the cost of government when the national government was no longer bearing the financial burden. On the eve of the destruction wrought on Jakarta (and Indonesia) by involvement in World War II as a vassal of the Japanese empire, the city had achieved remarkable progress in its development but had proved inept at including the majority of its indigenous inhabitants in that process. World War II merely delayed the inevitable battle for independence from the Netherlands that took place between 1945 and 1950.

Chapter 3 focuses on master planning for the metropolis which began almost immediately after independence with implementation of a plan for a new satellite city south of Jakarta, while newly formed planning units in national and local government, with the assistance of foreign consultants, prepared comprehensive plans to guide future development. It examines the ideas for planning Jakarta with attention to the influence of its political leadership and their reactions to the day-to-day needs of a metropolis growing by thousands of people each week. President Sukarno's vision for the new nation was wrapped into key projects in Jakarta, but these did not always mesh with those of the consultants and local planners brought in to convert broad ideas to practical strategies. The 1965 master plan for Jakarta, made unofficially under the governorship of Ali Sadikin represented a state-of-the-art scheme for the metropolis, and the basis for future plans. The chapter also examines the emergence of the concept of regional planning as expressed in the notion of a planning sphere beyond that of the city itself, and how the World Bank financed 'Jabotabek' (so named from the beginning letters of the cities of Jakarta, Bogor, Tangerang and Bekasi) approach to the greater Jakarta area anticipated the megacity phenomenon.

The day-to-day challenges of planning Jakarta involved addressing, among a host of infrastructure deficits, the need for a housing supply to keep up with an accelerating population. Chapter 4 examines planning for housing, neighbourhoods and the broader matters of urban revitalization through an assessment of the Kampung Improvement Program, efforts to control population growth in Jakarta, and the provision of new housing through urban redevelopment. The new housing provided through government support to private development came in the form of small-scale complexes as well as massive new developments involving thousands of units. The chapter also examines how land prices in central Jakarta forced much of the new low-cost housing to suburban locations, a trend that anticipated another key feature of the emerging megacity social structure.

The outward expansion of the urbanized area first to the less developed fringe of Jakarta and then beyond its boundaries deep into the periphery is examined in Chapter 5, 'Expansion, Revitalization and the Restructuring of Metropolitan Jakarta, 1970s to the early 1990s'. The two critical components of the mass suburbanization that occurred in the 1980s and 1990s were expansion of the toll road system and the creation of new planned suburban towns and cities to accommodate a growing share of the metropolitan population. Both were facilitated by generous government support for a small but powerful real estate development community. However development did not always conform to the plans for Jabotabek that sought to protect critical environmental areas and to cluster new settlements to reduce the costs of servicing these new communities. As a complement to the suburban expansion, there were efforts to preserve and revitalize sections of old Jakarta where the previously experienced pressures of population growth were eased by rapid growth in suburban locales. These early efforts at preservation and revitalization in the 1980s and early 1990s presaged a wholesale transformation of Jakarta from a collection of urban villages to a 'world city'.

This is the theme of Chapter 6, 'Urban Village to World City: Re-planning

Jakarta in the 1990s'. It examines a series of major projects planned (and in some cases later implemented) to elevate Jakarta into the ranks of world cities. This effort was derailed temporarily with the onset of the financial crisis in 1997, and the political revolution in 1998 that led to the ousting of the Suharto family from power. Loosening regulations to allow greater foreign investment, especially in commercial real estate, was one step taken prior to the 1997 crisis. Luring foreign investment to create a long overdue modern mass transit system for Jakarta was another. A third, reclamation of the North Jakarta coast, with the addition of several thousand hectares of land created by infill, was intended to produce a new 'waterfront city' which would, like the model set by its neighbour Singapore, provide residents with 'First World' amenities. These three schemes, and many more, were derailed temporarily by the fiscal and political crises, and the subsequent economic depression, of the late 1990s. But they spoke to a level of aspiration within Jakarta's leadership to achieve the grand vision of a world city. A new plan, known as the 2010 plan, set forth this vision. Yet, at the same time, Jakarta's planners continued to wrestle with the challenge of keeping the city accessible to people of all income levels, a challenge that proved even greater as prosperity returned after 2001 and the various 'world city' projects got back on track.

The final chapter, 'Planning in the New Democratic Megacity', incorporates the political changes since 1998 into the current processes of planning in Jakarta. As in the era when Ali Sadikin was governor under presidents Sukarno and Suharto, Jakarta's current governor, Sutiyoso, has demonstrated a strong, decisive and frequently controversial approach to addressing longstanding problems. He survived the financial crisis and the political revolution (both of which are examined in this chapter) while serving under five different presidents and in the face of a radically different approach to planning and decision-making. Sutiyoso's successes and failures in planning the megacity reflect the uncertainty surrounding how best to mesh democratic politics and decision-making with managing a city so large and complicated that meaningful input from all potential stakeholders might induce a policy paralysis that could only undermine its future prospects. Yet, as it demonstrates, the challenges posed by such profound change in the capital city over the past decade have given even greater urgency to the need to plan strategically for the future. It is no mean feat, as the conclusion suggests, that there is now a planning vision for Jakarta that states as its overriding objective the creation of 'a humane, efficient, and competitive capital supported by a participative, prosperous, well behaved and civilized society in a safe and sustainable environment'.[7] More than a century of effort on the part of Jakarta's planners, its leaders and its engaged citizens has gone into creating that vision. It is a history worth understanding, and worth telling. That is it what I attempt to do in the chapters that follow.

Notes

1. For an overview of the megacity phenomenon in these regions, Rakodi (1997); Gilbert (1996); McGee and Robinson (1995); Friedmann (2005).
2. There is one recent collection of essays that does attempt to examine how local and national elites influenced change in cities in Asia, some of which are megacities. See Nas (2005).
3. ROI, DOI (1989/90), p. 78; Jakarta, DKI (1992).
4. Heuken (1989), pp. 171–177.
5. See Anderson (1983), pp. 477–496.
6. McGee (1967); McGee (1997).
7. Jakarta, DKI (2002), p. 37.

Chapter One

Understanding Urbanization and the Megacity in Southeast Asia

Jakarta is the most populous city in Southeast Asia, the largest city in a nation and a region where cities account for less than half the total population. The rural village, not the urban neighbourhood, remains the dominant form of habitation and, according to some observers, Jakarta is really an overgrown cluster of villages. When measured as a whole, this cluster of villages makes up an urban area with nearly 10 million residents, which grows to nearly 11 million during the working day. Jakarta's rapid growth, as well as that of cities throughout the region, has largely been the product of the past half-century. In 1950, according to data from the United Nations, only 14.8 per cent of Southeast Asians lived in urban areas compared to 63.9 per cent in North America and 52.4 per cent in Europe. Only Sub-Saharan Africa had a lower rate of urbanization (11.5 per cent) although throughout Asia, especially if the massive rural populations of India and China are added to the equation, the overall percentage of urban inhabitants amounted to just 17.4 per cent.[1] Over the subsequent half century, however, the percentage of urban residents in Southeast Asia jumped to 37.2 per cent, pushing it ahead of Asia as a whole but still far behind North America, Europe, Latin America and North Africa.[2]

What is most distinctive about urbanization in Southeast Asia between 1950 and 2000 is its concentration in just a handful of urban places, creating a phenomenon that urban geographers refer to as *primate* cities. Their pre-eminence and centrality are in functions that strongly influence urbanization (e.g. jobs, transportation, services). Although the development of primate cities has been a global phenomenon, what happened in Southeast Asia in the second half of the twentieth century is a distinctive variation on primate city formation. Explosive urban growth, in terms of population concentration, economic development and spatial growth led, within a very short time span, to truly enormous urban places.

The term that emerged to distinguish those cities which reached the remarkable plateau of supporting a population of 8 million or more people was 'megacity', and during the 1990s Jakarta became the largest of Southeast Asia's 'megacities'. With a population of more than 11 million, Jakarta became one of the most populous cities in the world.[3]

Southeast Asia's other megacities are Manila, with a population of 10 million and Bangkok, with more than 7.5 million inhabitants. Singapore, the region's economic powerhouse, might have shared a similar glory in population growth were it not a small island nation lacking enough space to accommodate a megacity size population. Nevertheless, its more than 4 million residents make it the fifth largest city in the region, surpassed slightly in population by Yangon, Myanmar (4.5 million) although the former colonial capital of Burma is one of the poorest of the region's large urban places. Several other cities had multimillion populations by 2000 and were poised to gain entry into this elite grouping, including Surabaya (2.5 million) and Bandung (3.4 million) in Indonesia, and Ho Chi Minh City (4.6 million) and Hanoi (3.8 million) in Vietnam. In spatial size, Kuala Lumpur, Malaysia also exhibits megacity traits, especially in its spread, although the Malaysian national policy of encouraging urban deconcentration ensures that the capital city will not achieve megacity stature any time soon. Yet like Singapore, Kuala Lumpur's highly educated urban population of 1.4 million plays an economic role in the region far greater than would be predicted by its modest size.[4]

The official population figures for these large Southeast Asian urban centres do not tell the full story, however. The megacities are the nexus for much larger areas that include many more people than just those officially residing in the urban area. This uncounted population includes those who remain with one foot still firmly planted in rural agricultural life, but who have formed attachments through various linkages, usually economic, to the urban market. Because of the dual nature of these urban-related agricultural areas, Terence McGee aptly labelled them *desakota*, which literally translates from Indonesian as 'city village'. Together the *desakota* and the urbanized area make up what demographer Gavin Jones refers to as a 'mega-urban region'. As Jones notes, while in Western cities, there is typically a sharp division between urban and adjacent rural areas, in the Southeast Asian mega-urban region, densely populated rural enclaves lie beyond the confines of the metropolis, in some cases drawn into the urban orbit by out-migration of urban industries or through conversion to urban residential uses. But many serve as a labour pool for urban industries and services while simultaneously sustaining a rural lifestyle.[5]

'Extended metropolitan development' (another term used by analysts to describe the megacity and mega-urban region phenomena), has been a distinguishing characteristic of urbanization in Southeast Asia's developing countries over the past two decades. Accompanying this profound urban restructuring of large and intermediate cities has been a substantial research literature seeking to explain the phenomenon.[6] The megacity concept refers not only to population thresholds but also to the physical manifestation of an urbanization process where dense population and mixed land uses extend from 75 to 100 kilometres from the urban core. As McGee and Robinson put it, the 'megacity' encompasses 'the entire territory – comprising the central city, the developments within the transportation corridors, the satellite towns and other projects in the peri-urban fringe, and the outer zones [within] a single, economically integrated' territory.[7] On the basis of spatial development, five extended metropolitan regions had been identified by the 1990s – Bangkok, Jakarta, Kuala Lumpur, Manila and Singapore – although other candidates were poised to assume this status, including Bandung, Surabaya and Medan in Indonesia, Changmai in Thailand, Cebu City in the Phillipines and Ho Chi Minh City in Vietnam.[8]

The spatial configuration of the Southeast Asian megacity, like the sprawling metropolises of North America, has been depicted as 'amorphous and amoebic-like' owing to the rapid and irregular process of growth and change which it has undergone in recent decades. The megacity is typically characterized as an undesirable outcome of urban development. Critics point to environmental and ecological degradation, to the loss of precious agricultural lands, and to the increasing poverty among those who flock there from rural areas; its extremely dispersed settlement pattern which fosters inefficiencies in provision of basic services, and the nightmare confronting those charged with its management, have all been cited as reasons to thwart continued growth. Others laud megacity development as a visible manifestation of powerful economic growth forces in the region.[9] McGee contends that the advantages of spatial dispersion in megacities must be calculated alongside their obvious costs. Examples of advantages accruing from recent development include upgraded housing for workers, increased home ownership rates (as evidence of capital accumulation among consumers); improved environmental conditions through improved sanitation; clean water; increased open space that accompanies new peripheral development; improved job opportunities and wages (in large part associated with jobs that contribute to sustaining megacity development); and improved amenities for a broad segment of the population due to the wealth generated through megacity concentration. He regards as a myth that the size of the megacity is itself a problem, or that megacities cannot be sustained. He rejects the view that the megacities contribute to impoverishment, or that they 'are places of disharmony and poor quality of life'.[10]

As White and Whitney point out, the extended metropolis concept, with its accompanying 'greater dispersal of population', might help to 'overcome diseconomies of very large centers, diffuse economic activity more widely through regions and nations, and permit the environment to absorb better the wastes imposed upon it'. As they note further, the extended metropolis (or megacity) is a variant on the linear city, with the 'obvious advantage ... that it provides ready access to a string of urban centers without entailing the horrendously inefficient (time and energy consuming) pattern of daily expansion and contraction' which would be necessary with a single employment centre surrounded by residential areas.[11] The contention that unregulated urban development has created a desirable polycentric urban spatial pattern in the megacities of Asia offers the most extreme variation on the 'metropolitan growth is good' position. Taken together, these reassessments suggest that the growth and spatial dispersion of the urbanized areas in Southeast Asia yield results consistent with the objectives of a sustainable urban environment even with extended metropolitan area populations approaching 15 million inhabitants as in the case of Jakarta and Manila.[12]

What makes the case of urban sustainability plausible in the case of Southeast Asian megacities is that the rapid growth of the periphery has not undermined the vitality of the urban core as it seems to have done in so many North American cities. The absence of 'urban spatial abandonment' in the core areas of Southeast Asian megacities is one indication that the process of urban expansion at the periphery has not eroded critical urban core functions. Another factor is the emergence of a truly polycentric spatial and functional order. According to geographer Ira Robinson, polycentric metropolitan restructuring tends to offset certain economic costs associated with urban dispersion. As he notes, the 'polynucleated metropolitan spatial structure can relieve congestion costs at the centre without sacrificing the benefits of metropolitan-wide agglomeration of economies'. The polynucleated settlement pattern involves clustering multiple urban functions in order to reduce the length of trips and increase opportunities to make multipurpose trips over a shorter distance. By concentrating new development in a few locations, polynuclearity also reduces land consumption and preserves critical areas. While retaining interdependence with other components of the metropolis, these clusters can develop their own internal cohesiveness, enabling them to respond to service needs and to provide a community-based environment within the larger metropolis.[13]

Late in 1995, the journal *Indonesia Property Report* devoted an entire issue to examining the 'problems and prospects' for Jakarta's megacity development, focusing on the array of planned urban centres that had sprouted up along the expanding edges of the city. As the editors observed:

New Towns and Satellite Cities surrounding Jakarta seem to have grown like mushrooms

during the rainy season. Bumi Serpong Damai, Kota Tigaraksa, Lippo City, Lippo Village, Kota Cikarang Baru, Bintaro Jaya, Kota Legenda, and Royal Sentul Highlands, are only some of the new towns being developed near Jakarta.[14]

Their message was that these privately-planned large-scale developments relieved pressures on inner-city neighbourhoods to accommodate Jakarta's continuously expanding population. Not only were they proof of Jakarta's dynamic economy but they were the catalysts for restructuring the city from a highly centralized to a highly decentralized structure, so helping to usher in the 'megacity' era.

These privately planned residential towns, in combination with numerous publicly-financed (but privately-constructed) low-income housing projects led, in the 1990s, to wholesale transformation of land on the edges of Jakarta from agricultural to urban uses. Development pressures produced dramatic increases in land values close to the centre, thereby forcing moderate and low-income development to seek locations further out. The escalating land prices fuelled even greater expansion. As evidence of the housing construction boom, the national government's target of more than half a million new units to be built by 1999 was achieved ahead of schedule in 1997. Until the collapse of the Indonesian economy in the second half of 1997, it seemed as though the urbanized area of Jakarta would soon engulf all land within a 60–70 kilometres radius of the traditional city centre. While certainly proud of Jakarta's new status as a recognized global 'megacity', and determined to sustain the development momentum, Indonesia's planners also acknowledged the serious environmental, economic, social and political implications of this urban explosion.

Suddenly, in the second half of 1997, the economic bubble burst and 'formal' urban expansion ground to a halt. Prepared land sat vacant, partially-built structures littered the landscape, and completed residential and commercial structures remained unoccupied due to the sudden cessation of a previously insatiable real estate market. The long-term impact of the economic crisis on Jakarta remains a matter of intense speculation. What is clear is that the malaise that crippled Indonesia's economy hit, albeit unevenly, large and small cities throughout the region. Part of the explanation of this regional economic collapse was tied directly to the dynamics of growth in major urban centres. The rapid absorption of virtually all commercial and residential development during the boom time (typically referred to as the 'Asian miracle') fuelled further growth. At the peak of the boom in the mid-1990s, demand for a part of the growth was so intense that purchasers were willing to pay the full cost (and often an inflated cost) of a new home even before it had been constructed. When the economy collapsed, many who had already paid for their homes never got them. The assumption of never-ending demand represented a misreading of the urban growth process in Southeast Asia.

Peri-Urbanization

Terence McGee was the first scholar to study the peripheral growth areas of large cities throughout Asia (including Calcutta, Shanghai, Bangkok, Guangzhou and Jakarta) in order to identify common characteristics and development traits. He found these places typically had high population densities, usually cultivated wet rice, were most prevalent where the cities provided ample supplementary employment opportunities, were attractive to non-agricultural employment, and exhibited a highly diverse mixture of land uses created by the invasion of a range of urban activities. In calling these areas *desakota* (see above) he drew on the nomenclature used in the Indonesia 1980 census which refers to '*desa* urban' areas as those with a population density of 5,000 persons per square kilometre, 25 per cent or fewer agricultural households, and eight or more urban functions, such as schools, banks, hospitals, factories, shopping centres, roads that could be used by four-wheeled motor vehicles, public electricity and a market with buildings.

Indonesian planning analyst, Tommy Firman studied the census data for 1980 and 1990 and found increased urbanization in the rural districts (*kabupatens*) adjacent to all major urban areas on Java. This not only confirmed McGee's explanation of the transformation of rural areas in the widening orbit of a nearby large city, but that especially in the Jakarta metropolitan area there was an increasing conversion of agricultural land to urban uses. 'A rough estimate indicates', Firman noted, 'that in *kabupaten* Bogor, which borders DKI (*Daerah Khussus Indonesia*) Jakarta, approximately 2,000 of the 23,000 hectares of *sawah* (rice fields) that existed in 1986 have now been converted to industrial and residential uses'. The data pointed to the high incidence of urbanization squeezing out rural functions in the hinterland of Jakarta, and this further elevating the importance of the city within the region.[15]

But is this not just the most recent manifestation of a process that has been ongoing for centuries throughout Southeast Asia? Cities had a dominant position in Southeast Asian society long before the emergence of the modern megacity. Although several scholars have suggested that cities are modern and alien imports into a region which is best understood by its rural traditions, there is compelling evidence that urbanism is not new. As historian Richard O'Connor puts it, 'Southeast Asia's cities are indigenous in origin, function and meaning', and not an 'alien imposition as they are so often portrayed'.[16] In a region where such a vast array of local ethnic groups persisted, urbanism represented an essential means of social ordering.

What cities provided for Southeast Asia was a means to create a unitary society and a unitary culture, a 'larger whole', from the multiple ethnic traditions. Cities served to blend the disparate foreign elements with the indigenous. In creating an urban culture, Southeast Asia appropriated generously from many foreign influences, including China, India, the Middle East and the West, all of which had long standing economic engagements in the region. A distinguishing trait of Southeast Asian cities was acceptance of 'foreign borrowings as the idiom of urban rule', as O'Connor puts it.[17] The incorporation of the foreign elements served to undermine the local and to elevate the importance of urbanism, a phenomenon that reappeared throughout the development of Jakarta right up to the present.

While O'Connor suggests that one ought not measure the urban influence in Southeast Asia solely in terms of demographics, the size of indigenous cities (prior to Europeanization) was on a par with some of the West's largest cities, although not approaching the urban behemoths of East Asia, Peking and Edo, with roughly a million inhabitants each. Melaka, Ayutthaya and Demak on the mainland, and Aceh, on the island of Sumatra, Makassar on the island of Sulawesi, Surabaya and Banten on the island of Java, all boasted populations of between 50,000 and 100,000 or more in the sixteenth and seventeenth centuries.[18]

However, as historian Anthony Reid contends, the cities of the region differed markedly from those of the West and Far East. One difference was that Southeast Asian cities blended rural features into the city in such a way that 'the boundary between the city and countryside seemed almost non-existent'.[19] Fruit trees abounded not just for aesthetic reasons but because they were the true measure of wealth. For climatic reasons, open wooden houses, built off the ground were the preferred mode, whereas the Chinese and Europeans introduced stone and brick structures in tightly structured, treeless compounds that eventually were abandoned as the 'alien urban models' were modified to match indigenous forms. When, influenced by Europeans, some indigenous cities erected brick walls, only the nobles lived within the walls while most of the population resided outside. In the case of Aceh, the city remained wall-less, relying instead on the vigilance of its residents and courage of it warriors. As expressed in a seventeenth-century description of that north Sumatra trading city:

All the past rulers since the original ancestors of Sri Perkasa Alam have not fortified the capital (*kota negeri*) ... because God had given them stout hearts and strong character and sound judgement in fighting all their enemies... And this city (*negeri*) is not fortified as is the custom of other fortified cities because of the very large number of war elephants in this city.[20]

European incursions into the region, beginning in the sixteenth century, had a profound impact on indigenous urban places. When the Portugese captured Malacca and opened the door to the other European trading powers to enter the region, this led to the establishment of new cities. Some of the larger indigenous urban places lost out in competition with Europeans, notably Banten on the northwest coast of Java. Estimated to have had a population of nearly 700,000 within its sphere of influence in the late seventeenth century, and a menace to the nearby Dutch port at Batavia, Banten shrank into a small backwater town once its trading monopoly had been broken.

Colonial Influences

As mentioned in the introduction, the origins of Batavia preceded European contact, with evidence suggesting that it served first as a port for the Javanese kingdom of Pajajaran (whose capital was near the present day city of Bogor) known as Sunda Kelapa (established in the twelfth century) and then as a satellite of the Banten sultanate, known as Jaya Karta, and sustaining a population of approximately 10,000 inhabitants. However, in 1619 the Dutch Governor-General Jan Pieterszoon Coen razed the town to the ground and it was rebuilt on the European model of a walled and fortified city, served internally by a system of canals.[21]

Like Jakarta, most of today's major cities in Southeast Asia had pre-colonial origins, but were transformed significantly by the colonization processes from the seventeenth to the twentieth centuries. The most enduring impact of colonialism on Southeast Asia cities was to link them more fully within a global economic network. Simple indigenous urban places were transformed into cosmopolitan cities both in their make-up and in their outlook. The population composition of Batavia in 1673 points to this cosmopolitan character. Of the 27,068 residents counted in a local census, 2,024 were Dutch, 726 were of mixed European and Asian origins (Eurasian), and 2,747 were Chinese. Another large ethnic group was the 5,361 Moors/Marjikers, Asian-born of Portuguese descent, who had arrived from India and Malacca). Representing other areas in the archipelago were the 1,339 Javanese, 611 Malays and 981 Balinese, coupled with a mixed grouping of 13,278 slaves, many of whom were from South Asia but also some from the eastern islands.[22] The small percentage of Europeans within Batavia's population is noteworthy and typical of colonial cities throughout the region.

When Raffles set forth his plan for the physical development of Singapore in a thirty-two paragraph instruction in 1822, one of the key considerations was specifying exactly which spaces would be allocated to the settlement's diverse population. 'Raffles' decisions regarding the land and its occupants were based on his hierarchical social taxonomy and reflected a group's stage of civilization'.[23] The largest spaces were allocated for the European town and the Chinese settlement, although he separated the Chinese land area between the merchant class and labourers. He included an Arab quarter (adjacent to the European town) and a smaller allotment for the Chulia (manual labourers from India) to live near their workplace where they were most needed in a neighbourhood (*kampung*) north of the Chinese settlement. There was a separate *kampung* for the natives of Celebes, known as Bugis, who Raffles regarded as the least civilized and most dangerous to the social order, but who also needed a well-regulated space in the port city. The indigenous Malays were not provided with a designated zone; it was assumed that they would remain where they predominated in the coastal areas as they were largely engaged in fishing rather than commerce.[24]

This pattern was repeated in all the major cities of Southeast Asia touched by European colonialism, although there was wide variation in the way the social mix was translated into the spatial make-up of the cities. McGee identified three types of colonial city: the indigenous colonial city exemplified by Bangkok, with a pre-industrial walled palace city juxtaposed against the commercial city that expanded after the Treaty of Friendship and Commerce which King Monkut signed with the British in 1855; the planned colonial city which Raffles created on Singapore Island; and the 'grafted city' which the British built around the Sule Pagoda above the Hlaing and Pegu rivers in what is now Burma.[25]

The creation of a colonial capital by the French in Hanoi in the 1880s was by far the most radical urban reconstruction process undertaken by the Europeans. When the French civilian government took over in 1886, the Ancient Quarter, which had been constructed under Chinese colonial rule hundreds of years earlier, was opened up by removal of the old town walls and a process of street widening to improve access by the fire brigade, horse-drawn vehicles and troops. By the 1890s, the city's venerable citadel along with several important temples were torn down not because they presented a military threat but because they remained the most visible symbol of the former Vietnamese imperial rulers. A new Beaux-Arts Governor-General palace was constructed between 1901 and 1906 on 20 hectares of private land adjacent to the Botanical Gardens which had been confiscated, without any payment, from its native owners. Another importation of Parisian architecture was the Municipal Theatre, built between 1901 and 1911 and inspired by the Paris opera house constructed under the Haussmann regime by architect Charles Garnier. Although this was carried out on the orders of the new Governor-General, Paul Doumer, it was he who first recognized the mistake of dismantling the historically significant citadel. While unable to resurrect what had already been lost, Doumer established the École française d'Extrême-Orient to document and protect the city's heritage. The first successful test of its influence was in helping to reverse a decision by the Hanoi municipal council to remove the Thanh Ha gate, the last of the original city gates, in 1905. Doumer's efforts to construct a 'Paris de l'Annam' was celebrated in a grand exposition hosted in Hanoi in 1902. Although many of the civic improvement projects were still under construction, there was no further conscious effort to impose a European model on a long established Southeast Asian city.[26]

The cities most influenced by Europeans in Southeast Asia by the late nineteenth century, namely Bangkok, Batavia, Manila, Rangoon, Saigon, and Singapore, were also typically those places that developed most rapidly in the twentieth century, largely because of their role in regional and international trade. According to McGee,

[t]he most prominent function of these cities was economic; the colonial city was the 'nerve center' of colonial exploitation. Concentrated here were the institutions through which capitalism extended its control over the colonial economy – the banks, the agency houses, trading companies, the shipping companies and the insurance companies.[27]

They were also nodes in the transportation system within and between the colonies. Although these colonial cities offered the most lucrative economic opportunities in the region, the indigenous population remained outside the major trading, financial and professional occupations, and worked in marginal positions as skilled craftsmen or unskilled labourers, with some limited involvement in the colonial civil service. As McGee notes, 'some of the colonial governments did encourage the indigenous populations, through limited schemes of education, to take government jobs in the cities, but they remained a minority'.[28]

Positions in the hierarchy of Southeast Asian cities, based upon population size in 1900 went through a notable transformation over the final four to five decades of European colonial rule. The most populous cities in 1900 were Bangkok, Rangoon (234,881), Manila and Singapore. Batavia and Surabaya in Indonesia were significantly smaller (with only slightly more than 100,000 inhabitants each) along with Mandalay, Saigon, Hanoi and Georgetown. Rangoon grew steadily after 1901, with an annual growth rate of between 1.6 per cent and 2.3 per cent. This was much slower than it had been in the late nineteenth century. Nevertheless, by 1941 the city boasted a population of 500,000.[29]

Batavia emerged as one of the larger colonial cities, surpassing its eastern Java port city rival, Surabaya, which was actually larger than Batavia in 1900. Georgetown and Mandalay dropped far down in the rankings, largely because other colonial administrative centres were absorbing a greater share of economic and demographic growth than these secondary cities. This created distortions in national urban development patterns that would challenge policy makers and planners in decades to follow. As Dean Forbes contends,

the colonial period disrupted the economic and social geography of Southeast Asia. It brought significant changes to the distribution of economic activities, reinforcing the rise of the colonial port city, which in turn provided the foundation for the post-World War II surge in urbanization. These cities were dominated by the colonizers, whose needs generally came first, with the indigenous economy existing at the margins of the city.[30]

Urbanization in Southeast Asia after 1945 was influenced markedly by the related processes of decolonization and national development. Although there were varying rates of urbanization throughout the region, growth in the urban population significantly exceeded overall population increases in all nations.[31] McGee examined localities with 20,000 or more residents in select countries between the late 1940s and 1960 and found that the cities typically doubled (and in several cases tripled) the growth rates of the overall population (see table 1.1).

Typically, but not exclusively, the largest cities exhibited the most spectacular growth rates, at the expense of second tier cities. Phnom-Phen, Cambodia was one of the fastest growing cities in the region between 1936 and 1960. Its population grew at an annual rate of 14 per cent while the country's second largest city, Battembang, grew at just 3.2 per cent. A similar disparity in growth rates characterized Batavia and Surabaya between 1931 and 1961, although in Thailand (Bangkok and Changmai) and the Philippines (Manila and Cebu), despite substantial differences in overall population size, annual growth rates were comparable in the post-World War II decades.[32]

The main contributor to rapid urban population growth throughout the region was rural-urban migration. In some Southeast Asian cities, between 40 and 70 per cent of the population were post-independence migrants (and their offspring) from the countryside. According to McGee, political and economic instability in the countryside rather than the lure of the city, accounted for much of this migration. As he noted, 'the political instability which has resulted from the rebel movements in Malaya, Vietnam and Burma has brought about a massive influx of rural refugees to the main cities of these countries'.[33] The same can be said for Indonesia, given the ongoing conflicts in West Java, Sulawesi, East Java and parts of Sumatra that made overcrowded and ill-equipped cities preferable to the unprotected rural areas. Extremely high unemployment rates in cities throughout the region did not seem a deterrent to the migration process. Bidani

Table 1.1. Changes in the proportion of population (localities of 20,000 or more in select nations).

Country	Dates	Percentage of total population in cities of 20,000+	Percentage yearly increase in cities of 20,000+	Percentage yearly increase in total population
Malaysia	1947	17.1		
	1957	20.8	5.8	2.8
Philippines	1950	12.7		
	1960	14.2	5.3	4.0
Indonesia	1950	9.1		
	1960	11.2	5.3	2.4
Thailand	1947	5.1		
	1960	8.8	12.0	3.5

Source: McGee (1967), p. 79.

suggests that many migrants were attracted by false economic expectations and lacked proper information about job opportunities in urban areas. Another factor at work in many places, especially in Thailand, was the search for educational opportunities. Seasonal migration during the slack period in the agricultural cycle also introduced urban life to rural residents, which for many became permanent.[34]

Institutional Changes

The transformation of the social and political structure of the post-colonial city in Southeast Asia was not as radical as might have been expected from the rhetoric of change that accompanied nationalism. The transfer of power from the European elite to an indigenous urban elite, composed of a handful of wealthy businessmen and professionals, government bureaucrats, and military, sustained the hierarchical structure that had existed throughout the late colonial era. While vehemently anti-colonial, this leadership group helped to sustain Western values. The new Southeast Asian nations were:

urban-oriented, especially in relation to the capital city – not unlike the kingdoms of the traditional era. But the new elites could not resurrect the metaphysical and mystical nature of traditional government and often had more in common with former colonial elites than with their rural peasant constituencies.[35]

An increasing concentration of wealth, as well as political power within the urban elite accompanied the substantial increase in urban population, most of whom existed on the margins of society. At the same time, the proportion of foreigners residing in cities declined as the numbers and percentages of the indigenous population increased. Migrants from the countryside transferred rural customs to the cities with the result that the social and physical dimensions of village life were imposed on the cities. In Rangoon, for example, the housing shortage in the 1950s led to construction by in-migrants of squatter colonies (*kwetthits*) which were administered by headmen, accountable to city government, but fulfilling a function traditionally carried out in the countryside. Anthropologist Edward Brunner's examination of the social structure of Medan, Sumatra in the late 1950s underscored the intensification of urban heterogeneity in the aftermath of rural migration. As he observed,

Every national in Medan is, of course, an Indonesian citizen, but in terms of the language he speaks at home, the cultural tradition he follows, he is also a Javanese, a Malay, an Atjehnese, a Minangkabau, a Mandailing, an Angkola, a Simelungun, a Karo, a Pak-Pak, or something else. Medan consists of a series of separate ethnic communities as well as social enclaves of Chinese, Indians and Europeans.[36]

According to McGee, one outcome of the demographic diversity and increasing numbers of uneducated rural peasants in large Southeast Asian cities was the need for national governments to assume the functions of urban governance and urban planning in these cities.[37] Some consideration was given to transferring national capitals to places not associated with colonial governance. In the late 1950s Sukarno was enthralled by the idea of creating a new capital city for Indonesia in the heart of Borneo. He was inspired by Brazilian President Kubichek's plan to move the capital from Rio de Janiero to the new planned city of Brasilia located deep in the interior.[38] However, the preponderance of institutions needed to support the development of national identity that were already in the former colonial capitals made it too difficult to introduce such radical changes.

These former colonial capitals functioned as what Hildred Geertz referred to as 'metropoles', that is, places which played a dominant role in national development because of the breadth and sophistication of their institutional and social structures and, at the same time, provided a link to the external, global network. In Southeast Asia, the metropoles included Bangkok, Jakarta, Manila, Rangoon, Saigon and Singapore. These were distinguished from the 'provincial towns' which functioned within the context of regional development, with fewer foreigners and, typically, more stable and less diverse populations. McGee suggests a third layer of cities, the emerging metropoles that were smaller in size but otherwise shared many of the attributes of metropoles except to a lesser degree.[39]

The transition to the post-colonial city also introduced notable changes in the physical structure of Southeast Asian cities. These included the location of major economic functions, cultural institutions and residential patterns. In terms of economic functions, it is necessary to distinguish, as Clifford Geertz suggests, between the *firm-centred economy* which includes both domestic and international capital interactions through a set of impersonal institutions and the *bazaar economy* which revolves around traditional market places where face-to-face transactions occur between the suppliers and customers, and which support a lifestyle which does not rely on such advanced technology or imported goods. The traditional bazaar economy continued in Southeast Asian cities even as the role of the firm-centred economy expanded. There was an ongoing struggle between the two especially in controlling locations within expanding urban areas. In cases where the city attempted to replace traditional market functions with firm-centred enterprises, re-invasion by traditional markets in support of the indigenous population created challenges for local planners. Jerome Tadie's analysis of the modernization of one of Jakarta's traditional markets demonstrates how powerful the traditional bazaar market influence remained even when planned out of existence. Between 1962 and the 1990s, the Senen Triangle market area was cleared of all of its original Chinese shophouses and dwellings, as well as the open air market. It was replaced by a super block shopping mall, a five-star hotel, and condominium/office tower structures. But its social morphology changed little. As a magnet for vendors, prostitutes, and various indigenous cultural institutions, Senen did not reflect the modernism intended by its renovation. Moreover, it remained one of the most crime-infested places in the centre city.[40]

In terms of commercial and retail functions, Southeast Asian cities moved towards the creation of a central business district, some typically as an extension of the colonial urban patterns. But the Western-styled concentrations of offices, hotels, financial institutions, restaurants, and shopping facilities were often accompanied by nearby areas of Chinese or Indian merchants in what McGee refers to as 'the alien commercial centre'.[41] These areas usually comprised small entrepreneurs operating in specialized trades such as jewellers, tailoring, pharmaceuticals, food sales, hardware and small-scale finance, typically in structures which serve as the shop, when necessary as the place of manufacturing, as well as the residence of the owner. These 'alien' commercial centres functioned both day and night, and in conjunction with the mobile night markets.

In Southeast Asian cities, the role of public markets remained strong throughout the post-colonial period even as Western style supermarkets and shopping centres made inroads into the urban economy and spatial structure. None of these modernization efforts seemed to displace the bazaar economy that centred around the fixed public markets and the mobile night markets. The continued influx of low-income residents into Southeast Asia's large cities, coupled with the tendency of a sizable segment of the emerging urban middle class to continue to use traditional retail centres for day-to-day items, sustained this dual urban retail structure. The malls and the supermarkets serve as a place of leisure for those who can afford the price of imports.

Evers and Korff reject the concept of a central business district to characterize the economic spatial pattern of Bangkok. As they note,

> ... instead of a compact inner city, the commercial areas [of Bangkok] are spread along the major roads and streets. Even in the inner city one still finds free space, away from the main roads. The size of Bangkok and the integration of formerly outlying sub-centres leads to the emergence of several centres and to shifts of these centres.[42]

Moreover, the city developed a new market, Klong Thoey market, consisting of 1500 stalls and shops inside and alongside five large halls on land that had become a massive slum near the port. This 24-hour market has been linked to the city by a new highway, and so serves not only the low-income residents still situated around it, but is an attraction to those in all parts of the city and its hinterland because of its reputation for providing quality goods at cheap prices.[43] Similar markets exist side-by-side expansive modern retail areas in Manila, Singapore and Jakarta.

In manufacturing, the most consistent trend has been to create industrial estates on the outskirts of cities to accommodate new growth in this sector, although the port areas created during the colonial era remain a primary locus for processing operations, as well storage and shipping. What is most evident as a general trend in the post-colonial city is the wide dispersal of economic activity or, put another way, the lack of concentration (except around port facilities).[44]

In terms of the residential structure of Southeast Asian cities, the transformation in the post-colonial period has been more significant than the continuities with the colonial structure. What had been the low-density residential compounds of the Europeans initially became the neighbourhoods of the indigenous elite but later were more mixed as suburban settlements lured indigenous elites from the urban centre to the periphery. The massive in-migration of labourers from rural areas expanded the number and density of rural-like villages that were located in urban fringes, while also leading to increased densities in inner-city areas inhabited by working-class families. Ethnic enclaves for the Chinese persisted, although satellite settlements to accommodate the more affluent Chinese developed in the suburbs. What clearly distinguishes the Southeast Asian city from the Western model in terms of residential structure is the virtual absence of any clearly defined class distinctions related to location of residence and proximity to city centre. As McGee notes,

the patterns of residence of the Southeast Asian city which include a mixture of the poorest and wealthiest elements of the city in both the core and outer areas, represent some transitory phase which is developing between the patterns of pre-industrialism and industrialism.[45]

But it is not just a matter of a continuum on the road to industrialization that explains the unique residential configuration of Southeast Asian cities. For example, the need for sizeable numbers of low-income people to live near middle- and upper-income areas because of their continuing role in domestic service is one factor. Low income people occupying inner-city areas where environmental conditions preclude new high end development, and lack of enforcement of regulations against residing in those places, explains the persistence of slums and squatter settlements in the core areas of Southeast Asian cities. New Western-style suburban residential developments, alongside growing self-made indigenous villages in the fringes of the city, both induced by high land costs in the city centre, is another variation not explained by the pre-industrial versus the industrial city models. McGee concluded in the late 1960s that 'the rapid growth of the Southeast Asian cities has merely added new elements to the city rather than transforming the colonial residential pattern'.[46] Until the late 1980s that was probably still an accurate portrayal. The massive reconstruction of core and peripheral areas of Southeast Asia's megacities in the 1990s introduced such profound spatial reorganization that the remnants of the colonial city configuration are far more difficult to discern. The large-scale removal of slums and squatter settlements to make way for new commercial and residential development, as well as expanded transportation networks, radically transformed the urban landscape in all Southeast Asian cities.

The process of slum removal and urban redevelopment was directly connected to the changing land-ownership patterns in major urban areas and, what was a common feature throughout the region, land speculation. According to a United Nations study in the late 1960s,

Speculation in land in the very largest Asian metropolitan centres had indeed risen to such an extent that urban land prices are higher in the developing countries in Asia than even in the most developed countries.[47]

Land speculation followed positive economic growth trends that provided urban elites with the financial capability to invest in land. The control of land by speculators drove up prices while limiting the places where low income people could secure land for housing, thereby perpetuating the expansion of existing slum areas. Land speculation also affected housing opportunities for the middle class in the large cities by spreading from the inner city to the suburban land market. 'When with rising incomes through increased employment opportunities the middle class in Southeast Asian cities tried to improve their housing conditions', Evers and Korff note, 'they found that land on the immediate outskirts of cities had been bought up by speculators and land prices were rising fast'. Increased absentee ownership of the rural fringes of surrounding major cities by a combination of indigenous and expatriate urban elite was not a totally new phenomenon, but the extent of the absentee ownership helped to push prices higher. Evers and Korff contend that 'in the ASEAN countries the accumulation of capital has taken place largely in terms of land speculation and concentration of urban land in few hands'.[48]

The challenge for all Southeast Asian cities was to provide housing for their continuously expanding populations. During the 1960s and 1970s, 'housing conditions in the primate cities in Southeast Asia ... visibly deteriorated'.[49] Calculations of housing need, especially for low-income housing, far exceeded that which could be met by the private housing sector. The creation of national housing agencies in Thailand (1973), Indonesia (1974), Malaysia (1975) and the Philippines (1975) followed the lead of Singapore's Housing Development Board in provision of public subsidies for low-income housing.[50] While these organizations accelerated housing production through a variety of experiments, they did not reduce the need for self-built housing which remained the primary source of new shelter. It was an accepted policy to provide services to existing squatter settlements as necessary given the inability of government or the private sector to provide enough affordable housing.

Conclusion

Experiences in developing political and governance structures to handle not only housing shortages, inadequate infrastructure and ongoing problems of poverty, but also support for economic development varied widely throughout the region. So too did the level of success, ranging from Singapore's spectacular transformation to the demise of the once powerful city of Rangoon due to almost continuous political upheaval since independence. It was certainly the case with Jakarta that national political circumstances played a key role in shaping the planning and development processes throughout the second half of the twentieth century. Taken as a whole, the nations of Southeast Asia survived the challenges of decolonization and used independence as a springboard to development. As McCloud puts it,

the states of Southeast Asia have survived the pains of independence and outlived the disillusionment of unmet expectations. Preindependence hopes did not come to fruition, but these states did not collapse. Burma has shown that a Southeast Asian state can survive by itself; Vietnam has demonstrated that a Southeast Asian state can outlast, if not defeat, a superpower; and Malaysia and Singapore have demonstrated that states can survive without revolutionary fervor. Singapore and recently Malaysia and Thailand, with Indonesia not far behind, have shown that economic development is possible – perhaps without parallel political development. These states are demonstrating forms of political development, based in part on traditional, or at least non-Western, political values that will take them in different directions from those predicted by Western social science theories and models.[51]

Jakarta's transformation from the colonial capital of the Netherland Indies to the beacon of Indonesian nationalism, and the role planning played in this process is also not something that could have been predicted using Western social science theories and models. Yet the processes of urbanization and development were guided initially in the early twentieth century by individuals and institutions steeped in those Western traditions. But in so many instances these approaches were adapted to the unique environment of this Southeast Asian port. How modern Jakarta has developed is directly related to the formative influences of the late colonial period in the city's and the nation's history. It is to this part of the story that we now turn.

Notes

1.   See Ginsburg (1955) and Fryer (1953).

2.   United Nations (2001) *World Urbanization Prospects As Assessed in 2001*, cited in Jones (2002).
3.   Brunn, Williams and Zeigler (2003).
4.   Tyner (2003), pp. 387–389.
5.   Jones (2002).
6.   Dogan and Kasarda (1988); Richardson (1989); Ginsburg, Koppel and McGee (1991); McGee and Robinson (1995); Gilbert (1996); Firman (1999).
7.   McGee and Robinson (1995), p. x.
8.   See Jones (2002), p. 121. McGee (1991) refers to the mega-urban region as the extended metropolitan region, or EMR.
9.   See McGee and Robinson (1995).
10. McGee and Robinson (1995), pp. 20–22.
11. White and Whitney (1989), p. 42.
12. See Richardson (1989).
13. McGee and Robinson (1995), p. 88.
14. *Indonesia Property Report* (1995), pp. 3, 10.
15. McGee (1967); Firman (1996), p. 104.
16. O'Connor (1995), pp. 44–45.
17. *Ibid.*, pp. 35–36.
18. Reid (1980), pp. 237–279.
19. *Ibid.*, p. 240.
20. *Ibid.*, p. 243.
21. For a more detailed discussion of Jakarta's founding, see Abeyasekere (1989), pp. 4–19.
22. *Ibid.*, pp. 19–20.
23. Cangi (1993), p. 175
24. *Ibid.*, pp. 175–77.
25. McGee (1967), pp. 63, 67–69, 72–73.
26. Logan (2000).
27. McGee (1967), p. 56.
28. *Ibid.*, p. 60.
29. Than and Rajah (1996), p. 228; McGee (1967), p. 53.
30. Forbes (1996), p. 11; Sternstein (1984).
31. Bidani (1985), pp. 16–17.
32. McGee (1967), p. 81.
33. *Ibid.*, p. 84.
34. Bidani (1985), pp. 24–26.
35. McCloud (1995), pp.138–140.
36. As cited in McGee (1967), p. 99. See Brunner (1961), p. 513.
37. See Murphey (1957).
38. See Chapter 3 for a discussion of Sukarno's plan.
39. Geertz (1963), pp. 24–96.
40. Tadie (2002).
41. McGee (1967), p. 130. See also Ford (1993), p. 377.
42. Evers and Korff (2000), pp. 148 (including note 84).
43. *Ibid.*, p.151.
44. McGee (1967), pp. 136–138.
45. *Ibid.*, p. 140.
46. *Ibid.*, p. 141.
47. Cited in Evers and Korff (2000), p. 173.
48. Evers and Korff (2000), pp. 174, 181.
49. Yeung (1985), p. 50.
50. *Ibid.*, pp. 56–57.
51. McCloud (1995), p. 152.

Chapter Two

Fashioning the Colonial Capital City, 1900–1940

Batavia, as Jakarta was called under colonial rule, was the first foothold of the Dutch in the East Indies in the seventeenth century. Nearly 300 years of colonization and occupation produced only modest changes in the landscape of the original settlement. Only after 1900 did the Dutch begin to treat Batavia with the dignity and determination befitting their colonial capital city and by far the region's most important commercial centre. The period from 1900 through the 1930s witnessed, according to Lindblad, the 'political integration of Java and the Outer Islands into a single colonial polity' with Batavia positioned administratively and economically at the head of the regime. Through the military force of the Royal Netherlands Indies Army, tranquillity and order (*ruste en orde*) had been achieved in the colonies by 1910 and internal vigilance ensured the continuation of Dutch rule until the archipelago was seized by the Japanese in 1942.[1]

The glory of Batavia of the seventeenth and eighteenth centuries was not as a colonial capital, but as the nerve centre of an overseas economy directed by the privately-held Dutch East India Company (or *Vereenigde Oost-Indische Compagnie*) or, as it was commonly known, the VOC. Under the VOC during the seventeenth and eighteenth centuries, and subsequently during the nineteenth century under both Dutch and English control, Batavia was not so much a colonial capital as an international trading port. 'Batavia was outward-looking, and not keen to engage itself in territorial control of inner Java' let alone the vast network of Outer Islands.[2] It drew its population from overseas (Europe and China), it secured its wealth from overseas trade, and only tentatively did the city expand in the nineteenth century beyond the boundaries of the fortified commercial hub that had been erected at the mouth of the Ciliwungi River two centuries earlier. It was a place that modelled in its physical form the frugality with which the colonial administration attended to its needs. Its modest size was sufficient for the administrative and commercial functions it was expected to accommodate.

Batavia's population in 1900 was approximately 115,000, only slightly greater than its estimated size nearly a century earlier. According to the British Assistant Resident Thomas Raffles, the total population for the Batavia region, including agricultural communities located adjacent to the city, was 331,015 in 1810.[3] What proportion of this population could be ascribed to the city's residential base cannot be determined precisely, but it was certainly no greater than 50,000 since later Raffles claimed that there were just 47,000 residents in Batavia proper (although in this case he may not have been including those living in new suburban areas just outside the city limits). In any case, Batavia's nineteenth-century population grew slowly until 1870 when the pace of European arrivals to Java picked up considerably. Between 1900 and 1930, the population of the city increased from 115,000 to 435,000 which represented an average annual growth rate of 9 per cent. Five years later, through annexation of the previously independent adjacent municipality of Meester Cornelis, Batavia's population jumped to over half a million.[4]

Much of the city's population growth during this period resulted from immigration from rural areas and overseas and was accommodated by the conversion of agricultural estates to urban uses, together with higher densities in the native *kampung* settlements. A concurrent decline in Batavia's high mortality rate was also a contributing factor. Based on its population growth in the late

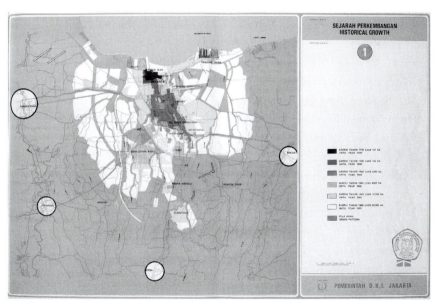

Figure 2.1. Growth of Jakarta from its origins in the seventeenth century (as Batavia) to the 1960s. (*Source*: DKI, Jakarta, Master Plan, 1965–1985)

1930s, and supported by a thriving local economy, Batavia could be described as a prosperous place in the early twentieth century, and with its ascent above rival Surabaya, the largest city in the Netherland Indies.

The spatial distribution of population within Batavia underscored the traditionally deep social divisions based on race, class and ethnicity. In turn, this reflected the uneven division of power in the colonial capital. In 1905, the European community represented just 9 per cent of the total population but occupied 50 per cent of the residential land, while the native population, which made up 71 per cent of Batavia's residents, crowded onto just 20 per cent of the city's land. That left the Chinese (and Arabs and Indians), who constituted 20 per cent of the population and occupied a more generous 30 per cent of the land.[5]

Colonial Policies

The role of Batavia as the leading port in the Netherland Indies in the eighteenth century and the seat of power of the omnipotent VOC, was lost to Surabaya, the eastern Java port, in the nineteenth century. However, the opening of a new deep water harbour at Tanjung Priok in 1886 and dramatic changes in government policy led to Batavia reclaiming dominance, and this increased between 1900 and 1940, making the colonial capital of Netherland Indies unquestionably the largest and most modern city in Southeast Asia. Given the improved economic condition of the city, there was expectation in the early decades of the twentieth century that this was the beginning of an era of renewed colonialism based on a new and enlightened approach to overseas governance, commonly referred to as the 'Ethical Policy'.

In a 1901 speech from the throne, the Dutch Queen Wilhelmina urged her government to take measures to raise the prosperity of the indigenous population of the colonies through an enlightened and interventionist approach. Queen Wilhelmina acknowledged that in the past the approach to the Netherland East Indies had been to exploit the colony's resources and its people, and that the Dutch owed something in return for the vast sums that had been withdrawn from these islands. One of the three pillars of the Ethical Policy was to help the indigenous population by increasing agricultural production though investing in infrastructure, particularly improved irrigation, and to reduce the out-migration from rural areas to cities. Improvements in education to create a better trained indigenous labour force, and greater local participation in governance were the other two components of this new policy.

Passage by the Dutch legislature of the Decentralization Law of 1903 represented the first manifestation of the Ethical Policy. This law set the legal framework for expanding local authority involvement in a vast new range of policy areas. Over the next two decades, other changes in the governance structure, especially in cities, provided both the indigenous Indonesians and the European and non-European populations a greater voice in colonial affairs. Within this milieu of enlightened colonial governance and expanded local autonomy, the idea of planning for the future development of the colonial city was introduced. Although the redistributive intent of the Ethical Policy was all but a dead letter in the public realm by the 1920s, it had helped to usher in a new colonial state 'that was firmly rooted and gave the outward appearance of having integrated the vast archipelago into one coherent whole'.[6]

Of all the colonial cities, Batavia benefited most from the policy changes initiated while the Ethical Policy was in force. This was a turnaround from the situation under previous policy initiatives. For example, the nineteenth-century Cultivation System had made East and Central Java the heartland of the Dutch plantation economy, while vast tracts in West Java (the immediate hinterland of Batavia) had been left out of cultivation. Surabaya became Java's leading city in terms of population in the nineteenth century. As late as 1929, it boasted greater imports and exports than Batavia. As a result of several factors, one being public investment in infrastructure and another accelerated private investment in the colonies after 1870, Batavia regained its dominance in economic activity on Java but not until the eve of World War II.[7] Between 1905 and 1921, as a direct outcome of the Ethical Policy, expenditure on public works and state enterprises rose from 20 per cent to 40 per cent of the colonial budget, while expenditure on military needs experienced a comparable drop. Although the economic recession in the aftermath of World War I forced colonial administrators to reduce funding for public improvements temporarily, overall investment under the Ethical Policy remained well above pre-1900 levels throughout the remainder of the Dutch regime and Batavia got the lion's share of this public investment.

The other important change in colonial Dutch policy was the creation of a modern bureaucratic state that initially administered a mercantilist economic policy but that after 1870 backed expansion of private investment, a move that encouraged large-scale migration from Europe to the Indies. The modern state, which had been initiated under the successive governorship of H.W. Daendels (1808–1811) and expanded in the English inter-regnum under Thomas Raffles (1811–1816), was consolidated following the success of the Dutch in the Java War of 1825–1830. After 1830, with the indigenous power base in Yogjakarta defeated, 'the Dutch could implement their policies in Java almost without restraint'.[8] The new Dutch governance system in the nineteenth century curtailed the authority of the Javanese district heads (*bupati*) and increased direct links between the colonial administration and the village heads. The position of assistant resident (or *controleur*) was established to handle day-to-day affairs with the indigenous local leaders. Although the number of assistant residents increased from 73 in 1825 to 190 in 1890, the overall European civil service corps remained just a few hundred. But backed by an army that grew from 10,000 troops in 1820 to more than 30,000 in the 1870s (an increase intended to enable the Dutch to respond to unrest on the Outer Islands, especially at Aceh in North Sumatra), the Dutch imposed system of governance was the unquestioned law of the land. Yet it is important to note that this was a dual system, with the indigenous population subject to traditional laws and governed by their own hereditary class of leaders. The government recognized in law three groups, Europeans, Foreign Orientals, and Natives, and each had its own governance system.[9]

Along with the establishment of a powerful centralized bureaucracy, the Dutch introduced a new economic system to solve the problem of inadequate tax revenue to support the costs of the expanded governance of the colonies. The Cultivation System, introduced in 1830 to replace the defunct VOC regulations, required the growing of export crops, such as coffee, sugar and indigo. Peasants had to provide land and labour for these crops in lieu of taxes. However, many peasants also had to pay taxes thus making the new system more, rather than less, burdensome than the previous one. The Cultivation System was made possible, in part, by accelerated growth in Java's population during the nineteenth century. Overall it proved a short-term economic boon for the colonial government but little benefit to the peasants. In his novel *Max Havelaar*, published in 1860, Multatuli (the pen name of Eduard Douwes Dekker) criticized the Cultivation System, revealing the abuses of local Javanese regents and the high level of colonial taxation imposed on the peasants. Criticism of the system mounted back home and when a Liberal Democratic government took power in The Netherlands in 1870, the system was abandoned. According to Day, the experiment of the Cultivation System demonstrated that 'the spirit of greed ruled the Dutch government as it had ruled the East India Company'.[10] Local government officials tended to worry more about yields and prices of crops since they, along with the land owners, and the local regents, all took a share (illicit as it was) of the proceeds.

The intent of the Agrarian Law of 1870 was to shift power from government to the landowners. While it was still possible for Europeans to lease rice fields from indigenous owners and to obtain waste land from the colonial government for cultivation, the 1870 law ended the forced labour of peasants on export crops. Although remnants of the Cultivation System continued after passage of the new law and even into the twentieth century, the privatization of agricultural production under what became known as the Liberal System increased production which in turn created expanded trade and processing. The Liberal System assumed that removal of restrictions on trade and production would stimulate private investment and that this was a better way to make the colony a viable business concern. Expanded processing and trade fuelled urban growth on Java, especially in Surabaya which was the leading port for the thriving sugar processing and export business, as well as the main Dutch naval base in the East Indies. In Surabaya, new machine workshops were established to manufacture and repair the equipment used in the sugar mills.[11]

While Surabaya thrived under the new economic system, Batavia benefited from the consolidation of centralized governance. Expanded government functions required new buildings and more space to accommodate them. This led to the transformation of Batavia from a compact walled fortress city of warehouses, shops and brokerage facilities into an open, more extensive urban area distinguished by large residential and government buildings on vast stretches of land. As Batavia expanded well beyond the confines of the early nineteenth-century port city, it became a place differentiated by ethnicity, class, and race as well as by its multiple urban functions. However, the most important change and the foundation for the colonial capital of the twentieth century was development of the European enclave of Weltevreden. While the old city centre, referred to as Kota (meaning 'city'), remained largely a commercial hub attached to port activities, Weltevreden emerged as the new centre of the colonial capital. Its development signalled the intention of the Dutch to elevate Batavia to a city on a par with the best in Europe.

Weltevreden in the Nineteenth Century

The suburban area south of old Batavia, commonly referred to as Weltevreden, was developed in the early 1800s by Governor General Herman Willem Daendels on the lands of a vast estate owned by a succession of wealthy predecessors. By the time the last Governor General of the VOC era, P.G. van Overstraten (1797–1801) had purchased it from his predecessor, Governor General P.P. van der Parra, it had become, as Heuken puts it, 'the official seat of the governor-general'. One of the motives for building in this area was, for the handful of colonial officials and business elite who could afford it, as an escape from the unhealthy confines of the old city. The initial migration to the suburbs of Batavia began in the aftermath of a devastating malaria epidemic in 1732.

Weltevreden functioned as far more than a palatial suburb. It was planned from the outset, according to Abdurrachman Surjomihardjo, as a place for the Dutch government to secure improved facilities. Its development more than doubled the land area of Batavia and created what by nineteenth-century standards was an extensive low-density city.

Daendels expedited the transfer of residential and governmental activities to the south of Batavia after 1811. He established a school of artillery in the southernmost district of Meester Cornelis, which later became the southern boundary of the city following annexation in the 1930s. He ordered the destruction of the original city wall to secure stones to build a new palace on the square in Weltevreden known as Waterloopein. This was one of a series of open spaces that gave a park-like character to this European enclave. Daendels's palace was situated on the north side of Waterloopein in the style of traditional Javanese palaces that would be situated similarly on the public square known as the *alun-alun*. Waterloopein accommodated not only the governor-general's palace (which later became a government office space) but also an elaborately ornamented Catholic Church, an army officers club (Concordia), the Freemason's Lodge and the High Court of Justice Building. Once the city walls were gone, the Chinese in the Glodok ghetto were no longer living on the outside but gradually merged into the traditional urban core. Following the infamous massacre in 1740, they had been ejected from the city proper and required to live in Glodok, between Kota and Weltevreden. Not until 1911 were they officially permitted to live outside the ghetto.[12]

Waterloopein was quickly overshadowed as the residential and cultural heart of the European community by a much larger public square, the Konigsplein. Occupying almost a square kilometre, it was shaped as a trapezoid rather than a square. While Daendels's palace was a two-storey colonnaded structure, the typical dwellings built around the Konigsplein were more compact single-storey residential buildings. The square's original function was as an exercise ground for government troops, a role it continued to play on and off throughout the nineteenth and early twentieth centuries. However it quickly became a space for both recreational and ceremonial functions for the expanding European enclave, a spacious civic centre ringed by two churches, the city's two leading hotels (Des Indes and Der Nederlanden), the town theatre (Schouwberg), and the main cultural institution of high European society, the Harmonie Club (built by Daendels) as well as many country houses. A racecourse appeared on the south-east section of the square during Raffles's administration in the early nineteenth century and remained there into the twentieth century.[13] Later in the nineteenth century a new governor's residence and new city hall were built on the south side. Adjacent to, but a block away from the square, were the main shopping streets and markets for the Europeans. Further to the south-east, in the Cikini area, was a botanical garden, a swimming pool, educational institutions, a hospital and an opium factory. Although the mansions and lush gardens of the most affluent surrounded the squares of Weltevreden, the European middle-class community extended southwards from Waterpoolein Square in a linear pattern along the post road and adjacent railway line into the areas known as Kramat, Salemba, Kebun Sirih, Prapaten and Pegangsaan.[14]

The development of the European community in Weltevreden more than doubled the urbanized area of Batavia. From the city's traditional harbour at Sunda

Kelapa to the north of the old town, the urbanized area extended southwards nearly 15 kilometres to Meester Cornelis (today called Jatinagara), following the post road and the railway that linked the port city to the mountain retreat of Bogor (Buitenzorf). Following the lead of Daendels, the Governors General typically conducted government business from a remote palace established there to provide an escape from the heat of the lowlands. The construction in the 1870s of the deep water port at Tanjung Priok, 9 kilometres east of the old town, served as another catalyst for urban expansion, in this case involving warehouses and other commercial facilities, as well as *kampungs* accommodating urban workers to the east along the flood prone waterfront.

The linear expansion of Batavia southwards from the commercial hub of the old town was facilitated by the establishment of a horse drawn tram in 1869. Converted to steam power in 1881, the tram was an essential means of transport beyond the old town area. It followed the road from old Batavia past Glodok, following the Molenveit canal southwards to Konigsplein to its terminus at the Hotel des Indes and the Harmonie Club. Visitors arriving at Tanjung Priok and making their way to Weltevreden's smart hotels experienced both the intensity of Batavia's commercial life in Kota and the seemingly more tranquil and expansive outer city. A visitor to the city in 1880 noted that 'everything in Batavia is spacious and airy'.[15] That would not have been possible to claim earlier in the century.

Figure 2.2. Steam tram in Batavia in front of the ironworks factory of Carl Schlieper, 1931. (*Source*: KIT Tropemuseum, Amsterdam)

The spaciousness of Batavia was not merely a function of the distance between the old city and Weltevreden but was accented in the layout of the suburban European settlement. The main residences of Weltevreden were colonial empire style single-storey structures set within spacious gardens. Even the public buildings surrounding the squares were designed to complement the wealthy residences and to blend into the domestic landscape. Life in Weltevreden centred on these residences or on the private clubs frequented by residents. Consequently, 'there was little that was public except street life. Even areas of the new town squares, the Konigsplein and Waterlooplein, were usurped by a European club in the former case, and by the activities of the army in the latter case'.[16]

There were sections in Weltevreden that accommodated a smattering of native and non-European elites, places such as Kebun Sirih, Tanah Abang and Senen. Class, not race, was what distinguished Weltevreden from the rest of Batavia.[17] But this was not by design. The initial development of the European settlements in Weltevreden did not follow a plan *per se*. Nevertheless, the designation of Konigsplein and Waterlooplein as public squares ringed by streets where government, civic and private residential structures were carefully positioned gave an orderliness and cohesiveness to the area that would suggest that planning was involved. In fact it was not until after 1900, with the development of a planned European enclave in Menteng south of Kebun Sirih, that a comprehensive neighbourhood design would be used to construct a new piece of the city. Although the development of planned residential suburbs in Batavia after 1900 were principally due to private initiatives, they were made possible by expanded local government functions that supported systematic urban development

What took place between 1900 and 1930, and largely within the precincts of Weltevreden, was the creation of a large European enclave within Batavia, not only detached from the native community (which had always been the case) but one that functioned almost as a city within the city to an extent not possible earlier in Batavia's development. As Furnivall put it,

In 1900 the European community was detached from native life but had no complete independent life; by 1930 it lived within its own world, with its own cultural interests and with its trade unions and labour politics, alongside, but wholly separate from the native world.[18]

Old Batavia was 'Downtown' whereas the European enclave in Weltevreden was referred to as 'Uptown'. The differences were quite stark. According to a description by a visitor to old Batavia in 1924,

One has not only gone down, but also gone back. One has gone back to the canals and the small streets with old facades of the past, where the simple citizens lived in their small town story houses with high roofs according to the old Dutch ways... Slowly one went uptown... The dignified people went to live in homes according to the Indies building trend, homes of one story with long gardens. The new city of Batavia became like one large park, with squares, lanes, lawns and forest-like gardens.[19]

In 1900, there was but a handful of social and cultural institutions to support the European community. By 1930, there were 35 daily newspapers, 54 weeklies and 91 monthly magazines and no fewer than 100 cultural, economic and political societies to support Batavia's expanded European world.[20]

Race Identity in the Colonial City

The creation of a European-styled city within Batavia needs to be understood within the larger context of the Dutch imposed system of racial separation and stratification that defined all levels of interactions. As Fasseur contends, 'racial classification was the cornerstone of the colonial administration'. What Fasseur suggests is that the system introduced in the nineteenth century was at least respectful of differences between European and indigenous institutions. Yet in the early 1900s, this system became the rationale for inequities that engendered intense resentment against the colonial regime. The origins of separate policies and judicial practices for Europeans and indigenous groups can be traced first to Daendels's administration from 1808 to 1811, but was reinforced under Thomas Raffles's governorship from 1811 to 1816. Raffles aspired to ensure fair treatment for indigenous people through a dual judicial system that recognized the importance of local laws, or *adat*. Well into the twentieth century, the progressive wing of the legal community in The Netherlands, based at the University of Leiden, supported the retention of *adat* law for indigenous people, and fought efforts to create a unitary system.[21]

The *Regeerrumreglement* of 1854 formally created the racial classification system which distinguished Europeans (and Indonesian Christians) from natives (and other foreign Orientals). The system became more fine grained and complex when in 1899, owing to international political pressures, the colonial government put Japanese on a par with Europeans, even though within Batavia (and other Netherland Indies cities) they occupied some of the more menial occupations (such as hairdressers and prostitutes). Batavia's Chinese community was outraged by this act which kept them outside the favoured European system, especially given their substantially greater role within the colonial economic system. This race-based system necessitated wholly separate governance systems for the indigenous communities, for the extensive Chinese community in and around urban areas, and non-Chinese Asians (including the Arabs and Bengalis). After 1913, non-Europeans became eligible for nearly all offices in the colonial administration and the army, but a three-tiered structure ensured that non-Europeans occupied the lowest rungs.[22]

Throughout the early 1900s, however, there was a push to reform the governance system. The Sonneveld Committee set up by the Dutch government in 1919 called for the elimination of the racial classification system through repeal of Article 109 of the 1854 Act. The idea was to replace the racial system with one of nationality, recognizing Dutch as one group and non-Dutch subjects as the other. But there was no agreement on this or any other reform despite a growing sentiment that 'equal treatment of all races is a principle that must find unconditional application'. The problem was that even the reformers were not prepared to abandon completely all the distinctions that had grown into the system over the previous century.[23] Even in the area of planning, there were arguments favouring retention of the racial classification system which were premised on the need for reform. Not until Article 27 of the Indonesian constitution of 1945 was the racial classification system eliminated, while for Batavia's Chinese community, a dual system remained in force long after that.

Political Reform, Municipal Authority and the Decentralization Law

When Queen Wilhelmina stated in 1901 that the Dutch owed their colonies a 'debt of honour', it set in motion an era of reform of relations between the indigenous population and the colonial administration. There is considerable debate concerning the motives behind the Ethical Policy as it was carried out in the colonies, although there is little doubt that the Queen's view reflected a prevailing sentiment in Dutch society that a more proactive government should support basic human development for those who had contributed so much to the prosperity of The Netherlands for nearly three centuries. According to historian Frances Gouda, the Dutch set out on a mission to govern with greater sensitivity and political skill than other imperial powers in Asia. The uniqueness of Dutch colonial policy in the twentieth century was how much attention was devoted to understanding and sustaining indigenous culture and customs. Led by the University of Leiden law faculty which studied and supported preservation of indigenous *adat* law, the proponents of the Ethical Policy sought to demonstrate that it was able 'to administer its empire with more wisdom and discretion than other colonizing powers'. Considered from another vantage point, Anderson suggests that the Ethical Policy was 'a huge extension of the state apparatus deep into the native society and a proliferation of its functions' in order to sustain the abundant revenue stream flowing from state enterprises.[24]

But as the Dutch government advanced its idealistic notion of colonial administration, it was contending with an emerging nationalist movement, beginning with the formation of several non-political organizations, *Boedi Oetomo* and *Saraket Islam* and soon a decidedly political movement organized initially around the communist party and later a nationalist party. The study of indigenous cultures became a key facet of the state's policing strategy, thereby corrupting the original intentions of the Ethical Policy. By the 1920s, the idealism of the Ethical Policy was:

overshadowed by a deep-seated fear of Indonesian nationalism, which tended to deflect the Ethical Policy's honorable intentions of creating more schools for Indonesians, delivering better health care, and bringing about political decentralization.[25]

In concert with its Ethical Policy, the Dutch government passed a landmark law to grant increased autonomy to municipalities. The Decentralization Law of 1903 made possible the formation of municipal corporations in Java, albeit with limited authority. The municipality (*gemeente*) was overseen by an appointed assistant resident and a local council. Regulations required a European majority on the municipal council, but there was representation by non-official Europeans, the indigenous population and foreign 'Orientals' (which basically meant Chinese). The expanded functions of the local government were rather sweeping in nature, including: provision and maintenance of roads, parks, cemeteries, markets and slaughterhouses, fire-fighting, public health, transport, street lighting, housing, water, waste disposal, and even site preparation for new urban areas. The most serious limitation on local intervention initially was the reluctance of the new city managers to embrace fully all the duties that the new law granted them, since to do so necessitated increasing local taxes to pay for these services.

The new local governance system took effect in 1905. One of the earliest initiatives of the new municipal council was to take a more aggressive role in the urban development process. A law passed by the Batavia Municipal Council on 5 June 1909 established the first codified 'regulations for building and demolitions in the municipality of Batavia'. The assistant resident position was replaced in 1916 by a mayor (*burgemeester*) drawn from local leadership, and the following year, the local council moved from an appointed to an elected basis. This was not intended to endorse universal suffrage, since voting was limited to those who had a satisfactory knowledge of Dutch and who paid a minimum income tax. Even those who met these conditions still could only vote for candidates from their own nationality. But it was during this first phase of expanded local authority that the city undertook systematic expansion of residential areas through the purchase of land and creation of a development corporation. The native population participated in the expanded governance system through positions in the civil service. Overall, there were about 250,000 natives on the state payroll in 1928, representing 90 per cent of the workforce. A small portion of this group was the educated Indonesians, many of whom assumed leadership positions in an independent Indonesia. While committed to independence, some never really broke with the policies and practices of their colonial mentors. Institutional continuities between the Dutch colonial and Indonesian government were commonplace.[26]

Local authority increased further through two subsequent amendments to the local government act. A 1922 reform law transformed the municipalities of Java from oversight by the colonial administration to fully independent status (*sladsgemeente*). A 1926 law allowed for creation of an executive council (*college van wethonders*) in addition to the existing legislative council (*gemeeteraad*), obviously in response to the expanded functions of the local government and the need of the mayor for a non-elected advisory body. According to Dutch legal standards, powers not explicitly granted to the local government were retained by the central government. But by the mid-1920s, Batavia was under the provincial government rather than the central government.[27]

Planning Batavia in the Early Twentieth Century

Under the 1909 'regulations for building and demolitions in the municipality of Batavia' permits were issued through the Municipal Works Department for all new construction, demolition or movement of structures. Subdivision and building lines were set by the Council itself. Later the same year the functions of the Municipal Works Department were expanded to include preparation of building designs and codification of acceptable building methods.

One of the new recruits to this office was a 28 year old architect, Frans Johan Louwens Ghijsels, recently arrived from Amsterdam with his new wife. He was, in fact, returning to his birthplace, having been born in Tulung Agung in East Java in 1881. He studied at the Technical University of Delft and among his peers were several other architects who later made significant contributions to planning and urban development in the Netherland Indies, such as Henri Maclaine Pont and his good friend Thomas Karsten (who will be discussed more fully later).

While 'pure architecture' was just beginning to emerge from the constraints of architects' basic training in civil engineering, no doubt that foundation in civil engineering enabled young Dutch architects like Ghijsels and Karsten to appreciate the necessity of planning on the larger canvas of the city scale. The Public Works Department was influenced, and at several junctures, led in the early twentieth century by members of the Dutch Social Democratic Party, virtually all trained at the Technical University of Delft. According to van Doorn, the development agenda of these engineers was progressive and

the indigenous population did interest them as a matter of care, but in a round-about way... Like all technocrats, these civil engineers were wholly concerned with the application of science in practice, with technical innovation and rationalization...They had a

Figure 2.3. Architect and planner, Johan Ghijsels whose practice contributed to Batavia's planning in the early twentieth century.
(*Source*: R.W. Heringa)

Figure 2.4. The staff of Batavia's municipal works department indicating the mix of European and Indonesian technicians. Ghijsels is seated third from the left.
(*Source*: R.W. Heringa)

pronounced admiration for productivity and for rationalization and planning springing from a dislike of traditional ways and capitalistic waste. The colonial system where engineers and planners were free to follow their own fancies offered these technocratic tendencies considerable scope.[28]

Ghijsels spent his first two years in Batavia in the Municipal Works Department before shifting in 1913 to the architectural division of the provincial government's

Department of Public Works. Ever since the administration of Daendels in the early nineteenth century, the Department of Public Works had been responsible for all government controlled construction. In 1909, they appointed an architect/engineer, Simon Snuyf, to head the architectural division to which Ghijsels was later assigned. Its primary task was to prepare building designs based on standardized designs that became the stock in trade of this agency. Ghijsels left the public works agency in 1916 to establish his own consulting firm, *Algemeen Ingenieurs en Architectenbureau* (General Engineering and Architecture Bureau, or AIA).[29]

Through his private practice, Ghijsels designed homes for the Municipality of Batavia (1918), the Menteng Property Company (1920–1921), for the state railway workers' community of Bukit Duri Manggarai (1918), coolie housing for the railway company (1919–1920) and for members of the Indo-Eurasian Association (1923) who had modest incomes. As Ghijsels wrote about the Indo-Eurasian Association commission, 'the living conditions of lowly civil servant or employee are poor. And if it [his house designs] can be proved to be possible, it could bring about a complete revolution. I shall use all my powers'.[30]

In 1916, the consulting firm established by Thomas Karsten developed a master plan for Semarang, by all accounts the first modern urban plan in Indonesia. Ghijsels helped to prepare plans for Bandung and Batavia in 1917 and 1918, respectively. The impetus for these latter two plans was the acknowledged need to establish a spatial framework for new residential development, which in the case of Batavia was already underway in Gondangdia, Menteng and the

Figure 2.5. The Freemason's Lodge at the Burgemeester Bischopsplein in Batavia in 1925, later to serve as the offices of Indonesia's National Development Planning Board (BAPPENAS). (*Source*: KIT Tropemuseum, Amsterdam.)

adjacent community of Meester Cornelis. Ghijsels prepared a portion of the plan for Menteng (discussed below) and designed a number of houses that were built there.[31]

The Batavia plan of 1918, which was finalized in 1921, was based on guidelines prepared by F.J. Kubatz, who was Director of the Municipal Department of Land and Housing in Batavia. Kubatz's plan altered the original plan of the larger area known as New Gondangdia (which included Menteng), and incorporated a new drainage canal (now Jalan Mohammad Amin) which served as a border between these two areas. The Kubatz plan modified the form of the original large square in Menteng in the original Mooijen design and created the smaller neighbourhood park, Burgermeester Bisschopplein (now Taman Suropati). The revised Menteng

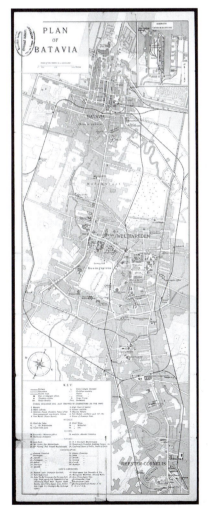

Figure 2.6. Plan of Batavia, 1910.
(*Source*: KIT Tropemuseum, Amsterdam)

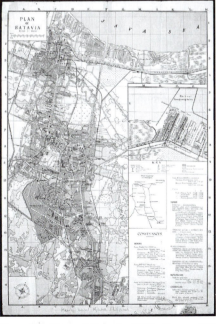

Figure 2.7. Plan of Batavia, 1930. (*Source*: KIT Tropemuseum, Amsterdam)

plan was considered superior to the original Gondangdia scheme in its design and character. According to a Batavian developer, G.E. Jobst,

New Gondangdia [was] cobbled together by incompetents, where no mortal can find his way [whereas] New Menteng has become an unusually beautiful residential district.[32]

This was due not only to the good circulation plan but also because it included only substantial houses.

The city was already prepared to meet the infrastructure needs of the expanding European residential community. In 1918, Batavia had formed the Local Water Supply Enterprise of Batavia (*Water Leidingen Bedriff van Batavia*) to manage a piped water distribution system that brought 89 litres per second of fresh clean water from nine artesian wells in the Ciomas-Ciburial-Bogor area south of the city to the European and other foreign communities. The local water enterprise extended the piped water system to some *kampungs*, particularly after the government agreed to fund part of a limited *kampung* improvement programme beginning in 1927. But the European residents received four times the amount of water delivered to native residents.[33]

The authority of the local administration to guide development of the city increased the legitimacy of the planners during the 1920s. From a planning standpoint, the most important provision of the 1926 law was that it gave preference to local authorities over third parties to acquire government land if they showed, through a structure plan (*geraamte plan*), that the land was needed for housing. This gave municipalities the impetus for planning and was 'the most important legal regulation on which the pre-war town planning activity was based'.[34] The new authority of local government not only expanded the planning function but led to improved services, especially in the European settlements.

By the mid-1920s there also was a growing Indonesianization of the local bureaucracy, with 'a small Indonesian elite ... in the municipal councils'. In Batavia, this introduced voices of dissent to the European orientation of public expenditure, and to the neglect of the needs of native *kampungs*. But this local government involvement did little to change local public policy which was to avoid any interference, or investment, in the indigenous areas.[35] Based on the 1907 law, the municipal administration did not have jurisdiction in the native *kampungs*, even those located within the municipal boundaries. Consequently, the 1907 act did not abrogate the policy of non-interference in native affairs that had been set forth in the Government Regulation (*Regeerings Reglement*) of 1854 (Article 75). That act had officially separated European and non-European populations in the colony and made the affairs in the *kampungs* the exclusive responsibility of native officials.[36] Indigenous communities were subject to traditional law (*adat*) administered through the village head. An attempt had been made to eliminate this in the constitutional reform of 1854, but it failed. Also outside the governance of the city were the extensive private landed estates (*particuliere landerijen*) that made up the majority of agricultural lands surrounding Batavia. In 1901, there were 304 private estates, 101 owned by Europeans and the rest owned largely by Chinese officials under the separate system of administration. These estates overall accounted for 800,000 peasant holdings.[37]

The Chinese Community of Batavia

The huge economic power of the Chinese community in Batavia, in contrast to that of the so-called native population, was both a creation of the Dutch governance system and a continuing challenge to that system. Under the racially-based Dutch governance structure in the Netherland Indies, the Chinese community was not only separated from Europeans but also from the indigenous population. The race-based system was hierarchical and stratified, with Europeans at the top, and separate branches below for the indigenous population (*Inlandsch Bestuur*) and for the non-native, non-European communities consisting of Arabs, Moors, Bengalis and Chinese grouped under the umbrella designation, *Bestuur voor Vreemde Oosterlingen*. As the largest of the non-native, non-European community, the Chinese community had its own system of local governance, the *Chineesch Bestuur*. Like all native and non-native groups, the Chinese had headsmen drawn from the community who were answerable to the colonial government for ensuring that Dutch policies were followed and taxes collected. The Chinese officials, known as *Kapitan Cina*, were especially important since they were responsible for governing both the largest and most affluent group. In the nineteenth century, the Chinese managed key segments of the agricultural system, especially the opium trade, which brought substantial revenues into the colonial coffers.[38] The largest proportion of Batavia's revenues came from land taxes and the Chinese were the largest land holding group. Although shifting economic policies undermined the advantageous position of the Chinese, their extensive land holdings and firm base in the urban economy helped to mitigate the negative effects of losing a monopoly position.[39]

The Chinese involvement in land in the Batavia regency was the foundation of their powerful economic position. In 1910, they controlled approximately 40 per cent of all private lands, although a policy of the Dutch government to purchase these lands reduced their holdings to only about 10 per cent by 1920.[40] The Chinese accumulation of land in Batavia had begun in the seventeenth century, and when Governor General Daendels initiated public land sales to fill the empty government coffers between 1809 and 1811, it was the Chinese who bought up the largest share of the offerings. By 1836, 83 of the 187 private estates in the Batavia regency were owned by Chinese. Although the Agrarian Law of 1870 closed off the opportunity for non-natives to purchase property, the Chinese land owners shifted their holdings into companies that operated outside the restrictions of the law and this enabled them to retain a substantial share of the land. And on these lands they grew various crops, but largely rice, for local consumption; they employed native labourers and tenants to cultivate the land and bring them profits. The move by the Dutch government in the early 1900s to reduce the amount of private land was initially aimed at the extensive holdings of the British, and in three separate purchases in 1906, 1910 and 1918, the influence of private British land owners was virtually eliminated. However, the plan to purchase lands in Tangerang and Meester Cornelis which were owned by the Chinese was 'to facilitate city development, where space was needed for transportation networks, railways, roads, bridges and an irrigation system'. Between 1912 and 1930, the Dutch government invested over 81 million guilders to repurchase 911,140 *bouws* (210,500 hectares) of private land.[41]

While there were Chinese communities scattered throughout the colony, the largest were in the cities of Batavia, Semarang and Surabaya. The best available estimates indicate that there were approximately 92,520 Chinese within the greater Batavia region, with more living outside the city than within it in 1905. Roughly one-third of this population, or 28,000, lived inside Batavia, mostly within the Glodok area. By 1920, the Batavia area Chinese population had grown to 116,525.[42] When the Europeans moved the major government institutions and their primary residential functions to Weltevreden in the nineteenth century, the predominantly commercially-based Chinese population expanded into the space that was vacated, and created its own institutional base, including Chinese temples, schools, hospitals, offices for Chinese organizations, and a great variety of business establishments.[43]

But the movements of the Chinese were closely regulated by a passport system that had been set up in 1835 which not only ensured strict residential segregation but made it possible to know who was coming and going from the community. A similar system operated within the native community. The Chinese officers working for the colonial government were responsible for enforcing the system, but technically were not employed by the Dutch since they received no remuneration. These officers were typically wealthy individuals whose income derived from their agricultural holdings or businesses in Glodok, and they served for indeterminate terms. From 1837 to the end of the colonial regime in the early 1940s, there were only five different 'majors' heading the Batavia Chinese community. Tio Tek Ho served as *kapitan cina* from 1896 to 1908, and the last, Khouw Kim An, served from 1910 to 1918 and then again from 1927 until the end of the system under the Japanese occupation in 1942.[44]

One reason for the time gaps in the ward master service in the early twentieth century was due to changing notions of colonial governance, and an aborted move to eliminate the separate system of headman rule in favour of a more unitary system.[45] Even when Batavia secured its own local legislative body under the 1907 municipal government ordinance, the Chinese community was still under the direction of the Chinese officers and a Chinese Council (*Kong Koan*). The Chinese Council functioned as the administrative arm of the officer system, handling all day-to-day matters in the Chinese community. It provided schooling for the Chinese poor and managed orphanages, charities, and mass ceremonies. It administered Chinese properties, such as farm lands, cemeteries, hospitals and temples, and handled the funds generated by these assets. At one point, the Chinese Council owned fourteen private estates in the Batavia region.[46] Because of the extent of its financial dealings within the community, the idea of the Chinese Council coming under European control was fiercely resisted and the Dutch never tried to implement a takeover.

The experiment with a system of local administration in the 1920s that eliminated the functions of the Chinese officers proved a failure. The plan was to replace the appointed officers with a system of ward masters directly in the employ of Batavia's government. The ward master system (*wijkbestuur*) was an attempt to abandon the segregation system that had been in place since 1828 which for the Chinese had provided for one ward master for every twenty-five households in a community. Rather than being recompensed with a percentage of the local tax revenues that they helped to collect as well as a compulsory fee for providing a night watch, the new ward masters would receive a salary from the municipal government. At the time the new system was being considered, there were seventy-four native, twenty-five Chinese and three Arab ward masters in Batavia. The Arab community protested the proposed new system citing that they would not accept anyone except a member of the Arab community as a ward master, which would not be guaranteed under the new system. In 1929, the Dutch government announced that they were going to eliminate the officer system throughout Java and Madura except for Batavia, and only in Batavia would the former system be preserved. In fact Khouw Kim An and his fellow officers had already been restored to their former positions in 1927.[47]

When the Japanese invaded the Netherland Indies, Khouw Kim An was put into a prison camp where he died in 1945.[48] After Independence, and under pressure from the national government, the Chinese Council was forced to sell its land holding to the city government in 1953 under provisions of Law 9/1953 entitled 'Necessity to Return the Private Land Properties to the Government'. This confiscation of Chinese private lands eliminated the financial foundation of the Chinese Council and the group dissolved after 1955.[49]

According to Nas, the growing power of Europeans in local affairs through greater local administrative autonomy from the Dutch government also led to a widening of their areas of intervention, not just in general local administration but also in taking on public improvements that had previously been outside the realm of the colonial government. One area of increased concern was housing conditions in the urban *kampungs*.

They [Europeans] more and more became conscious of the danger to their own health caused by the unsanitary conditions in the Indonesian villages (*inlandse gemeenten*) which were situated within the limits of their municipality, but which remained outside municipal jurisdiction.[50]

After 1925, the municipal governments in Java could undertake physical improvements in the *kampungs* within their boundaries, but only the East Java cities of Malang and Surabaya exercised this prerogative. The displacement of *kampungs* in Batavia was less systematic. In part this was a consequence of the 1911 law that allowed the Chinese to live outside Glodok. It was also as a result of development of new residential areas where *kampungs* previously existed but where residential densities were low enough to accommodate expansion. The absence of a full scale municipally-backed *kampung* improvement programme in Batavia, despite the stated intention of the Ethical Policy to address the welfare of the native population in crowded *kampungs*, was in part an example of the continuing indifference of the European dominated local government to local needs outside their own community. But it was also a matter of financial priorities, since there were insufficient local funds to meet the expanded local government responsibilities. Public funds went to meet the Europeans' demands for street improvements for the increasingly ubiquitous automobile and services for newly developed residential areas. As a result municipal involvement in *kampung* improvements did not begin in Batavia until 1938 at which time a *kampung* upgrading programme involved both municipal and central government Public Works Departments.[51]

The Planned Community in Menteng

The planned residential community of Menteng was one place where increased municipal infrastructure investment was targeted. Developed in response to the demand for new, well-designed housing to serve the expanding European middle class, Menteng was the most ambitious residential planning project between 1910 and 1939. As Thomas Karsten, referring to the development of Menteng and several smaller but equally fashionable residential subdivisions, noted in a 1938 memorandum to the colonial government, 'land development and the building trade have developed to such an extent that, except for temporary dislocation owing to unforeseen economic fluctuations, a normal and satisfactory provision for the housing needs of the well-to-do seems assured...'. He went on to point out that

real estate offices and the building trade have also turned their attention to the needs of the upper middle class – particularly those of the Europeans, but moreover those of the small category categories of the other population groups in that class [i.e. natives and foreign orientals, mostly Chinese].[52]

The initial development of Menteng took place between 1910 and 1918, based on a plan by Dutch architect, P.A.J. Mooijen, who had been practicing in Batavia since 1903. Mooijen was a member of a development group established by the

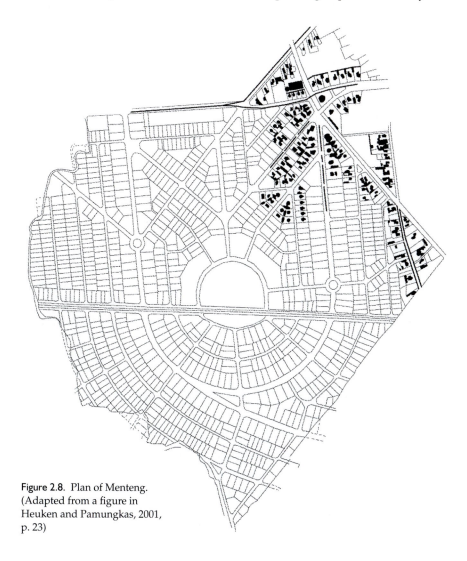

Figure 2.8. Plan of Menteng. (Adapted from a figure in Heuken and Pamungkas, 2001, p. 23)

Batavia city government, the *Commisie van toesicht op het Geheer van het Land Menteng*, which was responsible for planning and developing the larger area of Gondangdia *(Nieuw Gondangdia)* of which Menteng was the centrepiece.

The land for Menteng, which had been a privately owned estate of 73 hectares with 3,562 peasant inhabitants in the 1890s, was situated just south of the existing Kebun Sirih neighbourhood. Once it was evident that the city could absorb a significant new supply of middle-class housing, and to prevent illegal development from encroaching on this area, the city purchased the land and created the technical commission to oversee its development. Although Menteng was originally intended to be an exclusive community, there were, in fact, many modest houses built around its edges, perhaps to serve as a buffer, but also ensuring occupancy by a cross section of the European community of Batavia.[53]

Mooijen's original plan bore a striking resemblance to the garden city model of the English reformer Ebenezer Howard, in that it combined wide cross-cutting boulevards with concentric rings of streets and a central public square. At the northern entrance to the planned community, he designed an elaborate civic structure, the Art Center (Gedung Kunstkring), which became the cultural centre of early twentieth-century Batavia. Mooijen approached his architectural commissions in Menteng with an eye to bringing art to urban form. In fact, he was

Figure 2.9. Art Center (Kunstkring), the landmark Menteng structure designed by Mooijen. (*Photo*: author)

first secretary, and then president (1910) of the Bataviasche Kunstkring which was created to advance interest in the visual/plastic and decorative arts. The Gedung Kunstkring was made possible through the donation of the land by one of the construction companies that participated in building the neighbourhood. Through rental of the lower floor to commercial uses, the cultural centre generated a cash flow for its operations.[54]

Although planning for Menteng began in 1910, it was not until 1912 that Mooijen's revised plan was officially unveiled. From the outset, one key difference between the plan for Menteng and the garden city model was that the Batavia community was not intended to be a freestanding, self-contained place, but to link up with adjacent residential areas. For example, the broad boulevard (currently named Imam Bonjul) that bisected the community adjacent to the central square, connected Menteng to the adjacent Tanah Abang (with its important market place) to the west and Meester Cornelis to the east. Also the wide street, originally known as Jalan Jawa (now Jalan Cokroaminoto) was to serve as a north-south connector from Kebun Sirih adjacent to the Konigsplein to the southern fringe of Batavia. This southern boundary was marked by the line of a flood (*banjir*) canal which was included in the 1918 Batavia city plan and constructed in 1919.

Mooijen's plan was extensively modified by F.J. Kubatz as part of the city's next overall development plan. In the Kubatz plan, the street pattern was changed, and a small lake (Lake Lembang) was added to the east of the central park area, originally named Bishops Park (Bisschooplein) after G.J. Bishop who served as mayor of the city from 1916 to 1920. The Kubatz plan seems to have been the final say, since it accurately portrays the area as it developed during the 1920s and 1930s. Architects other than Mooijen and Kubatz contributed to the emerging character of the area through noteworthy structures. In addition to his house designs, Ghijsels designed the Paulus Church and the adjacent Logegebouw, which was the office of the *burgemester*. This office later served and continues to serve as the offices of Indonesia's powerful national development planning board (BAPPENAS). One of Ghijsels's colleagues in the AIA, architect J.F.L. Blankenberg, designed some of the more substantial residences in Menteng between 1926 to 1939 (after Ghijsel had returned to the Netherlands), including the home of the owner of Wallenstein, Krausse and Company; this eventually became (and still remains) the residence of the US Ambassador to Indonesia. He also designed the home of the Governor of Jakarta, and several lavish residences for local businessmen along Jalan Imam Bonjul. Several of these fashionable residences eventually became public places, including one that now houses the National Proclamation Museum.[55]

Not only in size but also in style, Menteng was the most important neighbourhood in the city and introduced into the urban landscape a diversity of traditional and modern structures that changed and enhanced the look of the city. Traditional Indisch style one-storey villas were intermingled with two-storey structures. There were three types of small villas, the Tosari, the Sumenep, and the Madura, all of which were designed with facilities to accommodate automobiles and house servants but were kept under 500 square metres. There was a sprinkling of Art Deco style houses and also innovative roof designs, including widespread use of the mansard roof.[56]

Menteng provided a continuous stream of commissions for the growing cadre of design and planning firms that had set up shop in the city. There were several large consulting firms in Batavia and other key cities that appeared after 1909 and functioned carrying out both design and construction. These included M.J. Hulswit, A.A. Fermont and Eduard Cuypers, Biezeveld and Mooijen, Bakker and Meyboom, and Ghijsels' 'trendsetting' AIA, all operating in Batavia; Karsten, Lutjens, Toussaint, and Henri Maclaine Pont with offices in Semarang, and C.P. Schoemaker and Associates the leading firm in Bandung.[57]

The prestige of Menteng within the context of colonial Batavia would eventually be transferred to the indigenous urban elite of Jakarta in the post-colonial period. Whereas many emblems of the colonial past were shunned, Menteng as a neighbourhood of prestige persisted. It provided a residential anchor for the central core of the city that remarkably withstood the pressures of commercial encroachment in later years. This should be attributed, in good measure, to the quality of the community's original plan, which effectively incorporated elements of interconnectedness with adjacent areas while preserving the area's spatial integrity through an ingenious system of streets and boulevards and contiguous structures that conformed to that system. Although escalating city centre land values exerted pressures on the edges of Menteng to convert to more intensive non-residential uses in later years, the core of the community became the focus of preservationists and re-greening advocates in the 1990s. The community plan of Menteng, and the lifestyle that it was intended to provide, endured as the city around it changed drastically.

Kampungs in the Colonial Capital

The development of new residential areas for the middle class through formal planning was not the only change underway in the urban landscape of twentieth-century Batavia. The rapid growth of the city from 1900 to 1940 also included the proliferation of informal settlements, often adjacent to new residential clusters. The development of new neighbourhoods produced an intensification of the distinctions between the European, Chinese, and native communities that had been less noticeable in old Batavia. The formal planning of new residential settlements for the affluent also affected the city's traditional informal settlement system of *kampungs* which previously existed outside the city (and outside Dutch regulations) but which became increasingly drawn, legally and functionally, into the city. The meaning of *kampung* is quite literally 'camp' and is applied typically only to native residential clusters. In the minds of the Dutch authorities, the *kampung* represented a lower-class urban settlement with the following attributes: a lack of modern amenities such as water and sewer connections or electricity; land relationships which were governed by traditional law or *adapt*; buildings which relied on informal construction methods (predominantly using bamboo); very high density development; and an intermingling of homes and workplaces. Further, *kampung* communities tended to be distinguished on the basis of race and ethnicity rather than class.[58]

Clustered along the edges of Batavia and comprising largely agricultural workers, these native communities were increasingly drawn into the urban orbit in the early twentieth century while retaining a strong link to their agricultural origins. Marcussen suggests that there were three distinct periods of transformation of *kampungs* in Jakarta, one beginning in the early 1900s when large areas were cleared to make way for new urban development (such as Menteng), and when the problems of sanitation and services for *kampung* residents were first given serious attention. The second phase occurred after Independence when large sections of traditional *kampungs* were added to the new Jakarta municipality, and all increased in size and density to accommodate mass migration from rural areas. The third period was after 1965 when the *kampungs* were integrated into the New Order's comprehensive administrative and socio-political system, and this included a massive programme of *kampung* improvement to bring a higher level of services to the vast majority of the city's residents.[59]

A fourth stage in *kampung* development may be added to Marcussen's periodization, a stage which runs from the late 1980s to 2000. This was the period when the scale of *kampung* removal throughout the metropolitan area accelerated, a direct result of an aggressive private redevelopment process that sought to usher in the modern metropolis full blown.

The 1910s and 1920s witnessed the first large-scale *kampung* displacements, when villagers were forced to move to accommodate residential expansion in the Weltevreden area, and when the emancipation of the Chinese in 1911 enabled that group to live legally outside the Glodok ghetto and to use their economic resources to secure lands that were occupied by *kampungs*. Also, there is some evidence that wealthy natives were buying up *kampung* lands from their poorer neighbours in anticipation of future land-use changes.[60] The net result was increased population densities in those *kampungs* not affected by urban expansion. In fact those beyond the areas of pre-1940 urban development, such as Kebun Kacang located south-west of Weltevreden, seemed to benefit from somewhat better circumstances.

Here the residents still functioned largely as an agricultural unit on the edge of an urban complex, and profited from the urban prosperity that had developed near their modest community. The expansion of the city would later draw Kebun Kacang into its web; first to accommodate an overflow of poor displaced from other rural areas and then as a slum area which was removed to make way for expanding commercial activities.[61]

Kampungs and Urban Reform

Consistent with the spirit of the Ethical Policy, the substandard conditions in most urban *kampungs*, especially unhealthy housing conditions, led to housing reform centred in the larger Netherland Indies cities, beginning in Semarang in Central Java and spreading to Batavia and elsewhere.[62] One result of the housing reform movement was a heightened sensitivity to the problems of the *kampungs* in general. After 1915, it was customary for visits by top colonial officials from the home country to stop in at least one 'bad *kampung*'. Data to assess health conditions in urban areas were just beginning to be collected at that time, but there was a general sense that diseases related to the environmental conditions in certain urban areas were a factor in public health. Mortality levels in Batavia were high in the early 1900s, averaging about 58 deaths per 1000 inhabitants from 1903 to 1911. Infant mortality (especially among those under one year old) was especially high.[63]

Henry Freek Tillema, a civic-minded pharmacist and philanthropist based in Semarang, was pivotal in increasing interest in urban health problems in the Netherland Indies. Building on a 1909 investigation of sanitary conditions in Semarang by K. Westerveld, a physician and member of the city council, Tillema compiled a six volume study of public health in the colony, entitled *Kromoblanda*, which was released in instalments between 1914 and 1923. What he added to the pioneering work of Westerveld was more data, more compelling illustrations of the many troubled urban districts, and a full-blown argument favouring systematic infrastructure improvements and better planning to create liveable places. Tillema was appointed to Semarang's city council in 1910 and then won election to that body in 1911 on a pro-public health platform. He was especially concerned about the quality of urban housing and in 1913 wrote a treatise entitled *On the Subject of Housing and Accommodation, About Building Construction, Home and Garden*. He favoured increased local authority and better planning to address these problems. But his major writing on these subjects came after he left the Netherland Indies in 1914, returning only for a brief visit in 1924 to check on local conditions. According to Joost Cote, Tillema's passion for improved public health did not lessen despite no longer being in the Netherland Indies. Yet his concerns about urban housing were coloured by a view of the indigenous society as defective and helpless and in need of outside intervention. This view is emphasized in his later writings where his arguments for housing improvements shifted from reforming native housing as a social objective to reform as a necessary step to ensure the survival of colonialism. He actually wanted to expand colonial rule but to do so through more enlightened social policies. Tillema lived until 1952 and thus witnessed the colonial system he so fully embraced give way to an independent national government.[64]

He energetically pushed his research on *kampung* conditions in Semarang to convince the colonial government that it was necessary to address *kampung* problems. Initially, the government refused on the grounds that it was not its role to interfere in *kampung* matters. Together with Thomas Karsten, he organized a housing reform movement to put pressure on the government to take some action. Tillema and Karsten pointed to two key factors, primitive building techniques in *kampung* – housing and the intensification of land use leading to over concentration of the poorer inhabitants – as deficiencies that could be addressed through better planning.

The new responsibility for local affairs growing out of the decentralization movement also helped to fuel the *kampung* improvement effort. Annual meetings held after 1911 to discuss the challenges of government decentralization became a forum for highlighting *kampung* problems. At the Eighth Decentralization Congress held in Batavia in 1918, the mayor of Semarang, D. de Jongh, presented a report on the housing conditions in his city and his efforts to institute improvements. He identified several constraints on the provision of good housing for the expanding population, and also the danger of removing poor housing in dilapidated condition because this would only tighten the housing market further. He noted the dual challenge of upgrading *kampungs* and providing new housing for more affluent residents, efforts that sometimes were in conflict. That same year the Social Technical Society was founded to develop a public housing programme. The Society organized the First National Housing Congress in 1922 at which the leading planners in the Netherland Indies, including Karsten, Maclaine Pont and Gerhard Jobst, focused on the provision of infrastructure as a way to combat sanitary problems in indigenous communities.

A national housing law and expanded local building regulations were also on the planners' agenda. At the Second National Housing Congress held in Batavia in 1925, the central theme was how to facilitate new housing construction and to improve the building standards for the more affluent. Discussion of low-income housing focused on the benefits of encouraging self-help building. The participants noted that strict building regulations were more a threat than a benefit to the low-income neighbourhoods. Yet the widespread use of indigenous materials, such as palm leaves for roofs and bamboo for walls, was a problem since these materials could not insulate against the spread of contagious diseases and were a constant fire hazard. Instead, manufactured components that owner builders could use to construct more permanent structures were preferable. Accompanying the use of improved housing building materials should be mandatory cleaning of the *kampungs* by their residents on a regular basis.[65]

Those at the housing conference advocated that the government intervene not only to establish building standards and to enforce hygiene efforts, but to develop new residential areas. The creation of limited liability housing companies, with capitalization shared by the central and local governments, was first experimented in Semarang in December 1925. Within the next couple of years, the practice spread to cities off-Java. Batavia's limited liability building company was created in September 1926. Few houses were built by these organizations and those that were built for the native population were, as one Dutch observer noted in 1927, like 'barracks where an occupant felt as one of a number of fellow sufferers looking for the first good opportunity to find shelter in a normal *kampung'.*[66] Efforts to improve conditions in the existing *kampungs* led, in 1925, to the first Native Housing Congress. One outcome of this gathering was an organized *kampung* improvement programme. The programme's emphasis was less on improving existing settlements than on finding ways to prevent further deterioration. The Native Housing Commission that was created by delegates to the Congress proposed a government-financed programme of housing for low-ranked government employees, most of whom were natives.

While the colonial government did not respond immediately to the demands of the housing reformers, some *kampung* improvements were undertaken during the 1920s and 1930s. Indonesian members of the Municipal Council in Batavia kept the issue alive and convinced a financially tight-fisted municipal government to invest in *kampung* improvements. In 1927, the colonial government agreed to cover one-half the cost of improved services in *kampungs*. And the following year, a comprehensive plan for *kampung* improvement for all Java cities was drawn up. But the economic depression of the 1930s, coupled with the prevailing view among the European and Chinese members of the Batavia's Municipal Council that *kampung* improvement was not a high public priority, severely diluted the effort. In 1932, the proportion of Batavia's budget dedicated to *kampung* improvement was a mere 1.25 per cent. European and Chinese members voted down a proposal by an Indonesian member to increase the allocation.[67]

The call for improvements in *kampungs* gradually gained political backing and during the 1930s programmes were underway in the twelve largest of Java's municipalities. These were confined to physical improvements, such as upgrading roads, construction of gutters, bridges and culverts, and the provision of new public services such as facilities for laundry, bathing, toilets and street lighting.[68] Unlike later *kampung* improvement efforts, there was no resident participation in the planning for these improvements. The programme was defined and directed by municipal officials. The design of the *kampung* improvement programme was prepared through the city's planning department and executed through public works, although the funding from the local level came from the public health budget. The programme was formalized in 1934 through the *Kampung* Improvement By-Laws (*Kampung Verbeeteringsordonnantie*, 1934).

An Emerging Planning Agenda and the Role of Thomas Karsten

Three years later, with no actual *kampung* improvements undertaken in Batavia, a new programme was set up to study the conditions of native residential areas. In the tradition of Tillema's efforts in Semarang, this programme was focused on the collection of detailed data about the quality of life in *kampungs*. Tanah Tinggi neighbourhood near the Senen market and near, but separate from the European areas in Gondangdia, Batavia was selected for investigation. The study reflected not only concern about the health conditions in the native *kampungs*, and how these conditions might impact surrounding areas where the Europeans resided, but also a growing appreciation of the need for environmental planning to ensure proper development of the city. The notion of planning as more than laying out subdivisions and infrastructure was being advanced from many fronts as the colonial capital rapidly developed in the 1920s and 1930s. And in the work of the professionals studying the ward of Tanah Tinggi, this broader notion of planning figured prominently (as discussed more fully below).

The most influential figure in research on urban issues in the Netherland Indies, and in the development of a modern planning system and new thinking about the role of planning in urban development, was Thomas Karsten. The son of a professor of philosophy and Vice-Chancellor of the University of Amsterdam, Karsten studied architecture at the Technical University of Delft from 1904 to 1908, a place where Dutch architecture students were also introduced to planning concepts. While there, he became involved with the Social-Technical Society of Democratic Engineers and Architects which was interested in housing and planning issues. This affiliation eventually led him to a connection with the Amsterdam Housing Council (1909). Although there is no evidence that he participated in the newly created international housing and planning movement, from later writings when in Indonesia it is obvious that he was well versed in the leading issues in housing and town planning in Europe and the United States. In 1914, a friend from student days, Henri MacLaine Pont, invited him to work in the Dutch East Indies. He accepted the invitation and, except for several holiday visits to the Netherlands, he was a permanent resident in the colonies until his death in a Japanese internment camp in 1945.[69]

His initial work was with Pont's Architectural Bureau. By 1916 he was already working as a planning advisor in Semarang and prepared the plan for the expansion of the city into the hilly area to its south. He quickly assumed a prominent position in the fledgling planning movement in the colonies which dated from the 1913 International Housing Congress held in Scheveningen, Netherlands, where Tillema presented a paper on the poor housing conditions in the Semarang *kampungs*. Through his work with Semarang's Public Housing Service, Karsten gained an in depth understanding of the critical planning needs in Javanese cities. Given his support for Indonesia's political independence, he brought to his planning work not only the technical expertise of the architect but also a keen interest in understanding urban conditions from the native population's point of view. He was active in the annual decentralization congresses (first held in 1911) where the local civil service corps discussed how to strengthen local capacity to address urban needs.[70]

Karsten prepared a report on planning in Indonesia in 1920 which was not only a study of planning as it related to urban development in the Dutch East Indies but also a basic text on the subject. It was the first comprehensive discussion of planning in Dutch since the 1912 publication of *Modern Town Planning* (*De Hedendaagsche Stedenbouw*) by a local legislator from Utrecht. Karsten pointed out that in the case of most urban societies, there were multiple social groups with differing needs and aspirations. In the case of Java, he identified three separate races (European, Indonesian and Chinese), although others added a fourth group (Euro-Asians, which was a sizable component of Batavia's population). In his view the object of planning was to help create an organic whole out of these ethnic groupings and this required active intervention by government through a planning process that was much more comprehensive than that advanced by the architects who dominated the colonial planning movement. He stressed the need to integrate buildings, road systems, squares and open spaces, and to take into consideration aesthetic as well as economic, technical and hygienic considerations. Cities were dynamic places and their planning could not be approached as a static process. Planning was the means to organize, and had a special duty to serve the economically weak. Karsten's commitment to planning that served the masses was part of his basic social philosophy which inspired him to decorate his office with pictures of Lenin and Gandhi.[71]

Contrary to prevailing practice, Karsten contended that planning should not be used to divide cities by race but on the basis of economic class. This breakdown applied to types of houses as well as the classification of streets. Karsten also stressed that the architecture and landscaping of cities should be consistent with a tropical setting, with low-rise structures predominating amidst extensive plantings. He paid particular attention to 'townscape' because he regarded the goal of planning as the creation of places both unified and distinctive in character. Instead of advocating detailed plans, Karsten urged the creation of what would later be termed a 'concept plan' which identified the main features to be considered (transportation lines, distribution of building types and uses, the general location of open spaces, as well as future development areas). Although conceptual in nature, the plan should take into account the detailed implementation which might lead to changing local circumstances.

In his writings from the 1930s, Karsten expanded his planning scheme to the regional scale and even contemplated a national plan, especially one related to economic development. However, he never surrendered the centrality of the planner to the planning process. In his view, the planner's role was to coordinate all the activities associated with city development. As he noted in 1935, 'town planning as a technical subject has its own character and … it not only concerns itself with building but also with assemblage, organization, and cooperation'.[72] He wrote extensively on a range of planning issues in the journal *Locale Techniek* which was launched in the early 1930s. He also trained the first generation of native planning experts through his practice in the local governments of Semarang and Malang, and later as a consultant. He established a Planning Study Group in 1939 that eventually became the Indonesian Association of Planners and accepted a lecturing post in planning in 1941 at the Bandung University of Technology, an assignment cut short by illness and by his internment after the Japanese seized the Netherland Indies.

A town planning ordinance for municipalities on Java, and an accompanying 'Explanatory Memorandum on the Town Planning Ordinance for Municipalities on Java', the first systematic exposition of planning in Indonesia, were largely the work of Karsten. These provide a benchmark to judge the extent of city planning in Batavia in the 1930s. The central government had created a Town Planning Committee in 1934 to develop recommendations for a planning system to address the needs of municipalities in the East Indies. It was chaired by J.H.A. Logemann, a professor in the Law School in Batavia. Karsten was the leading authority on planning on the committee which also included his Indonesian protégé, Susilo, and the Dutch planner, J.P. Thijsse. Karsten used this committee assignment to advance understanding of, and support for, planning in Java. His 'Memorandum' constituted a sort of handbook for planning in the colonies. A planning ordinance that grew out of the work of this committee was adopted in 1948 during the Dutch restoration period, and remained the legal basis for planning after Independence. It provided a valuable link between planning in the late colonial era and the emergence of Indonesia's approach to planning for urban development in the new nation.[73]

The 1935 draft clearly reflected Karsten's progressive vision of planning in a multi-racial society. Article 8 of the original draft (which was not kept in the final 1948 bill) read as follows:

The town-plan and town planning regulations arrange the layout and building by both the local authority and by third parties, so as to ensure town development in line with its social and geographical characteristics and possible growth, and complies to the needs of the various races, and strives for a harmonious functioning of the town as a whole and in sympathy with its surroundings and general function.[74]

The 1935 draft planning law also specified the need to use zoning to organize urban uses. However, the general plan prescribed by this act was not legally binding although the detailed plan was enforced through a system of development permits and building regulations. As Nas points out, the basis for the planning legislation was not derived from contemporary planning theory but was based on a detailed understanding of urban problems in the Netherland Indies which needed to be addressed through public regulation and intervention. The major problem was the layout, density and extremely poor conditions in native *kampungs*, coupled with similar environmental problems in the traditional Chinese settlement in Glodok. Karsten expressed the view that the situation for the middle class had been rectified through aggressive new development since the early 1900s. So planning must, as a first priority, address the *kampung* and low-income housing problems, especially in the already built-up areas (or what he referred to as 'town planning after-the-fact').[75]

Karsten considered the *kampung* problem out of control and likely to get worse even with *kampung* improvement, since that process would inevitably lead to another problem, namely displacement. To forego this, it was necessary to reserve enough land for *kampung* expansion and to do so in the context of suitable space for individual homes for the poor. He regarded multi-family publicly-constructed housing as useful only for the lower-middle class. But this view did not gain wide support in the colonies. Bogarers and Ruitjen contend that one of the key differences between planning in the homeland and in the colonies was that in the former, efforts to address housing needs were at the core of an expanded planning function. In the Indies, despite the efforts of Karsten and his colleagues to make housing a higher priority of local government, it remained predominantly a private sector function.[76]

Karsten's planning also focused on commercial development, which he believed should be regulated both in terms of location and height restrictions. The lack of regulation of commercial and residential development, a complicated and contradictory system of land ownership (government ownership, private estates with native rights attached, and unregistered lands thus owned by government by default), and the legality of planning regulations posed further problems that needed to be addressed through a new planning act. Karsten also recognized that the public improvements required to support new development actually cost more than the additional revenues collected from the development itself, meaning that the public sector was sharing equally with the private sector in urban development. This was placing significant fiscal strain on the municipality. He also noted the need to extend municipal control of development to the adjacent semi-urban and semi-rural areas.

He approached planning not just as a response to a set of physical, economic and legal problems but also as it related to the complex and conflict ridden social network of colonial Batavia. Planning had to contend with a highly stratified society, with Europeans at the top, and native neighbourhoods at the bottom, and two intermediate groupings of Chinese and Indo-Europeans. According to one contemporary authority, these four groups had very little common culture and thus approached life in Batavia with very different aims and often in relation to very different legal systems:

They live, work and build in completely different ways, and in those respects have dissimilar needs, potentialities, and ideals: to some extent they even have dissimilar legal institutions.[77]

Karsten expressed the view that the Chinese population was indifferent to the needs of the city, and viewed its involvement more as temporary and perfunctory. Because of 'such diverse strengths and such divergent aspirations', it was not surprising to Karsten that Batavia developed in 'a confused and disorderly way'.[78]

Based on his knowledge of urban problems in Batavia and other large Javanese cities, Karsten devised a set of planning principles to guide the colonial authorities. First, there was a need for strong governmental intervention in town development; this should recognize the intrinsic differences between buildings and neighbourhoods, and preserve internal order and harmony within these areas. He specifically regarded zoning as the way to accomplish this. Planning should address social equity problems: 'the urban masses, evidently badly off, deserve particular attention because this semi-rural population should become urban, but also needs to be protected in the unequal struggle'. Planned intervention should anticipate and guide development in order to control costs. Moreover, planning should take into account Javanese town traditions rather than simply applying modernist ideas. Planning should be supported by ongoing research in the area of urban development, and the cities needed trained local leaders to guide that process. But as Nas observes, Karsten was not thinking about a participatory planning process but a process that was 'top-down'.[79]

Urban Environmental Planning and the Study Ward Project

The creation of an intensive public health research project in a typical Batavian *kampung* in 1937 reflected growing concerns about the hygiene conditions in these expanding native neighbourhoods and complemented Karsten's research on urban planning problems. The origins of the local public health programme can be traced to the establishment of the Public Health Services by the Netherlands' government in 1911. Yet it was not until the 1930s that local governments had the authority to implement health standards. Given the absence of data about conditions in the *kampungs*, which previously were outside local authority, it was not known how best local governments should intervene in these native residential areas. The establishment of the Study Ward for Hygiene in Batavia in 1937 was intended to increase knowledge of conditions in densely populated urban areas in the city. As one of the researchers noted,

… our knowledge of conditions of a far off tribe in New Guinea is greater than of a great section of the population in densely populated Java, in particular in towns … a fact which can indeed be explained but cannot be denied.[80]

Even though the majority of the native population remained rural, 'there exists a strong and continuously progressing growth of the towns' and these towns 'have, moreover, a significance for the whole country which far exceeds that expressed in percentages of the total number of inhabitants'.[81] The data collected in the study ward would give local officials a better handle on the changing demographics of the *kampung* dwellers.

The 1937 Study Ward project was modelled on several similar research efforts in the United States, one being the East Harlem Health Center in New York City and the other a comparable public health project in Baltimore where post-graduates from the Johns Hopkins University medical college studied living conditions in one of the city's poorer neighbourhoods. There were several antecedents to the Study Ward project in the Netherland Indies, most importantly a one time study of health conditions in Batavia carried out by W.J. van Gorkem in 1911, as well as another programme in Central Java aimed at bringing hygiene to rural villages. Van Gorkem documented the high mortality rate in several Batavia neighbourhoods. For a year, he collected data on disease and mortality in Mangga Besar, a *kampung* area between the old city and the new European enclave in Weltevreden. He kept a register of sick people and also carried out post-mortems. Van Gorkem published the results of his study in 1913, and that seemed the end of the matter until the 1937 study, which had a much broader research focus.

The 1937 study was planned by Dr. E. Walsh in 1934, but he died before it got underway. However, it continued for 6 years in the Tanah Tinggi area. Originally intended to encompass an area of 10,000 inhabitants, the eventual study area covered a population of more than 25,000. The Tanah Tinggi study differed from van Gorkem's work not only in the size of the area but the comprehensiveness of its approach. The 1937 study kept track of disease and mortality, but also much more. It took into consideration 'care for the environment in the broadest sense', which meant also '*good houses* ... built on proper sites [and] houses should have a supply of *reliable drinking water*. The sewage, faecal matter, urine, refuse, and drainage water should be arranged so that they cause *no pollution* to the surroundings'.[82] The comprehensiveness of the research effort in Tanah Tinggi was unmatched by any effort in Europe or the United States and was well supported, with funds from the Public Health Service, the Queen Wilhelmina Jubilee Foundation, and the Rockefeller Foundation.[83]

Tanah Tinggi was a 2.34 square kilometre area located east of the railway line running from the old city area of Batavia to Meester Cornelis. Part of the neighbourhood had stone shop buildings and new brick and concrete homes, but most of the population resided in less commodious structures, with many living in *pondok* complexes (literally meaning a building arranged for shared living) 'where from 50–100 people lived together surrounded by muddy gardens and neglected gutters'. The community population composition reflected, at least in part, the social diversity of Batavia in the 1930s. It included a mix of 'natives of varying position', a relatively more affluent Chinese population, and some lower class Europeans (in contrast to the middle class who lived in nearby Weltevreden and Meester Cornelis). The 2,500 Chinese, 1,000 Europeans (but most likely predominately Eurasians) and other 'Asiatics' accounted for less than 4,000 of the area's 22,000 residents.[84] Tanah Tinggi was considered a stable neighbourhood, with a majority being permanent residents. Yet in the first year of the study, there were 1,115 changes in occupants in the community's 4,721 registered dwelling units. Certainly a portion of the turnover was explainable by a death rate which was comparable to the estimated average for the city. In terms of overall housing quality and general liveability, Tanah Tinggi was probably slightly above the average for Batavia's *kampungs* at the time.[85] In Tanah Tinggi's most densely populated *kampungs* there were wooden dwellings with tile floors, some of them large *pondoks* constructed of bamboo. But there was also a 'fairly large number of newly built dwelling units of molded concrete', many of which had been built between 1938 and 1940 after the study began. These new homes had water and sewerage connections, an improvement which was reflected in rents that limited their accessibility to only the more prosperous. The availability of these serviced rental units indicated a demand for better housing.

In Rawah *kampung*, in the Tanah Tinggi neighbourhood on the eastern side of the Sentiong canal, the houses were in much poorer condition, although substantially larger, than the *pondoks*. This area was a mix of European, Eurasian

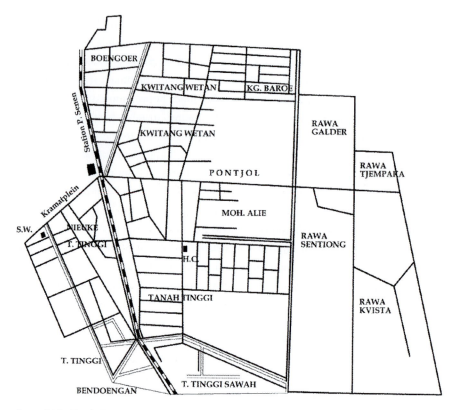

Figure 2.10. Tanah Tinggi Study Ward near Senen Market, 1937. (Adapted from Tesch, 1948)

and Javanese of moderate prosperity who preferred the spaciousness of a rural setting rather than access to urban services since it was officially outside Batavia's municipal boundary. Other sections of Tanah Tinggi had benefited from the growing interest in planning residential areas in Batavia, boasting straight and paved alleys and pathways that included gutters to remove rain water. Except for the newly constructed rental dwellings, the water supply for most of Tanah Tinggi was by means of taps from the municipal water system, although Chinese merchants sold water (that they secured from the municipal system) to residents and many others continued to rely on private wells and river water.[86]

The population density in the Study Ward in the most intensively built-up areas was approximately 550 persons per 100 square metres. According to Tesch, this was less dense than in Berlin and roughly comparable to the residential density of The Hague. Yet in those European cities, this level of residential density was made possible by multi-storey buildings while in Tanah Tinggi virtually all housing was single storey. Overall, 85 per cent of the housing was described as primitive construction, that is with bamboo walls and roofs of woven palm leaves. Nine per cent (approximately 400 units) were built either of brick or concrete while another 6 per cent (260 units) were wooden framed (with bamboo walls). The exception was in Rawah *kampung* where only 58 per cent (339 units) were primitive, with nearly 40 per cent (235 units) rated by the study survey as 'better' and a handful as permanent. But taken as a whole, Tanah Tinggi reflected the generally poor condition of residential areas for the native population, where 'conditions in the dwellings do not attain even moderate hygienic requirements'.[87]

Urban Transformation in the Late Colonial Era

In addition to Karsten's efforts to advance housing improvement and town planning, there was also a nascent urban preservation movement in the prewar years. In 1931, the central government enacted a Monument Ordinance (*Monumentenordonnante*) to protect historic buildings from demolition. This act was prompted by those who were concerned by the extensive 'demolition and replacement of historic buildings during the twenties' in the old Batavia area. Even with the historic preservation ordinance, the pressures of new development constantly threatened the urban fabric. As late as 1936, H.A. Breuning, the National Buildings Engineer in the Dutch East Indies, decried the continuing demise of Old Batavia.[88] The commercial expansion of the 1920s that centred on Old Batavia was largely responsible for the construction boom, but there was also a direct link to the emerging planning movement and efforts to revamp the physical structure of the city.

Architect Hendrik Petrus Berlage drew up a redevelopment plan for the old city hall complex in Fatahillah Square in 1923 as part of a new plan for Batavia. His plan called for a 'townhall square as a civic forum for Batavia' surrounded by bulky, European-style public buildings with strong façades, and a square pinned at the corners by bushy trees (waringins). The historic axis of the old city connected Fatahillah to the original fort, and the Berlage plan sought to re-establish this aesthetic and functional link. The area just south of Fatahillah contained several important new commercial structures, including the planned union railroad station, Stasiun Kota (1929), designed by Ghijsels, an Art Deco factory building for the Netherland Trade Company (1929) and the Javasche Bank building (1929). All these were within the boundaries of the Berlage plan and were built, although the transformation of Fatahillah Square was not undertaken. While devoid of the aesthetic splendour of Berlage's plan for Fatahillah, the square in front of Stasiun Kota, created by the intersection of several broad streets, became the new commercial centre of Batavia. The more unified conception in the Berlage plan exceeded the expectations, and perhaps the available resources, of Batavia's leadership.[89]

As the Kota area of Batavia modernized as a result of the commercial construction boom in the 1920s, a concurrent development process was transforming the Konigsplein area from a quiet suburban retreat into an intensely used civic centre. Like the Fatahillah area in old Batavia, the Konigsplein became the focus of a major planning effort, this one by Karsten. Completed in 1937, the Karsten plan for the Konigsplein called for the square's remaining few open spaces to be carved up to support a variety of new urban recreational uses. The Karsten plan seemed to signal the final stage of the Konigsplein's transformation from an army parade ground, as it was laid out under Daendels in 1808, to what it had become by the 1930s, the centre of the European civic and community life. With the largest and still growing concentration of European housing shifting southwards into the Menteng and Gondangdia areas, it was possible to consider

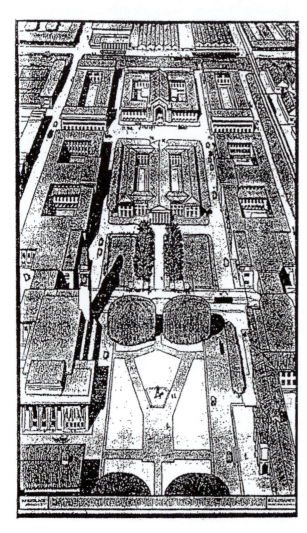

Figure 2.11. Berlage Plan for Batavia's Civic Center, 1923. (*Source*: Berlage, 1931)

Figure 2.12. A view of Batavia's main railroad station, Stasiun Kota, designed by Ghijsels in the 1920s. (*Photo*: author)

uses for this area that might have been less acceptable when it served as the front lawn of private residences. The adaptation of its Indisch buildings to various civic, governmental and commercial functions was already well underway by this time, and without destroying the aesthetic integrity of this important space.

The transformation of Konigsplein that the Karsten plan envisioned had started even before it ceased to be the primary residential area for Batavia's European population. In 1909, a telephone office had been built on one corner of the square, and four years later a movie theatre was placed on the eastern side. A fountain was added to the southern segment of the one kilometre square and that spot became the venue for an annual trade fair that continued until its sudden removal in 1990. The facilities for the Batavia Sports Club, a horse track built in 1905 and a bicycle track added in 1936, took up a substantial portion of the eastern side of the square. But it was also development around the square that reinforced transformation of its function. On the west side of the square a Law School was built in 1928 and adjacent to it (to the north) were the offices of the Nederland and Rotterdamsche Lloyd shipping company and a building for the Netherlands Indies Broadcasting Corporation (which is still used for communication by the Radio Republik Indonesia). The Batavia Municipal Council occupied the former official residence of the Director of the Bank of Java, and adjacent to it was the office of the Governor of West Java, both of which were historic buildings, while new buildings (out of character with the predominant Indisch style) were added for the Netherlands Colonial Petroleum Company (now Pertamina), the Batavia Petroleum Company and the Dutch Inter-Island Lines shipping firm.[90]

Following Independence, Konigsplein was redesigned as Freedom (Merdeka) Square – a process that would become a consuming national project. Around the square, the newly independent Indonesia situated its most prestigious structures, including the Presidential Palace and some of the most important ministry offices. As in the late colonial era, it served as the locus of power, but with a new leadership and by the removal of the more than half a century of accumulated structures, and through landscaping carried out first by Sukarno and then again under the Suharto administration in the 1990s, the square was transformed back to an open, civic space much as it had been in 1808.[91]

Dark Days for the Colonial Capital

The growth of Indonesian nationalism in the 1920s and 1930s was not a political movement that emanated from squalid conditions in Batavia's sprawling *kampungs*, although some notable local native political leaders, like M. Husni Thamrin,

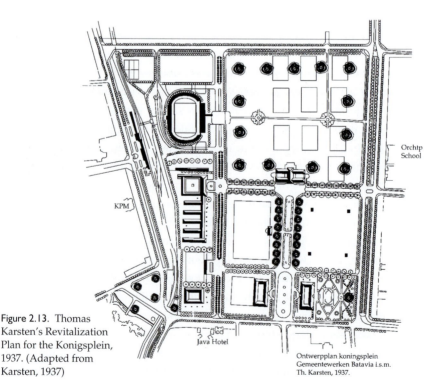

Figure 2.13. Thomas Karsten's Revitalization Plan for the Konigsplein, 1937. (Adapted from Karsten, 1937)

had pushed the Batavia Municipal Council to address *kampung* improvement seriously. Nationalist sentiments simmered in the city at several levels, and not just among those radicals like Sukarno who embraced a coherent anti-colonial ideology. Schumutzer contends that in the 1920s there was another nationalist strain, 'a growing awareness of a political identity among the Dutch, native, and other inhabitants of the colony' that can best be described as 'a nationalism of The Netherlands Indies'. This was reflected in the vision and demand 'for a measure of self-government and self-determination of the dependency'.[92] It was a nationalism reflecting some common aspirations but with two very bitterly and fundamentally divided contingents. There co-existed a 'native nationalism' which

Figure 2.14. Building of the fair, Pasar Gambir, located on the Konigsplein, 1934. (*Source*: KIT Tropemuseum, Amsterdam)

was inspired by 'a mix of religion, social, Marxist, and pan-Asiatic discontent' and a 'Holland-oriented white national movement that came to oppose the liberal ethical policy, and stressed law and order, systematic education and development from the bottom up'.[93] It was the failure of the pluralistic, neo-liberal approach to running society, including decentralization, improvements in education, *kampung* improvement, the welfare policies of the Ethical Policy, and engagement in the economic life of Batavia, that led to the irrevocable division of local Dutch and the Indonesian elite into separate political parties and socially and economically separated societies within Batavia 'between which communication stagnated and adverse emotions flourished'.[94]

The occupation of the Netherland Indies by the Japanese temporarily removed any possibility that these conflicting versions of independence could find common ground. Initially, native leaders thought that the Asian-led removal of European colonialism would hasten independence but quickly discovered that Japanese occupation was the substitution of one form of repression for another. Under Japanese occupation, all improvements to Batavia that had been underway were put on hold, with many of key individuals either in exile or in prison camps. The one notable exception was the institution by the Japanese of a system of local administration that created a hierarchy of officials reaching from the central command all the way to the *kampung* level. This system would be retained by the Indonesians after Independence as a means for a highly centralized government to maintain effective linkages with, and to exert control over, the urban masses in the *kampungs*.

During the four decades leading up to the demise of the Dutch colonial rule in the East Indies, many of the challenges confronting the growing capital city had been exposed. Key components of Batavia's planning agenda for the post-war city had been unveiled during this period, and would remain to be addressed long after both Japanese and Dutch occupations ended. Projects, such as the development in Menteng, revamping the Konigsplein, initiating a preservation movement, and establishing comprehensive planning must be seen as laying the groundwork for the post-colonial city. However, what was notably lacking in Batavia's colonial planning legacy was the sort of grand, comprehensive visions for the city that were so prevalent elsewhere in the world. Thomas Karsten's thoughtful analysis of the needs for Batavia and the other Dutch colonial cities was highly pragmatic, but did not rise to the level of a visionary scheme, even by contemporary standards.

Perhaps it was the mistaken expectation on the part of the colonial leadership that there was plenty of time to work at the planning process and to create the dignified colonial capital that they desired. Since the Dutch had been in Batavia for more than 300 years, few would have expected their colonial empire to crumble in the matter of a few years. Interestingly, in the aftermath of World War II, when the Dutch sought to regain control over Batavia and its other East Indies colonial possessions (despite Indonesia already declaring its independence), the pace of planning for reconstruction of the capital city picked up markedly. But it was much too late to preserve Batavia as a colonial capital city. The world had changed radically as a result of the war and out of this emerged both the nation of Indonesia and a whole new set of expectations for Batavia, now the renamed city of Jakarta (in honour of its origins). Those expectations required more than piecemeal interventions, but rather a master plan to transform the colonial capital into a national capital.

Notes

1. See Lindblad (2002), p. 111; Anderson (1983), p. 478.
2. Cobban (1976), p. 55.
3. Raffles (1817), Vol. 1, p. 63.
4. Abeyasekere (1989), p. 88.
5. Hugo (1980), pp. 114–115.
6. See Lindblad (2002), pp. 111, 117–119.
7. Dick (2002), pp. 157–158.
8. Houben (2002), p. 57.
9. *Ibid.*, pp. 60–61.
10. Day (1904), pp. 289–290.
11. Abeyasekere (1989), p. 82; Furnivall (1939), p. 175.
12. Surjomihardjo (1977), p. 39, p.41; Milone (1966), p. 305; Soesilo (1936), pp. 73–74.
13. Milone (1966), pp. 311–312.
14. Surjomihardjo (1977), pp. 50–51; Abeyasekere (1989), pp. 54–57.
15. Cited in Abeyasekere (1989), p. 52; see also Vos (1887).
16. Milone (1966), p. 563.
17. Milone (1966), pp. 318–320; also map in Breuning (1936), p. 20 compared to Vos (1887).
18. Furnivall (1939), p. 406.
19. Quoted in Merrillees (2002), p. 14.
20. Furnivall (1939), pp. 415–417.
21. Cribb (1994), pp. 33–37, 41.
22. Fasseur (1994), pp. 38, 41.
23. *Ibid.*, pp. 45, 50.
24. Gouda (1995), pp. 23–24; Anderson (1983), p. 489.
25. Gouda (1995), pp. 23–24.
26. Anderson (1983), p. 480.
27. Milone (1966); Nas (1990).
28. Doorn (1982), pp. 26–29.
29. Akihary (1996), pp. 10, 14–15.
30. Quoted in Akihary (1996), p. 101.
31. *Ibid.*, p. 14–15, 19–23, 94, 98.
32. *Ibid.*, p. 98.
33. Argo (1999), pp. 50, 52.
34. Bogarers and Ruijter (1986), p. 77.
35. Abeyasekere (1989), p. 124; Nas (1990), p. 9.
36. Argo (1999), p. 43.
37. See deVeer, W. (1904) cited in Marcussen (1990), p. 74; see also Day (1904); Furnivall (1939).
38. Batavia was exempt from the Cultivation System.
39. Lohanda (1994), p. 247.
40. *Ibid.*, p. 247.
41. *Ibid.*, pp. 268–274.
42. *Ibid.*, p. 229; Lohanda (2002), p. 17.
43. Lohanda (2002), p. 39.
44. Lohanda (1994), p. 71.
45. *Ibid.*, p. 73.
46. *Ibid.*, p. 118.
47. *Ibid.*, pp. 306–314.
48. *Ibid.*, pp. 317–318.

49. *Ibid.*, pp. 133, 276.
50. Nas (1990), p. 9.
51. See Wertheim (1958).
52. Cited in Marcussen (1990), p. 80.
53. Heuken and Pamungkas (2001), pp. 12–20.
54. Bellen (1995), pp. 106–107. Jessup also points to the influence of garden city principles on planning and design in Batavia. See Jessup (1989), p. 67.
55. Heuken and Pamungkas (2001), pp. 88–93.
56. *Ibid.*, pp. 45–63.
57. Akihary (1996), p. 12.
58. For a careful analysis of the historical and multiple meanings of the *kampung* in Indonesian cities, see Nas, Boon, Hladka, Sudarmoko, and Tampubolen (2005).
59. Marcussen (1990), pp. 76–77.
60. Wertheim (1958), pp. iv *et seq.*
61. Jellinek (1991), pp. 1–4.
62. Polle and Hofstee (1986).
63. See Tillema (1915–1922).
64. Polle and Hofstee (1986), p. 117; Gooszen (1999), pp. 188–192.
65. Cote (2002).
66. Cobban (1993), p. 893–894.
67. See Tesch (1948); Living Conditions of Municipally Employed Coolies in Batavia in 1937, in Wertheim (1958), pp. 85–224; Cobban (1993); Abeyasekere (1989), pp. 120–122.
68. See Flieringa, G. (1930), cited in Polle and Hofstee (1986), p. 119.
69. See Bogarers and Ruijter (1986), pp. 71–88.
70. *Ibid.*, pp. 71–77.
71. *Ibid.*, pp. 78–79.
72. *Ibid.*, pp. 80–81.
73. For an English translation of most of Karsten's memorandum, see Wertheim (1958).
74. Bogarers and Ruitjer (1986), p. 83.
75. Nas (1986), p. 91.
76. *Ibid.*, p. 88.
77. Toelichting (1938), p. 81 quoted in Nas (1986), p. 94.
78. Nas (1986), p. 95.
79. *Ibid.*, p. 99.
80. Tesch (1948), pp. 26, 31.
81. *Ibid.*, p. 31.
82. *Ibid.*, p. 17.
83. *Ibid.*, p. 38.
84. *Ibid.*, p. 49.
85. *Ibid.*, pp. 40–41.
86. *Ibid.*, p. 53.
87. *Ibid.*, pp. 88–93.
88. Breuning (1936), cited in Gill (1995), p. 65.
89. Gill (1995); Akihary (1996). Henrik Petrus Berlage (1856–1934) was the foremost Dutch architect of his era and was credited by many scholars for ushering in the modern movement known as the Amsterdam School. His most noted building was the Amsterdam Stock Exchange. But he also prepared a number of plans for Dutch cities, including schemes for South Amsterdam and West Amsterdam. Moreover, he conducted lectures on urban planning at the Technical University of Delft where so many notable architects who migrated to the Netherlands Indies received their training. He lectured there in 1908–1909 and again in 1913–1914. He travelled to the Netherland Indies on several occasions, once in 1913 in conjunction with designing the overseas headquarters of one of his leading clients in Amsterdam, De Nederlande van 1845 Insurance Company. His visit in 1923 for approximately four months (at the age of 67) was both for sight seeing and to provide consultation on Batavia's city planning process.

This led to his design for the civic centre of Batavia. Berlage was an ardent socialist but rejected calls for violent resistance. His planning and design style was modelled on the Renaissance and Baroque traditions, as expressed in the replanning of Paris in the late nineteenth century. He felt that 'this type of urban planning proves … that a sense of space combined with a regular street plan can create great beauty, as long as it satisfies a primary need for high density'. Yet he was also much influenced by a visit to the United States to view the work of Frank Lloyd Wright, Louis Sullivan and Henry Richardson. See Rossem (1988), pp. 52–56; Polano (1988), p. 235; Berlage (1931); Singelenberg (1972), p. 174; Reinink (1970), pp. 163–174.

90. Surjomihardjo (1977), pp. 55–59.
91. For a discussion of the efforts of Sukarno and Suharto to refashion the former colonial community space, see Chapter 3 .
92. Schmutzer (1977), p. xii.
93. *Ibid.*, p. xii.
94. *Ibid.*, p. 116–12.

Chapter Three

Plans for the Modern Metropolis, 1950–1970s

Djarkarta is growing fast. There will be more parks, monuments, fountains. There will be more spacious buildings for the people to live and work in as well as gay establishments for amusement and recreation. There will be much more beauty and attraction. Djakarta is becoming a big, modern city though not modeled after some other big city elsewhere in the world.

Sri Budojo, Executive Director, Indonesian Council for Tourism, February 1962

The Colonial Backdrop

The Dutch colonial leadership in pre-independence Batavia undertook a variety of development initiatives but none seems to have considered the tremendous changes underway in the city as a whole. Plans were prepared but they were simply detailed mappings of existing uses and went out of date almost on a daily basis. Batavia had grown to 800,000 by 1940, with a near doubling of the land area of the city through development of suburban Weltevreden, and its formal annexation (along with the adjacent residential enclave, Meester Cornelis) into the city in the 1930s. These crucial decisions to enlarge the city were undertaken without reference to any scheme for the desired outcome. The only plans were those for specific sub-areas of the city, such as the residential development of Menteng, the proposed revamping of the Fatahillah civic area and the redesign of the Konigsplein. In fact Batavia progressed using the tradition of municipal-level regulation of the city's development that began in 1909. This typically involved laying out the expanding city's street pattern to accommodate new European residential areas such as Menteng and Gondangdia. The so-called Kubatz plan of 1918 consisted of a single city map with the most up-to-date inventory of the existing infrastructure and the proposed street network for the Menteng neighbourhood.

Given that there were ample precedents for a comprehensive approach to city planning, how was it that such a piecemeal approach characterized the situation in Batavia in the early twentieth century? It was not that the city's small but energetic band of planners and architects failed to keep abreast of what was going on elsewhere. As noted in Chapter 2, the leading advocates of better planning in Batavia were well connected to the international planning movement. Perhaps the best explanation is that at that time there was no planning tradition in The Netherlands to serve as a model for such an approach. Planning in Holland in the early twentieth century was principally a matter of regulating land development to address the immediate housing needs of the nation; its essence was street platting and subdivision design rather than the monumental schemes that had come out of the nineteenth-century tradition of city planning in Paris and were implemented in so many United States cities in the first three decades of the century.[1]

Another notable factor was that Batavia apparently lacked powerful, wealthy and enthusiastic planning sponsors to back and possibly even fund preparation of a plan. Those who were the leading advocates for better planning in Batavia were a handful of architects, and not the business elite, and these professionals were in many cases constrained in their advocacy by the need to make a living. To rally support for public planning was incidental to their primary work of designing residences and commercial structures.

In Western cities, particularly in the United States, local business and professional communities were often the key sponsors of local plans. In the absence of public planning institutions, civic leaders provided both financial and political backing for the initial preparation of plans and powerful support to local government intervention to all aspects of city improvement. When local government budgets were slashed and projects ended during the great depression of the 1930s, the United States government created housing, community development and infrastructure programmes aimed at alleviating the economic crisis, but which also sustained the planning movement. By comparison, the colonial government's attempts to plan for Batavia at this time seem paltry and there was no real pressure from the business community to assume a more positive approach to the challenges of cities in the colonies.[2]

There was little chance that a movement for civic improvement could spring from indigenous sources in Batavia. For one thing, its commercial-civic elite was divided along race and ethnic lines. The existence of two separate commercial groupings, one based in the Chinese community and the other dominated by the Europeans, prevented the city's business community from galvanizing into a force for civic improvement of any kind. Under the colonial regime, planning for the needs of the city stuck to the bare necessities. The key challenges faced in the 1930s, such as the increasing number and size of substandard *kampung* housing areas and the need to improve services to the expanding European enclaves, would have benefited from an integrated and strategic approach, but each was dealt with separately and incrementally. Perhaps the reluctance to invest heavily in the reconstruction of Batavia was related to the fact that The Netherlands government was aiming to transfer the functions of the colonial capital from Batavia to Bandung, the cool hill city some 150 kilometres south-east of the port. The Ministry of Public Works and the telecommunications ministry were moved there in the 1930s, but the outbreak of World War II diverted attention and resources from this project. When the Japanese took control of the Netherland Indies in 1942, the capital building effort in Bandung ceased. The new occupiers reasserted the role of Batavia as the administrative centre of the archipelago. Later, it was the locus of the struggle to create a new nation on ashes of the former colonial capital. At that point, planning for the future began to matter.[3]

Planning for Reconstruction

Reconstruction of Batavia following the Japanese withdrawal from Java in 1945 and the Dutch reoccupation provided the initial impetus for an aggressive and more comprehensive approach to planning urban development. In the midst of the turmoil accompanying its attempt to reassert authority over the Indonesian islands, and despite the declaration of Indonesian independence in 1945, the Dutch government embarked on infrastructure planning for post-war recovery. In 1947 a Central Planning Bureau (CPB) was set up within the Department of Public Works and Traffic and under the leadership of Jacques P. Thijsse, a civil engineer who later became Professor of Physical Planning at the Technology University of Bandung (now known as the Institute of Technology Bandung). His staff began to churn out plans in rapid fashion, focusing initially on eastern Indonesia because the war between the Dutch and the Indonesian nationalists was fought principally on Java and Sumatra, making planning there impossible. The CPB prepared plans for Ambon, Makassar, Kupang, Ternate and Menado. A separate planning bureau was later set up for what was to be the state of Eastern Indonesia, but the anticipated partitioning of Indonesia into multiple, independent states did not occur. The CPB in Jakarta continued to work towards establishing a legal foundation for planning, and one of its committees drafted a Physical Planning Act based on the preliminary work of the Loggemann Town Planning Committee from the 1930s.

When national sovereignty was officially transferred to the Indonesians in 1950, Thijsse resigned as head of the Central Planning Bureau. Nevertheless, he continued to work the new Physical Planning Act into a legal document until he left for the Netherlands in 1954, ending a career in the Indies as a civil engineer, planner and academic which had begun in 1921.[4] Since the Physical Planning Act was not enacted at this time, government agencies and private developers jumped into the post-war rebuilding efforts with neither a plan nor a legal framework to guide urban development.

Kebayoran Baru, the Satellite City

In 1948, at the height of the conflict between the newly created Indonesian republic and the Dutch restoration government, Professor Ir. V.R. van Romondt from the Institute of Technology Bandung drew up a bold scheme for a new satellite city, to be called Kebayoran Baru, adjacent to Batavia. As Abeyasekere notes, 'the Dutch were so confident' that they were going to restore their control over the Indies 'that they began planning for the future growth of Batavia'.[5] The site, a 750 hectare (1,801 acre) tract of fruit groves 4.5 kilometres south-west of Batavia, had previously been designated for a new airport. It was a pear-shaped section of high ground bordered by two rivers, on the east by the Kali Krukut and on the west by the Kali Grogol. These rivers and the adjacent underdeveloped land were to serve as a so-called 'greenbelt' around Kebayoran Baru, both to establish a natural development boundary and in recognition that the land, which was subject to regular flooding, was best preserved as open space. Remarkably, van Romondt's plan was retained by the Indonesian planners. Its implementation was quite true to the original design although within two decades the proposal to preserve the greenbelt gave way to unregulated development. As the original planners predicted, this area regularly flooded when the 'rainy season' struck Jakarta.

The Kebayoran Baru plan, approved by the Central Institution for Reconstruction (*Centrale Stichting Wederopbouw*) in August 1948, was intended to provide a quality residential community for civil servants and other white collar professionals, supported by a new local market, and linked to the employment centres in the city by a new highway. Inspired by the garden city and new town models so widely used in post-World War II European urban reconstruction, Kebayoran Baru was closer to the garden suburb model than to the self-sufficient garden city conceived by Ebenezer Howard. Yet unlike the post-World War II new towns sprouting up in the United Kingdom with projected populations of 25,000, Kebayoran Baru was designed at a far larger and denser scale. It was planned to accommodate a population of between 50,000 and 100,000 when fully built, but the final population of its core area was closer to half a million.[6]

Thomas Karsten's protégés, the Dutch planner Thijsse from Bandung, and the Indonesian Susilo, played key roles in the preliminary implementation of the Kebayoran Baru plan through the CPB based in Bandung. Groundbreaking took place in March 1949, months before the final transfer of full authority from the Dutch to the Indonesians. While planning for the project remained under the jurisdiction of the Ministry of Public Works (renamed the Ministry of Public Works and Power under the Indonesian government), construction of the new city was put under the direction of a special Kebayoran Baru Authority, headed by Srigati Santoso. This new agency undertook all of the site preparation work and installation of the infrastructure, which included constructing a 4.5 kilometre long highway (24 metres wide) that connected Kebayoran Baru to Jakarta, as well as the 120 kilometres of the street network within the new city itself.[7]

The community's master plan called for the construction of 7,546 housing units (especially for civil servants), government offices, schools, markets, churches, mosques and theatres. Between 1950 and 1953, 4,630 housing units were constructed, ranging in size from a 68 square metre three-bedroom *perumahan rakjat* (people's house) to the more substantial *pemandangan muka* (85 square metres) and the slightly larger *rumah koppel*, providing 110 square metres of living space, including three spacious bedrooms, bathroom, kitchen, a single grand living and dining area, as well as space at the rear of the house for live-in help. There were 183 of these larger residences for high government officials. In addition, Kebayoran Baru boasted 559 grand houses, *rumah partikulir*, distinguished from the government-designed models by having nearly twice the living space (many were two storey) on larger lots, and each boasting a unique design. The style of the larger houses built in Kebayoran Baru was consistent with the 'Indisch' architectural tradition so widespread in Jakarta's traditional European enclaves.[8]

While the use of Indisch design reflected the persistence of colonial influence, the vast majority of the houses in Kebayoran Baru were smaller government-designed models, including clusters of semi-permanent structures for construction workers, domestic help and various service workers. The head office of the national police force was one of the larger employment centres built within the new city. However, where the Kebayoran Baru community surpassed all other urban residential developments in Jakarta built since the early 1900s was in its modern infrastructure. Although it did not have an enclosed sanitary sewer, it boasted 12,302 metres of drainage channel for waste water, and 50,283 metres of channelling for rain water. The original plan called for a central water system linked to a water purification plant but from the outset houses were supplied water through artesian wells located within the community.[9]

Development of Kebayoran Baru necessitated displacement of about 10,000 local fruit growers. While still under the Dutch government authority, the intention was to negotiate with local land owners to purchase the land required. When land owners pressed for higher compensation, the Dutch abandoned the process of negotiation and exercised their legal right to set the level of compensation. The land was quickly secured and construction was well underway before the Dutch exodus in 1949.

Figure 3.1. Original street plan for Jakarta's first satellite city, Kebayoran Baru. (*Source*: ROI, MPWP, 1953)

The first step for the new Indonesian government was to incorporate the new satellite city into the capital. The land on which Kebayoran Baru was built formed the major component of a massive annexation of peripheral areas around Jakarta in 1950. President Sukarno had created an advisory committee to identify the appropriate boundaries of an expanded metropolis, or 'Great Jakarta' (Djakarta Raya). The addition of Cenkareng (the future site of the international airport) and Kebun Jeruk to the west of the city, Mampang Prapatan, Kebayoran Lama, Pasar Minggu, Pasar Rebo and Kebayoran Baru to the south, and Pulo Gading to the east fulfilled this objective. The 1950 annexation more than doubled Jakarta's area. The building of the new city, as well as the incorporation of the other new sub-districts into the city proper, constituted the first step in a massive expansion of the urbanized area over the next two decades, predominantly but not exclusively in a southerly direction.[10]

The Concept and Outline Plans for Jakarta

In March 1950, a committee of Indonesian and Dutch planners within the new Ministry of Public Works and Engineering was formed to consider how to devise a master plan to guide future development of the capital of the newly independent Indonesia. An initial report prepared in August 1950 introduced the idea of a 'metropolitan region and metropolitan concept under the name Jakarta Raya', which was consistent with President Sukarno's vision of the national capital.[11] Lambert Giebels, the Dutch planner who was later among a group of foreign consultants who helped to develop the regional planning scheme for the area commonly referred to as Jabotabek, offers the only known reference to the report of which no copy has been discovered. The ideas in the report were fleshed out more fully in what was termed a 'concept plan' for Greater Jakarta prepared in 1952.

The concept plan set forth development principles for Jakarta, drawing on the garden city scheme which had figured so prominently in the design of Kebayoran Baru. In this case, it was a garden city scheme writ on the whole of the expanded metropolis. The concept plan conceived of Jakarta expanding in concentric layers, with the former Konigsplein (renamed by the Indonesians as Merdeka or Freedom Square) at its core, partitioned by a series of ring highways, and encased within a greenbelt which defined the outer limits of urban development.[12] According to Robert Cowherd,

many vestiges of the thinking of this original plan remained lodged in the thinking of Indonesian planners and bureaucrats, eventually finding their way into built form, despite concerted efforts made to get away from concentric development models.[13]

This thread of conceptual continuity in Jakarta's plans extends from the 1950s all the way into the 1990s.

With assistance from the United Nations, and with the additional goal of upgrading the capabilities of Indonesian planners, a consulting team led by British town planner Kenneth A. Watts, drafted a more detailed plan for Jakarta in 1957, which was accepted by the Municipality of Greater Jakarta in 1959 'as a basis for the future development of the city'.[14] Commonly referred to as the 'Outline Plan', it examined in greater detail than any previous study the infrastructure, housing and urban facility challenges facing a city undergoing spectacular population growth.

According to Watts, a survey of local conditions determined that at least

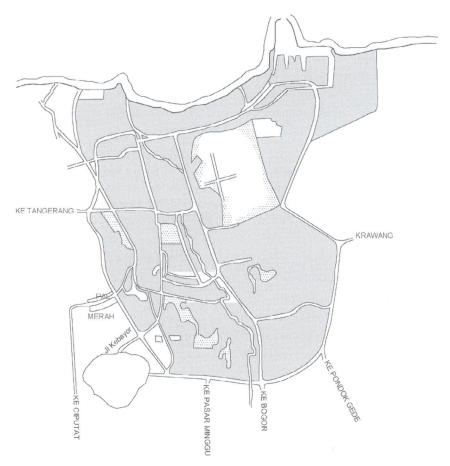

KE TANGERANG

KRAWANG

MERAH

Jl Kebayor

KE CIPUTAT

KE PASAR MINGGU

KE BOGOR

KE PONDOK GEDE

Figure 3.2. Concept Plan for Jakarta prepared in 1952. (Adapted from Surjomihardjo, 1977)

300,000 persons needed improved housing; that the road system of the sprawling urbanized area was completely inadequate for the more than 70,000 motorized vehicles that now plied the 230 miles of paved streets; that because of inadequate school facilities (as well as family deprivation) as many as 40 per cent of children between the ages of 6 and 12 did not attend school; and owing to inadequate infrastructure and services, Jakarta was unable to accommodate the heavy industry needed to provide employment for its labour force. The Outline Plan proposed a development programme, with a price tag estimated at 182 million *rupiah* (approximately US$5 million based on early 1950s exchange rates), which could be financed largely through loans from central government, and only partially supported by increased local taxation.

While Watts conceded that 'the level of expenditure on housing is extremely low' compared to the need, it was a key premise of the plan that public development funds did not go into housing. Government investments should be devoted largely to expanding 'social overhead, namely a universal water supply, drainage, [and] roads to open up new land' and that the provision of housing should be handled largely by private builders. Watts contended that meeting the housing needs of Jakarta through a permanent housing programme was beyond the scope of available funds, and as an intermediate strategy, the city should allow temporary housing to accommodate the rapid growth of the population. As he put it,

people who are migrating into [Jakarta] preserve their rural outlook, and it will take two or more generations for them to form urban attitudes. Is there not perhaps some wisdom in allowing the majority of structures to be built in short life materials, during the period when these people are becoming accustomed to city life? Will it not allow them to decide for themselves what mode of life they wish to adopt, and what permanent buildings will express this best?[15]

The Outline Plan reaffirmed the importance of Merdeka Square and Benteng Square (in front of the former governor's palace and now the main offices of the Ministry of Finance) as the civic core of this expanded metropolis, a view consistent with subsequent efforts, first by President Sukarno and then in the 1990s by President Suharto, to reassert their importance through major redesign efforts. The Outline Plan also called for land conservation on Jakarta's North Coast to support new recreational uses, and proposed moving the city's zoo to a remote location in South Jakarta.

To accommodate new residential areas, the core concept of the plan was to focus future development around three strategic locations, the town of Tangerang to the west, around Bogor (the former retreat of the Dutch Governors General going back to the Raffles regime in the early nineteenth century and still a favourite of Sukarno) to the south, and Bekasi to the east.[16] This regional approach to Jakarta's development expanded on the ideas set out in the 1952 concept plan but was far more place specific concerning the future growth of the urbanized area. The plan assumed an annual population growth rate of 4 per cent. In fact, Jakarta's population growth rate between 1948 and 1952 was closer to 25 per cent per year, and remained at an average of greater than 7 per cent between 1952 and 1965. Undoubtedly, it was impossible to project, on the basis of a concept plan and population estimates using flawed historical data, the precise level of population growth or to address adequately the city's existing crisis situation with regard to housing, jobs, services (especially water and sanitation), road improvement, schools and health facilities.

How Much Had Jakarta Grown?

There was no more vexing issue for the local administrators and planners, and their consultants, than deriving accurate figures for the population of Jakarta, and its rate of growth due to natural increases and the seeming flood tide of migrants to the city in the 1950s. Since there had been no population census in Indonesia since 1931, and given the tumultuous circumstances during the Japanese occupation and the subsequent war with the Dutch, gauging Jakarta's population size was little more than guesswork.

H.J. Heeren, a former member of the Faculty of Economics at the University of Indonesia, undertook a study of Jakarta's population growth in the early 1950s using a sample of 11,700 households. He not only sought a more reliable population figure for Jakarta but also to identify how many of the current population were either long-term Jakarta residents or recent migrants, and to determine from where the migrants were coming. He estimated a base population of 1,174,252 in 1948, and an average annual migration of approximately 110,000 thereafter. Coupled with natural increases, he estimated the city's population at approximately 1.8 million in 1953. He suggested that migration accounted for 85 per cent of the city's annual population increase, and that nearly one-half (49.2 per cent) of the population in 1953 had arrived since 1949. Approximately 7.7 per cent came during the Japanese occupation and another 23.3 per cent arrived between 1946 and 1950, meaning that only around 20 per cent of Jakarta's population could trace its urban roots to residency in the city before 1942. He also determined that the majority of new migrants (approximately 60 per cent) were from nearby rural sections of West Java, whereas migrants who came from Central Java and East Java (which made up the next largest contingent) were more likely to have migrated to Jakarta from an urbanized area in that region. And those who came to Jakarta from off-Java were even more likely to be from a city.[17]

The Watts planning team chose to use a significantly lower figure (80,000) as the total annual population increase. While this proved to be well short of the mark when the results of the 1961 census were available, the annexation of the peripheral areas in 1950 certainly accounted for a sizeable spike in the city's overall population. On the basis of the Watts team's estimate, and given

Table 3.1. Population of large Indonesian cities, 1931–1971 (000s).

City	1931	1961	1971
Jakarta	533.0	2,907.0	4,576.0
Bandung	116.8	972.8	1,201.7
Surabaya	341.7	1,007.9	1,556.3
Semarang	217.8	503.1	646.6
Medan	76.6	479.1	635.6
Palembang	108.1	474.9	582.9

Source: Central Bureau of Statistics, Population Census of 1930, 1961 and 1971. Cited in Wirosardjono (1974).

a continuation of current migration trends into the future, Jakarta was likely to reach as many as 4.5 million persons by 1977. In fact, the city reached that population plateau by the time the 1971 census was completed.[18] Watts believed that there were probably greater numbers of migrants in the early 1950s but that, as he put it in his report, the annual migration had probably dropped to 40,000 to 50,000 per year. This was not, however, a reason to relax. He regarded the problem of the unassimilated masses flocking to Jakarta the gravest challenge to the city's planning. 'Unless the whole problem of surplus population is satisfactorily dealt with', he concluded, 'the success of these physical plans will be seriously – even completely – jeopardized'.[19]

The problem was even worse than he had estimated. According to the 1961 census, Jakarta's population had grown to 2.9 million, which constituted an increase of nearly 1.8 million since 1948. This translated into an average annual overall increase of 133,000 over this period. In fact, the rate of annual population growth would grow even more in the ensuing decade, rising to approximately 167,000 persons per year between the 1961 and 1971 censuses. No matter what was the precise figure, there was no more discussed issue among Jakarta planners and local leaders throughout the 1950s and 1960s than how to deal with the seemingly unstoppable flow of migrants to the city and the increasing inability of the city to accommodate them. A widely cited solution was to make improvements to those rural areas the migrants were leaving so as to make the trek to the capital city less attractive. That was one reason why Heeren took pains to assess the place of origin of the migrants.

However, in his 1953 survey Heeren found that the majority of migrants believed they were better off in their new Jakarta home. While some were more overwhelmed by their new urban poverty than the situation in their home villages, a greater proportion seemed to have made some modest gain, although Heeren readily admitted that his conclusions were not really scientifically verifiable. But what they suggested was that despite uncertain (or non-existent) employment opportunities, inadequate housing, higher costs of living, and the difficulty of surviving in a chaotic urban environment, there seemed to be no effective way to discourage the flow. For Jakarta's planners, the test was handling this sustained population increase both in the short run and in terms of long range improvements to the city.

Administrative Leadership in Jakarta

Neither the administrative relationship between Jakarta and Indonesia's central government nor the city administrators' functions were clarified in the legal structure of the new nation. For this reason, coupled with the powerful personalities of Indonesia's two presidents whose tenure spanned nearly the first five decades of national development, it was never entirely clear who had the controlling hand in the urban development and planning of Jakarta. The city's first post-independence mayor, Soewirjo, was elected on 30 March 1950, nearly 5 years after Sukarno first tapped him for that position at which time he had to relinquish it following the Dutch reoccupation of Jakarta in late 1945. His second try was as abbreviated as the first when, slightly more than a year after taking office, the Representative Council of Jakarta, its transitional legislative body, selected Sjamsuridjal as the new mayor in June 1951. Soewirjo moved into the national government as deputy prime minister. Sjamsuridjal's most pressing problem, and one that was to challenge Jakarta's leadership over the next four decades, was control of land occupancy in the face of mass migration from depressed rural areas. He initiated the preparation of a city plan to guide the resettlement of squatters where there was evidence of illegal occupancy and to clear areas which were intended to accommodate future development. The focus of his land regulation efforts was the densely packed residential areas in the Kebun Kacang *kampung* near where the Hotel Indonesia would later be constructed.[20]

Land was bought and cleared of the temporary structures, the displaced residents being pushed to other parts of the city, where in some cases the government built new replacement housing.[21] In 1952 alone, ten housing projects were initiated to provide shelter for the more than 35,000 people displaced by the clearances as well as to provide housing for a growing army of civil servants. An equally daunting problem for the Sjamsuridjal administration was to upgrade water and electrical services, both of which lacked the capacity and reliability for such a rapidly growing city. None of these initiatives kept pace with the growing housing demand and, despite Sjamsuridal's aggressive clearance programme, slum areas expanded faster than the government could remove them.[22]

Sjamsuridjal's short but active administration was followed by one of the longest of any Jakarta mayor. Sudiro took office in 1953 and remained until 1960. In 1958, his position was changed to that of governor, which reflected not only the elevated status of the metropolis but also the intention of President Sukarno to treat the city as an extension of the national government under his new national programme of Guided Democracy. However, Sudiro's long tenure was not indicative of a powerful administration, rather he seemed to serve largely as a figurehead as President Sukarno assumed closer control of city affairs not only through his own direct intervention, but through involvement of other national government agencies. The Ministry of Public Works oversaw development of the Kebayoran Baru satellite city, and the Ministry of Communications controlled both the port facilities at Tanjung Priok and the city airport at Kemayoran.

Moreover, the city had grown so quickly that it was necessary to divide it administratively into three separate cities, Jakarta Utara (North Jakarta), Jakarta Tengal (Middle Jakarta) and Jakarta Selatan (South Jakarta). By 1966, Jakarta had expanded enough to the east and west to warrant two more separate cities, Jakarta Timor (East Jakarta) and Jakarta Barat (West Jakarta). Sudiro made the administrative change unilaterally (but most likely at the behest of Sukarno), only seeking approval from the Ministry of Internal Affairs afterwards. To strengthen the links between the government leaders and the communities and neighbourhoods, Sudiro introduced a new system of local administrative units, a scheme borrowed from the experience of the Japanese occupation during the 1940s. The *Rukun Tetangga* or RT and the *Rukun Kampung* or RK (which would later became known as *Rukun Warga* or RW) were set up to ensure some level of dissemination and enforcement of government regulations right down at the neighbourhood and block levels.[23]

But what distinguished Sudiro's administrative tenure was how Jakarta was reshaped so decisively by the intervention of President Sukarno in major planning and development decisions. Several of the key initiatives associated with Sukarno's grand scheme to recast the face and functions of Jakarta began during Sudiro's administration. One major project was the construction of a national monument on the Konigplein (Merdeka Square). Adjacent to this national monument, the Sukarno government constructed a new national mosque. A modern highway connecting the port facilities at Tanjung Priok to the southern edge of the expanding metropolis, the removal of electric streetcars from the city streets, a large urban redevelopment project at Krekot Bunder, construction of a flood control canal, and the clearance of an area near Kebun Kacang for the high-rise Hotel Indonesia, were all undertaken while Sudiro was Jakarta's mayor and governor. All, according to most scholars, represented the handiwork of President Sukarno.

The difficulty of administering the city during a period of such rapid population growth was made even more challenging because the heavy hand of the president often intruded in even the most mundane matters. Another problem was the belated recognition that, although Jakarta functioned as the capital city, no official action had been taken to legalize that role. The city had been designated as the nation's capital in the preliminary constitution in 1945, but the detail of ratifying the initial decision was overlooked in enacting the permanent constitution. This was not a problem for Sukarno, especially as he was toying with the idea of moving the capital from Java to Kalimantan (Borneo). Yet even with its lack of official standing as the nation's capital, Jakarta was unquestionably the primate city of the nation and that status increased almost on a daily basis.

Sudiro's involvement in planning the metropolis was subordinate to the role played by the Ministry of Public Works and the intervention of President Sukarno. The Outline Plan of Jakarta was produced during Sudiro's tenure as a conceptual scheme to guide urban development. But his boss, Surkarno, did not really want the type of structured advice that a conventional plan afforded nor to be constrained in his actions by the advice of foreign consultants. Further, he did not want to be obstructed by appointees such as Sudiro. Several times when Sudiro asserted his will, such as in a plan to preserve the electric trams running between Jatinegara via Matraman and the line from Kramat to Senen, the mayor was overruled by the president. Sudiro thought the tram system was essential to support the petty traders working in those areas. Sukarno disagreed, and wanted all vestiges of the decrepit Dutch tram system removed in favour of modern cars and buses. So Jakarta's trams disappeared suddenly and completely. Sudiro also wanted to preserve the building at No 56 Jalan Pegarysaan Timor, where Indonesia's proclamation of independence had been read out in 1945. Sukarno preferred a new and modern structure to celebrate this monumental event. After Sudiro left office, the old building was torn down and a new one, Gedung Pola, was built as Sukarno desired.[24]

Sudiro's successor, Soemarno Sosroatmodjo, a medical doctor and army brigadier-general (and later Minister of Internal Affairs) shared Sukarno's vision of Jakarta as a beacon of Indonesia's rising national status. During his four year term (1960–1964), the city was officially made the nation's capital under Law 10/1964. Soemarno worked tirelessly to prepare Jakarta to host the Asian Games in 1962, and to do this helped to complete some of Sukarno's signature capital improvements. The *Djakarta Guide* produced in 1962 for tourists described the capital as 'A year-round Vacation City' and pointed to the continuous process of physical transformation that was underway. As tourism director Sri Budojo noted in the preface to the guide,

the face of Djakarta is rapidly changing. A small street you pass through today will have become a broad avenue tomorrow. An obscure residential quarter will have turned into an important business centre of towering buildings the next year.[25]

Soemarno embraced this approach and cleared the obstacles to urban modernization with a rapacious scalpel. For example, the land designated for the Senayan sports complex in South Jakarta required removal of 8,000 houses and construction of replacements elsewhere. Modest replacement housing (*rumah minimum*) was built near office and shopping centres throughout the city to put workers near to their workplaces. Soemarno believed that the provision of housing for workers made up for the losses necessitated by clearance and was a vital function of government. It was under his administration that one of the larger government-supported housing projects at Cempaka Putih was undertaken. An even more ambitious mixed-income community at nearby Pulo Mas was planned and later constructed, but not as originally conceived. Soemarno's administration also built new markets at Pasar Cikini and Pasar Senen and established two government development firms: *PT Pembangunan Jakarta Raya* to finance commercial developments in Jakarta prior to the explosion of privately financed efforts in the 1980s and 1990s; and *Bank Pembangunan Daerah*, a regional development bank that provided financing for city projects and helped to manage city funds. It was also during Soemarno's governorship that work was undertaken on Jakarta's comprehensive plan, which was nearly completed when Ali Sadikin took office as governor in 1965 and which covered the period from 1965 to 1985.

Although Sukarno actually appointed Sadikin, the last governor to serve under Sukarno was Henk Ngantung, an unlikely candidate for the position as he was a painter, not a soldier or a politician. Henk did have experience in government as the deputy governor under Soemarno, and in that role he worked to introduce cultural elements to the capital. He was responsible both as deputy governor and for a year as governor (1964–1965) for designing many of the monuments that became such iconic features of Jakarta's landscape. He designed street overpasses for pedestrians and bus shelters for commuters. In small, but important, ways Henk helped to realize Sukarno's quest to fashion a more orderly and beautiful national capital.[26]

Sukarno's Urban Vision

The recommendations of the Outline Plan to address the long-term infrastructure needs of the rapidly growing population were not entirely consistent with the expectations of the city's most influential resident, President Sukarno. His vision for Jakarta is central to understanding the motivations behind the master planning for Jakarta in the early years of the republic and during his so-called Guided Democracy era from the late 1950s until he fell from power in 1965. According to some scholars, the extensive investments made by the government in Jakarta between 1957 and 1966 were a direct outcome of Sukarno's intention to transform the colonial capital into a symbol of Indonesian national unity. His quest to recapture the unity of the powerful colonial state through loyalty to the nation required a range of strategies of which the two key were to share power with conflicting political factions and to provide patronage in return for loyalty. Sukarno's patronage was rampant, with the civil bureaucracy growing from 250,000 in 1940 to about 2.5 million by the time he left office.

Others suggest that Sukarno's urban modernization drive was a way to camouflage the most glaring weaknesses of his regime, such as failed economic strategies, the continued threats of dissolution of the republic emanating from the outer regions, rampant corruption, and a quest for global recognition.[27] Boddy suggests that the grand plans for rebuilding Jakarta were intended to reinforce

Sukarno's authoritarian regime. Yet within this authoritarian framework the modernist development projects financed by the national government in the early 1960s, such as the Senayan sports complex and the redesign of the Konigsplein into Merdeka Square, were intended by the president 'to foster a national unity and identity for the Indonesian people'.[28]

Kusno contends that Sukarno's modernist projects were not meant as a slight towards traditional culture but were expressive of a connection to pre-colonial spatial structures. This suggests that Sukarno was "both a progressive national unifier and a reinforcer of traditional values'.[29] In the judgment of Lambert Giebels, who worked on Jakarta's plans throughout the 1950s, it was not just flawed population data that undermined implementing the plan for Jakarta. Rather, the whole plan implementation process was hijacked by President Sukarno's priorities, which were oriented to showcase capital projects and not the mundane matters of growing the low-income housing stock, upgrading dilapidated *kamungs*, and improving basic services. However, other planners who also helped to prepare and implement the city's master plan, offer a contrasting and more favourable view of accomplishment during Sukarno's regime, both in terms of preparing plans, securing approval from the city council, and creating local institutions to support expanded planning education.[30]

Actually, Sukarno was not fully committed to Jakarta as the key to binding the divided nation into a more unified whole. At one point he considered scrapping Jakarta altogether as the capital and selecting a new locale. As previously noted, in the 1930s the Dutch had begun a process of moving administrative offices to the mountain retreat of Bandung, but World War II interrupted that move. The issue of what would serve as Indonesia's official capital city remained unresolved during the 1950s even though most administrative functions remained in Jakarta. In 1957, the Sukarno government sponsored a conference in Jakarta to discuss the creation of a new capital city. In his travels, and in discussions with leaders of other politically developing nations, Sukarno had become intrigued by the idea of building a new capital city from scratch. At the 1957 gathering, participants discussed the bold idea of shifting Indonesia's capital from Java to a more remote location.

It was not to Yogjakarta that Sukarno looked, the place of retreat for the unrecognized Sukarno government in the 1940s when the Dutch troops returned to unseat the new Indonesian government, and where the cultural capital of the Javanese would persist over the next half-century. It was to a remote interior area of Borneo (now Kalimantan) where he proposed building a new capital city. As in the case of Brazil where President Kubichek was moving the capital from Rio to Brasilia, a new city being built deep in the interior, or in Pakistan which intended to move the capital from the port at Karachi to a planned new

city known as Islamabad, Sukarno contemplated a similar capital transition in
Indonesia. Following the 1957 conference in Jakarta, a plan was developed, and
site preparations begun, for an area in central Kalimantan to serve as the new
capital city, a place to be known as Palangka Raya. The plan for this new capital
was prepared by the Ministry of Public Works. The city was designed and built.
However, none of the functions of the nation's capital were moved to this remote
location.[31]

The fact that Sukarno even contemplated the creation of a new capital city
on a remote Kalimantan site indicates his indifference to the day to day affairs
of Jakarta, as well as his proclivity for large-scale capital projects. His desire to
construct the Senayan sports complex, the Hotel Indonesia, and even the new
ring highway to connect the port of Tanjung Priok with South Jakarta, should
not be understood simply as ill-conceived urban initiatives in lieu of efforts to
deal with more pressing problems. Sukarno believed that national projects were
most appropriately located in the capital city to support both a national and a
local development agenda. Although Sukarno abandoned the idea of moving the

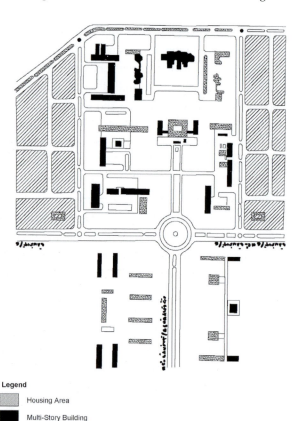

Figure 3.3. Concept
Plan for the proposed
government complex
to be built in the
remote central area
of Kalimantan at
Palangkaraya.
(*Source*: ROI, MPPW,
2003)

Legend

Housing Area

Multi-Story Building

Non-Multi-Story building

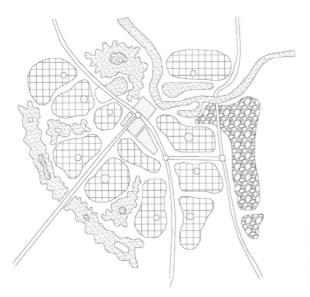

Figure 3.4. Urban concept plan for the proposed capital city of Palangkaraya. (*Source*: ROI, MPPW, 2003)

capital from Jakarta to a new planned city in remote Borneo, he did not abandon completely the idea of creating a new capital city. Instead of carrying out this plan in Kalimantan, he was going to do it within the former colonial capital. As he noted in a speech delivered on the city's 435th anniversary on 22 June 1962:

Building up Djakarta as beautifully as possible, build it as spectacularly as possible, so that this city, which has become the centre of the struggle of the Indonesian people, will be an inspiration and beacon to the whole of struggling mankind and to all the emerging forces. If Egypt was able to construct Cairo as its capital, Italy its Rome, France its Paris and Brazil its Brasilia, then Indonesia must also proudly present Djakarta as the portals of the country.[32]

Sukarno's virtual silence on the problems of the rapidly growing capital city is instructive in what it suggests about his approach to planning. But it also means that it is not just to the quixotic president that one must look for urban strategies in this critical period in the city's development, but also to the government planners who were addressing the challenges of a rapidly expanding metropolis on a daily basis. The planners held a view that Jakarta had been short changed by its colonial mentors, as compared to other cities in the region. But whether the city warranted investments to compensate for this neglect or abandonment as a capital to start over with a clean slate was a key question in the 1950s. As noted in a Department of Foreign Affairs publication, Jakarta had been neglected during the early Sukarno presidency because of:

the belief that sooner or later Djakarta would be abandoned for a better place, more worthy of being the seat of the central government. It has been for that reason that the capital of Indonesia, ever since the state gained international recognition in 1950, has on the surface, retained the look of a small and unambitious provincial Dutch town.[33]

Its appearance was 'depressing' compared to other colonial urban projects such as Saigon and New Delhi which had been conceived by the colonial rulers 'with great vision and imagination, characterized by handsome and impressive government buildings, beautiful parks and broad tree-lined boulevards'. The Indonesian foreign affairs office assessment went on to reinforce the prevailing negative image of Jakarta:

Indonesians themselves were the first to admit that their capital was ugly and flat, with narrow streets and empty squares that are not parks, and with that disturbing Dutch-made canal system winding through the city. To demonstrate this ugliness, a foreign correspondent once took a picture of a Djakarta back street, and flashed it around the world with a caption saying this was the main shopping center of Djakarta.[34]

But by the early 1960s this critical attitude had changed, and Jakarta's leadership offered a more upbeat assessment of the city's place in Indonesian development:

Djakarta is determined to become beautiful, but to see her best is to see Djakarta as the living symbol of a tolerant but determined nation among the newly emerging forces of this century, struggling for a just and peaceful world.[35]

The guiding principle for the city was 'Indonesian Socialism', which would help to define responses to its many problems and which justified a massive public investment in urban infrastructure. 'During the next eight to ten years', it was noted in 1962, 'there are about seventy major and minor projects of physical development with a budget of some four thousand five hundred million *rupiahs*' that would radically transform key sections of the city. These included the 14-storey Hotel Indonesia, a six-lane Jakarta highway bypass, the removal of *becaks* and the introduction of a new bus system, and 'the removal of ill-planned *kampungs* and overcrowded slums by housing arrangements conducive to a community spirit and human comfort'.[36]

The impact of Sukarno's distinctive imprint on the built and social environment of Jakarta has been the subject of a variety of conflicting interpretations by scholars and public officials. One plausible explanation for his penchant for monumentality in the projects he favoured for Jakarta, especially from the late 1950s until his fall, was to reflect in the city's architecture the power he wielded over the nation. The institution of his one-man authoritarian rule under the banner of 'Guided Democracy' coincides with the beginning of his vigorous engagement in capital reconstruction work. Another explanation offered by scholars, and in many instances bolstered by Sukarno's own pronouncements, is that these civic building works, using a modernist, international architectural motif, were an exercise in raising national prestige to blot out the lingering images of the colonial past. Sukarno's expectations went far beyond throwing off colonialism and securing an independent nation. With Jakarta as the 'beacon' of a powerful new nation, Sukarno had his sights set on creating a model of the just and well-cared for state. As he put it in one of his addresses:

Comrades from Jakarta, let us build Jakarta into the greatest city possible. Great not just because of its skyscrapers, great not just because it has boulevards and beautiful streets; great not just because it has beautiful monuments, great in every respect, even in the little houses of the workers of Jakarta there must be a sense of greatness… Jakarta is becoming the beacon of the whole of mankind. Yes, the beacon of the New Emerging Forces.[37]

Yet it is also obvious that by listing all the physical improvements that he had initiated, he wanted credit for forging greatness out of the humble fabric of the city.

As an inveterate traveller, Sukarno saw, admired, and sought to emulate those features of other capital cities which could add to the lustre to Jakarta. His ego and sense of personal destiny, his penchant for built objects due to his training as a civil engineer, and his desire to accelerate the nation's position as a regional force, helped to fuel the quest to modernize the capital. In his own terms, Sukarno was doing great things for the Indonesians even if these projects diverted the nation's precious few resources from other needs that would have had less visibility in the international arena.

An example of Sukarno's use of large-scale projects to convey the desired image can be seen in Indonesia's exhibit at the 1964 New York World's Fair. The US$2 million expended on the pavilion, designed by R.M. Sudarsono of Jakarta, in concert with the US team of Max O. Urbahn and Abel Sorensen of New York, was a relatively substantial sum for a struggling underdeveloped nation. Sorenson had a track record for important government commissions in Jakarta under Sukarno, including the National Housing Development Corporation building (1960) and the State Development Bank building (1960). He claimed that his modernist style reflected Indonesia's desire to show its 'progressive aims and cultural art forms'. As the architect of the Palace of State in Bali, Sudarsono's role was to ensure that the Indonesian pavilion at the World's Fair was appropriately grounded in traditional design elements. And there was another message intended by this international exhibition. Sukarno personally selected the site for the pavilion when he visited the fair grounds in 1961. According to Nicoletta, 'he wanted to be sure [it] would be halfway between those of the U.S. and the U.S.S.R'.[38]

The completed pavilion was 'overwhelmingly modern in appearance, but was flanked by two eighty foot, hand-carved replicas of Balinese towers'. Nicoletta contends that 'the prevalence of modernism at the fair demonstrated the ambivalence towards breaking free from western modes of architecture and colonial hegemony, especially for new nations' like Indonesia. 'The postwar modernism they incorporated in their pavilion reflected the dominance of the style after the war, its association with democracy and capitalism, and desire of new nations to be players on a global scale.' However, a quarrel ensued with the US government when it sold military equipment to Indonesia's enemy, Malaysia. This prompted Sukarno to retaliate by refusing to pay the 1965 rent to the fair corporation. As a result, after being open only for a few months, the pavilion was seized by the fair corporation and shut down.[39]

Another possible explanation for Sukarno's intense focus on Jakarta's modernization, according to planning historian Kusno, is that Sukarno was appropriating modernist architecture and design in Jakarta to create a national centre of power derived directly from the 'political culture of traditional Java ... an authoritative center akin to the Javanese spatial concept of power'.[40] In this way, he was not just looking to Indonesia's role in the international realm but to consolidating the disparate parts of the new nation into a single whole. This is consistent with political scientist Benedict Anderson's interpretation of traditional concepts of power in Southeast Asian culture which places a premium on concentrating power within a centre rather than dispersing it spatially or functionally. Thus, Sukarno wanted not just to put Indonesia on the world stage but also to strengthen national unity, to counter the forces of disintegration that were threatening the new nation, something Sukarno recognized in the opening years of the new republic.[41]

A key component in realizing Sukarno's vision of a greater and more carefully planned Jakarta was to bestow on the national capital greater authority over its own development. By a Presidential Decree in 1959 (6/1959), Jakarta was elevated to the status of a province, and Mayor Soemarno made its first Governor. In 1961, another Presidential Decree (2/1961) provided Jakarta with full autonomy, although the governor was still directly accountable to the president. In 1964, the Capital City Special Territory was created, correcting a noteworthy legal oversight in that Jakarta never officially had been made Indonesia's capital in 1949. In 1965, Soemarno was promoted further, this time to become one of Sukarno's ministers.[42]

The structural changes in the leadership of Jakarta were significant because they contributed to the growing influence of the central government over the Municipal Council to set policy priorities and to undertake project implementation in the capital city. The Municipal Council, initially established by the Dutch in the 1920s, was now a body appointed by the central government through the Minister of Internal Affairs. Like the governor, the council was subject to influence from the central government. In the early national period, the mayor and the council exercised shared responsibility for general administration, and because of this worked closely. But the elevation of Jakarta's mayor to the status of a minister, in concert with the designation of Jakarta as a special district comparable to a province, diminished the administrative functions of the local council. A small consultative body, *Baden Pemerintah Harian*, helped the governor to carry out executive functions and this group remained entirely responsible to the governor. Under the Sadikin governorship, there was a reassertion of local prerogative for a brief period. Sadikin combined central and local government offices in Jakarta under a single administrative structure which he headed. This helped to ensure that the execution of daily functions through the local government offices (*dinas*) would not be overruled by counterparts from the central government in comparable units. This structure was unique to Jakarta and persisted during Sadikin's tenure, but the way the governance structure typically operated in the capital city, meant that full autonomy was never achieved.[43]

The 1960 Master Plan

According to the view of the foreign consultants who prepared the Outline Plan (which was adopted by the Jakarta municipality), and the subsequent master plan which was completed in 1960, the implementation process fell far short of expectations. For one thing, the 1960 plan was never granted official status. It was a relatively brief document, running to just sixteen pages, and set forth what its authors regarded as a broad framework for action, but did not contain action strategies *per se*. It conceived of Jakarta as having three distinct functional parts, an inner city of 2,000 hectares with more than a half of this dedicated to residential functions. The rest was used for unspecified 'working', 'livelihood' and 'recreation' functions. Beyond the inner city was the central city of similar proportions, but with lower residential densities and more intensive commercial and industrial activities. The third layer, an outer city, made up nearly 60

Figure 3.5. Senen Market area before modernization. (*Source*: KIT Tropemuseum, Amsterdam)

per cent of urbanized area would be primarily residential and recreational. Encompassing an area of approximately 6,000 hectares, the outer city could absorb half of Jakarta's anticipated population of 2.5 million and with substantial lower residential densities.[44]

The conception of Jakarta divided into three concentric zones did not mesh at all with the historical pattern of development in the city. Rather than expanding in concentric rings, the city's growth had been linear, following the high ground between the thirteen waterways that flowed northwards from the mountains into the Bay of Jakarta. Within this linear development pattern, Jakarta had supported several distinct and separate commercial centres while at the same time accommodating population growth through high densities on those sites less prone to flooding. Even with this compact development pattern, a distinctive characteristic of Jakarta was its polycentric character. The architects of the 1960 plan seemed either to have overlooked or to have denied that attribute of the city. What they offered instead was an urban model that mimicked the standard Western concept of 'urban decentralization' in a city that evidenced dense clusters and centralization irrespective of proximity to the inner, middle or outer zones.

To achieve this new urban structure, the 1960 plan advocated an aggressive restructuring of the urban fabric through a combination of redevelopment of old buildings, street improvements (including improved drainage to address the perennial flooding problem), improved sanitation, and improved urban services, including new market areas. It identified thirteen priority areas – Rawamangun,

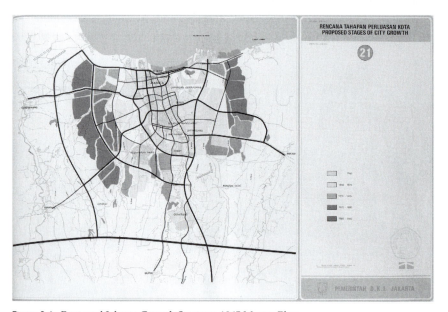

Figure 3.6. Proposed Jakarta Growth Strategy, 1965 Master Plan.

Pasar Minggu, Tebet, Polonia Dalam, Slipi, Tomang, Cempaka Putih, Pluit, Rawa, Sari, Sunter (Sumar Batu), Karet Kuningan, and Petamburan – in which to target these improvements.

The plan also called for slum clearance in the dense neighbourhoods and market areas that were encroaching on the traditionally prestigious neighbourhoods in the former European quarter of the inner city as well as some in the expanding southern section near Kebayoran Baru. These neighbourhoods and market areas included: Pasar Cikini, Planetarium, Gajah Mada, Jalan Sabang, Pegangsaan Barat, Krekot Dalam, Pasar Tebet, Pasar Grogal, and Wisma Niaga (in Blok M). The detailed identification of the various urban market areas and run down *kampungs* earmarked as a priority for improvement suggests that the plan-makers were far more cognizant of the realities in Jakarta in the 1950s than was suggested in their conceptual model. Areas to accommodate new growth in industry, agribusiness and residences were situated largely to the south and west of Jakarta where the annexation of 1950 had added new territory. The plan recommended an intensive community development programme to serve low- and moderate-income residents on the eastern and southern edges of Jakarta, which were to be opened up by means of a highway connecting the harbour at Tanjung Priok to the southern edge of the city. The plan identified Pulomas (270 hectares) in eastern Jakarta, Cipete Cilandak (500 hectares), Pasar Minggu (500 hectares) and Cipanang Galur (3,000 hectares) in South Jakarta, and Cengkerang (200 hectares) in West Jakarta as areas to be developed to accommodate the greater portion of Jakarta's rapidly expanding population. It was estimated that these developments could provide housing for an additional 400,000 residents.[45]

The 1960 Master Plan was largely a public works agenda and, except for its simplistic delineation of Jakarta's land-use structure, did not give a coherent spatial vision for the capital city. By identifying specific *kampungs* with acute problems for redevelopment and renewal, it re-energized the *kampung* improvement concept that had been shelved with the outbreak of war in the 1940s. It was, nonetheless, the opinion of the two foreign consultants who contributed to its formulation, Kenneth A.Watts and G.H. Franklin, that there appeared to be little indication either from the Jakarta leadership, or from the central government, that the planning process was valued. The 1960 Master Plan was never officially adopted by government. Even so, the lack of official standing was not a true measure of the plan's impact. A number of its recommendations, including highway developments, location of new residential settlements, and upgrading infrastructure in the worst *kampungs* were soon under way. Although the Sukarno government might have seemed indifferent to the rigours of the plan-making process, it is obvious that planning overseen by the local administration contributed to the vision of Indonesia's changing capital city.[46]

Plan for Pulo Mas Community

One innovative component of the replanned capital city that followed the recommendations of the 1950s was development of Pulo Mas. Located in north-east Jakarta, Pulo Mas was intended initially to function, like Kebayoran Baru, as a stand alone satellite city offering a carefully planned environment for its residents. But what distinguished it was that its high-quality environment was intended to support the 'masses', not the elite. What began as a student project emerged as a serious response to the challenges of the expanding low-income population. In 1961, three young Indonesian architects were given scholarships to study town and regional planning in the School of Architecture of the Royal Danish Academy of Fine Arts in Copenhagen. The three were Herbowo, who later served as Vice Governor of Jakarta, Radinal Moochtar, a future Indonesian Minister of Public Works, and Kandar Tisnawinata, who later served as Director of City Planning of Jakarta from 1977 to the late 1980s, making him the capital city's longest serving planning director.

Besides gaining further professional training in planning and urban design, the mission for the three was to bring back with them a plan for a second new city for Jakarta as the next stage in implementing the Outline Plan. To undertake the project, they determined that it was necessary to collect and collate better data on Jakarta (and Indonesia) as a 'tool for future planning'. As in the case of urban demography, data on Jakarta's changing spatial, economic and social circumstances over the previous two decades was non-existent. Together with a fourth student from Canada, they prepared a 161 page compendium of urban and architectural data on the 'nation', the 'region', the 'town' and 'housing', drawing on all the sources they could find, which included the Watts Concept Plan of November 1957 as well as a follow-up survey Watts conducted in 1961 through the Division of Regional and City Planning at the Institute of Technology Bandung.[47]

There were also several housing studies that were important sources of data and inspiration for the Pulo Mas plan, such as 'Urban Mass Housing for the People of Djakarta', prepared in 1961 by Philip A. Arctander, Director of Research at the Danish National Institute of Building Research and consultant to Indonesia from 1957 to 1961; G.H. Franklin's memorandum, 'The Planning Aspects of the Provision of Prefab, Multi-Storied Mass Housing for the People of Djakarta' (September 1961); Mary R. Doebele's social survey of the Krekot Dalam Housing Project (prepared in June 1959), and Hadinoto's 'Housing in the Sphere of Socialism in Indonesia' (1961). Their preliminary plan, which Governor Soemarno praised, called for construction of a large moderate- to low-income housing community as one of the additional regional settlement centres suggested in the Outline Plan. As the students described its function,

The Pulo Mas Project is designed for the purpose of initiating urban housing for the masses in Indonesia and in particular for the relief of the housing problems in Djakarta.[48]

They believed that the Pulo Mas plan could serve as a prototype for a citywide community development initiative. They stressed that the more mundane matter of addressing urban housing needs through projects like Pulo Mas

is ... a worthy successor to the ASIAN GAMES, redirecting the energy released during the execution of that great enterprise. Its successful completion should enable it to be used as a model for the development of other areas in Djakarta as well as in other Indonesian towns.[49]

Like Kebayoran Baru, Pulo Mas was intended initially to be a 'self-contained' settlement linked to the rest of the city through the new ring road.

Located on a 270 hectare site in East Jakarta adjacent to the ring road and within reasonable proximity of the Tanjung Priok harbour, Pulo Mas was an

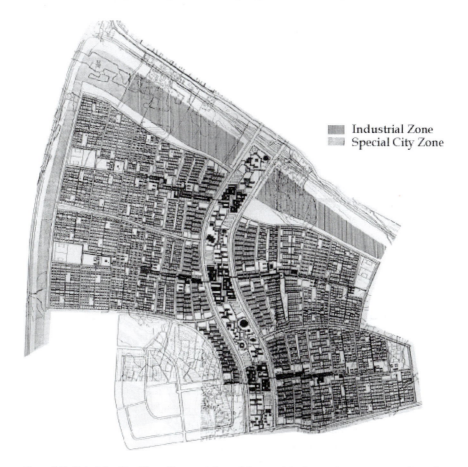

Figure 3.7. Pulo Mas Site Plan. (*Source*: Adapted from original copy in possession of Kandar Tisnawinata, Jakarta)

ambitious plan for social housing which was anticipated to accommodate about 50,000 people when complete. Most of the land was still in rice cultivation, and the limited displacement of indigenous residents (compared with the development of Kebayoran Baru) was consistent with the project's main goal of addressing a dire shortage of decent housing for low-income residents rather than compounding the problem through large-scale displacement. The plan proposed a series of interconnected neighbourhood units (or *lingkungan*), each accommodating about 3,000 people. Groups of houses were clustered around small open spaces. Like the neighbourhood unit so widely used for community planning in the United States at this time, especially in public housing projects, the residential units in Pulo Mas were linked together by community institutions, such as a primary school. In common with worker housing complexes in European cities but not in public housing developments in the United States, there were also neighbourhood shops. A combination of several neighbourhood units would make up a *kelurahan*, the community level organization of local government.

What is noteworthy about the Pulo Mas plan, and obviously a consequence of its authors' experiences overseas, was how it adapted international planning concepts to the unique cultural, spatial, economic and political circumstances of the Indonesian city. In addition to small shops to serve the neighbourhood units, the plan proposed a ribbon-shaped commercial corridor, flanked by wide roadways, which was to serve as the civic core of the Pulo Mas community. The 'elongated form' of the central commercial area was intended to encourage interactions between both the eastern and western sections of the community through a system of pedestrian passages. The project designers distinguished between the community centres and the main centre:

In community centers are the shops, the primary and secondary schools, the *Lurah's* office and an open space. In the main center, the principal shops are to be found, with the high school, offices and other public buildings.[50]

One of the defining features of the Pulo Mas scheme was the proposed state-of-the art infrastructure, beginning with clean public water taps to support residents and the intention of later bringing water into individual dwellings. The plan also included a system of closed sanitary sewers connected to each dwelling, and linked to a sewage treatment plant which would provide primary treatment before being discharged into the Sunter River. A system of surface drains would handle rainwater, taking the runoff through open ditches to a reservoir, in order to prevent flooding especially during the rainy season.

The greatest possible separation of pedestrian and vehicular traffic was also a feature of the plan. While most of the housing was to be permanent, the plan did not rule out the possibility that initially some structures might be of the semi-permanent variety found in *kampungs*. Self-built housing clearly was acceptable. As long as the basic street pattern and land-use configuration were adhered to, the plan emphasized flexibility in how the area was built.

Not until Ali Sadikin replaced Soemarno as governor in 1966 was the Pulo Mas project begun and, much to the regret of the project designers, what was constructed diverged fundamentally from the original concept of a model community for the masses. Two key decisions undermined the plan. One was that the original plan to use public funds to develop the community was abandoned because of the dire state of the Jakarta city budget. The new governor, Ali Sadikin, had an alternative approach: to use public power to secure the land and private developers to finance construction. Under the leadership of Kandar Tisnawinata, who was assigned the task of implementing his group's project by Governor Sadikin, private investors were secured and construction began in 1966. As Tisnawinata quickly discovered, the mass housing scheme he had helped to devise was not financially feasible from the private sector perspective without public subsidy. What was feasible was more upscale housing for the moderate-to middle-income market at significantly lower densities, and that was what was supplied by the Pulo Mas project when built.

The second significant change in the project design, and one that struck directly at both the design and social integrity of the plan, was the insistence by Jakarta's Vice Governor that a horse race track, rather than the proposed commercial and civic centre, be placed in the middle of the project site. The race track, Pacuan Kuda, was built, and with it Pulo Mas lost its claims as a model for inexpensive housing (*projek model perumahan murah*). It was not a collection of coherent neighbourhood units but one continuous low-density housing complex. In addition, an industrial area was added between the residences and a new expressway to the west. The race track and an adjacent park, Taman Pasadenia Pulo Mas, consumed more space than was originally allocated to the commercial-civic centre, and reduced substantially the space available for housing.

Rather than providing a link between the eastern and western residential sections (the latter, Pulo Gading, built later as another low-density neighbourhood and in a separate *kelurahan*), the race track and the park became permanent barriers. Pulo Mas proved to be a successful real estate development, but it was a failure as an experiment in social housing so desperately needed in Jakarta, and a major disappointment for Tisnawinata. Apart from a small housing complex north of the race course, known as Rumah Susun Pulomas, what was built in Pulo Mas and Pulo Gading were middle-income neighbourhoods along Jakarta's developing periphery. There was a modest concession to the original intentions of the Pulo Mas project years later. When Moochtar became a senior official in public works, he made an effort to correct the situation by having a massive low-income housing project constructed in the Kebun Kacang neighbourhood within a short walk of Sukarno's newly built Hotel Indonesia.[51]

As the Pulo Mas plan was being developed, it was already evident that the demographic assumptions used to prepare the Outline Plan were flawed. The rapid tempo of population growth in Jakarta required a more aggressive approach to housing development than the plan envisioned. The Outline Plan called for the addition of three satellite cities (in addition to Kebayoran Baru) in southern Jakarta, where the greatest population growth was anticipated, and besides Pulo Mas in east Jakarta there was to have been a fourth satellite city in the north-west quadrant which was not built.

Kenneth Watts, who not only helped to prepare the Outline Plan but also worked with the Indonesian students and their Danish instructors to prepare the preliminary plan for Pulo Mas (under a contract with the United Nations) had other suggestions on how to meet the need for more housing. He was a fervent advocate of developing the existing towns surrounding Jakarta, especially Tanggerang to the west, Bekasi to the east, and Bogor to the south, as growth poles. In a 1961 survey of planning issues in Jakarta (which the Indonesian students used as a background piece for the Pulo Mas plan), Watts underscored the 'problem of surplus population' as the one factor that could seriously jeopardize all physical plans for Jakarta. Rather than create new towns like Kebayoran Baru or Pulo Mas, he suggested a two pronged alternative approach: increase the use of transmigration of Javanese to Sumatra which could easily absorb the surplus new population, and build up the existing small towns around Jakarta rather than establishing new ones. To build up the areas around Tanggerang, Bekasi and Bogor required an ambitious road development scheme to provide access to existing employment centres in Jakarta as well as to facilitate the dispersal of new employment opportunities to the periphery. In words that sounded much like a rationale for 'planned sprawl', Watts concluded that Jakarta should be allowed to expand by 'a process of peripheral development' and an expanded road network would enable this to take place.[52]

The recommendations in the Outline Plan, coupled with the ongoing consultation by Watts and others, became the basis for a far more practical and detailed scheme to guide development of the expanding metropolis, the Master Plan of 1965. While drafted in the waning days of Sukarno's increasingly embattled regime, it was presented to Jakarta's Regional Council in September 1966 by Ali Sadikin. Sadikin, who would serve as governor for the next 11 years under the new president Suharto, was an unlikely proponent of an ambitious planning initiative for Indonesia's largest city. As he later admitted, he had given precious little thought to urban matters prior to becoming governor. But the 40 year old Major General in Indonesia's Marine Corp quickly became the single most important political figure in the emerging megacity of Jakarta, and an unequivocal proponent of an interventionist and comprehensive approach to planning in order to improve urban conditions. Under his administration, and for the first time in the city's history, state of the art master plans in the form of detailed assessments of conditions and elaborate blueprints were prepared by his planners. His intention was to transform the big city of villages into a modern Indonesian metropolis.

Sadikin and the Master Plan of Jakarta

Ali Sadikin was appointed governor by the lame duck President Sukarno in March 1966. In September, he presented for approval by the legislature of the special district of Jakarta *The Master Plan of Djakarta, 1965–1985*. Obviously, this was not a document that he had played much of a part in crafting, and he readily credited others with conceiving the basic framework of the plan. Yet, in the foreword to the plan, Sadikin urged the Jakarta Regional Council to adopt it quickly,

so that it could be implemented and further developed for making it the planning basis for well-formulated City Detail Plans with their aspects of Ordering, Renewal, and Expansion of the city.[53]

As governor, Sadikin was also Chairman of the Regional Council, so it is no surprise that the plan was adopted in May 1967. It was not just a plan for a large city but one that took into account Jakarta's special role as a capital city. This role had been confirmed by the passage of Law 10/1964[54] and the language of the resolution officially accepting the plan picked up on this theme. It indicated that the goal of the plan was not only to 'develop city life in accordance with modern technology', but

to transform Djakarta into a city/region capable, and being capable to place itself as the Country's Capital and as an International City up to proper and universal standards, and be the vessel of national as well as international aspirations.[55]

The idea of Jakarta as an aspiring international city reflected the continuing influence of Sukarno's lofty vision. Also, the concept of Jakarta as the centre of a regional complex, which was first articulated in the Outline Plan, was elevated to one of the key organizing principles of the 1965 plan. The unstated assumption underlying the plan was that it was only through an aggressive and engaged public effort led by the newly appointed and greatly empowered leadership of the special district of Jakarta, that the vision could be realized. In the person of Governor Sadikin, Jakarta had a new chief administrator intent on addressing 'the disappointing physical condition of the present city'.[56]

The plan identified five major problems facing Jakarta that demanded immediate attention; most involved basic services and infrastructure. One was the flooding problem, which had plagued the city since its founding 350 years earlier in a low lying coastal area bisected by thirteen rivers. The Dutch government had partially addressed this through the construction of flood canals along the southern and western edges of the city, but the annual flooding of poor communities located in low areas throughout the city warranted a 'comprehensive flood-control plan', including regulation of new settlements as well as additional infrastructure to improve the drainage. Jakarta's flooding problem was regional in scope and needed to be tackled at that level.

Improved sanitation, especially removal of solid waste, was also a pressing concern that demanded both short-term amelioration and some long-term strategies. The plan offered no specifics on the short-term approaches but indicated that improved waste management at the community level as well as a better overall system of collection and disposal would greatly reduce the problem. Traffic congestion was another matter demanding immediate intervention. According to the 1965 plan, the transport problems emanated from a combination of mixed land uses, poorly designed road intersections, the existence of surface rail lines crossing major thoroughfares, and the recurring flood conditions. The 1965 plan acknowledged that the number of vehicles was expanding faster than road improvements were taking place, and 'inadequate mass-transportation facilities' only compounded the problem. Its references to mass transit needs were oblique but improvements in mass transit were definitely part of the long-term strategy.[57]

Another critical need was for the city to take an active role in addressing

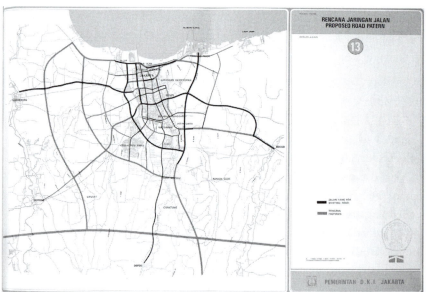

Figure 3.8. 1965 Master Plan.

inadequate housing and community facilities, especially for the expanding low-income population. Squatter settlements and slum areas were increasing, and many of these areas were not served sufficiently by markets, schools, clinics or transport facilities. The identification of improved low-income housing and community development as planning priorities would frame two notable initiatives of Sadikin's administration. These were the restoration of a *kampung* improvement programme and the first serious effort to create public housing for the needy.

According to the 1965 plan, all the problems confronting Jakarta revolved around the control and use of land, much of which was controlled by government agencies. Each agency operated as an independent unit and none was accountable to the city's leaders nor were they required to run their projects past the local planning authority for approval. As a result, land planning and development in Jakarta was not under the control of the city's administration but rather could be undertaken by many different government actors, or by private developers acting on the authority of these other government units. Ensuring that development did not take place in areas set aside for open space, on land needed to recharge the aquifer, on rights of way, or on agricultural land, as well as coordinating land development with other infrastructure investments, was critical to proper development of the metropolis. What was necessary, but which the plan itself could not ensure, was that in 'developing the lands of the capital, well-coordinated policies and actions between both the Central and Regional Governments should be effected'.[58]

Shortly after approval of the 1965 plan, initial steps were taken to prepare another planning analysis based on the assumption that the development of the capital city should be carried out on the basis of regional considerations. The result was the creation of a plan and an administrative body for what came to be known initially as Jabotabek, drawn from four contiguous places, Jakarta, Bogor, Tanggerang and Bekasi. Although planning for Jabotabek formally began in the early 1970s, the Jabotabek approach would not exert any real impact on Jakarta's planning and development processes until later in the 1980s and the 1990s. In Jakarta in the late 1960s, the focus was on how much the Sadikin government could do to address immediate development needs of the core city and its expanding periphery.

Sadikin's predecessor, Soemarno, had played a key role in overseeing Sukarno's aggressive building agenda, which concentrated largely on the commercial zone and civic centre connecting Merdeka Square with the new sports complex at Senayan to the south of city, and building Indonesia's very first highway overpass and cloverleaf. Construction of a six-lane boulevard running from the south-western corner of Merdeka (in front of the Bank of Indonesia) to a new welcome

Figure 3.9. Aerial view of Jalan Thamrin (south of the Hotel Indonesia roundabout) from the early 1970s. (*Source*: KIT Tropemuseum, Amsterdam)

statue positioned in the centre of a roundabout in front of the Hotel Indonesia began in 1961. This provided a distinctive urban gateway that would be extended an additional 4 kilometres southwards to the Senayan sports complex. Locating the Hotel Indonesia at the roundabout helped to anchor this emerging commercial corridor.

Under Sadikin's governship, the remaining parcels on the circle and along the newly built boulevard named in honour of Jakarta's famous legislator of the 1920s and 1930s, Mohammed Husni Thamrin, would be filled with more hotels, the British, German and Soviet embassies, a string of government and private offices, and the Sarinah department store. One of the buildings which Sadikin completed was Jakarta's first office tower, Wisma Nusantara. It was planned by Jakarta's development company, *P.T. Pembangunan Jaya*, in 1964 and built across from the Hotel Indonesia on the north-east edge of the roundabout under Sadikin's watch.[59]

The 1965 plan provided city leaders with a more coherent vision of how to address key problems but it was, in the end, as one Jakarta planner noted, just a set of drawings. It reflected the best current advice about how to guide development of the capital city but it was a very different creature from the detailed plans that developers would use to get things done. Needing to show results quickly, Governor Sadikin and his planners did not feel constrained by the somewhat 'academic exercise' reflected in the 1965 plan. It proved to be a relatively accurate guide to the forthcoming infrastructure investments, however. Unlike the Outline Plan, which had proposed an extensive network of new satellite cities, the 1965 plan opted for a broader range of strategies to address local needs.[60]

Continuing the lead of his predecessor Soemarno, Sadikin favoured an incremental approach, with some large-scale undertakings, such as the construction of Pulo Mas and the even larger Cimpaka Putih housing estate, an infrastructure improvement programme that eventually blanketed most of the *kampungs* in Jakarta, and a significant amount of new road construction (including

Figure 3.10. Hotel Indonesia roundabout during Sadikin governorship, 1971. (*Source*: KIT Tropemuseum, Amsterdam)

road widening). But Sadikin also undertook many smaller but visible initiatives such as adding new bus shelters and improving public markets. Given the paucity of Jakarta's development budget in the late 1960s, Sadikin relied heavily on private sector engagement in key projects, such as with Pulo Mas, and also experimented with other techniques for generating revenues, such as permitting gambling in the capital. The city's own development company, *P.T. Pembangunan Jaya*, was a holding company for a number of related enterprises tied to specific development projects (such as *P.T. Pembangunan Jaya-Ancol* for the Ancol Amusement Park) or to related industries, such as building supplies through *Jaya Aluminum*). These private-public partnerships drew needed private capital into the city's development work. But the secret weapon that Sadikin wielded was an inexhaustible supply of persuasiveness.

To secure land for street widening, which often involved individuals surrendering up to a quarter of individual parcels, Sadikin used a combination of persuasion and charm. He persuaded land owners, such as those along Jalan Gadja Mada and Jalan Hayam Wuruk, that it was in their interest to donate land for the road widening. As he pointed out, modernizing the road way, even if it involved giving up a portion of their land, would stimulate the land market, since the clearance of the older structures would provide space for new development and increased land values would follow (which would more than make up for what they lost). The land owners along these streets, as well as along the planned new boulevard through Kuningan, Jalan H. Rangkayo Rasuna Said, marched to Sadikin's tune and donated the right away in expectation of increased land values (which in fact ensued).

The charm factor was evident when he personally invited to dinner at the governor's house all who had contributed through donations to Jakarta's development. One of the most trusted staff members who was responsible for implementing Sadikin's development projects, including land acquisition, was architect and planner, Wastu Chong.[61] Sadikin felt that the citizens of Jakarta needed tangible proof that the government was making real efforts to improve their circumstances. The loyalty that the outspoken and demanding Sadikin earned from his staff was matched by his popularity among the people. The name Ali Sadikin was synonymous with the development of Jakarta into a modern capital and especially with the *kampung* improvement programme (discussed in Chapter 4).

Jabotabek and the Emergence of Regional Planning

While Sadikin's planners focused on meeting the everyday needs of Jakarta's burgeoning population, Indonesia's United Nations-financed consultants, who had helped prepare the Outline Plan and the subsequent 1965 master plan, kept the spotlight on long-range development challenges. In a section of the master plan entitled 'The Future of D.C.I. Djakarta', the idea of regional planning was introduced. The plan recommended an aggressive expansion of the administrative boundaries of Jakarta to accommodate the growing population which had already consumed all of the vacant land made available through the 1950 annexation. The proposed expansion was not precisely delineated in the 1965 plan but was described in general as the area beyond the 'greenbelt', meaning Tanggerang to the west, Depok and Tjibinong (Cibinong) to the south and Bekasi to the east.

This expansion of the official boundaries of Jakarta was not to take place but the recommendation underscored the view of the consultants that Jakarta's urbanized area would greatly increase in all directions in the ensuing years. Not surprisingly, the Dutch consultants lapsed into familiar discourse, referring in the English translation of the 1965 plan to an idea they had propagated earlier, the *'Gewest Batavia en Ommelanden'*, or the 'Jakarta District and Environs.[62] This 'planning region' encompassed an area well beyond the proposed enlargement of Jakarta's administrative boundaries. As the 1965 plan noted,

In the future planning of Djakarta where the principles of decentralization in development will be used ... not centralizing development within the city which would unduly burden the city itself ... it is clear then, that a wider regional scope should be used than the boundaries of the D.C.I.[63]

The outer limits of the planning region were defined by the watersheds of the Tjikarang (Cikarang) and Rjisadane (Cisadane) rivers to the east and west respectively, and the mountain range that provided the city's water sources to the south of Bogor. This planning region was what would eventually be known as Jabotabek, a contiguous urbanized area that extended up to 65 kilometres in all directions from the centre of Jakarta.

The initial formal Jabotabek regional planning study was undertaken by the Ministry of Public Works through its bureau for planning and human settlements, *Cipta Karya*, in 1973. It was done with technical assistance from a team of Dutch planners, including L. Giebels, from the Dutch National Physical Planning Agency, and several local planners. The initiation of the Dutch technical assistance began under Radinal Moochtar, at the time Director General of *Cipta Karya* and later Minister of Public Works. His leadership explains why the Dutch consultants who had been used for earlier planning assistance reappeared to help to expand the planning functions. One of the Indonesians who assisted Moochtar to develop a new legal framework for urban planning was Supangkat, a former clerk in Batavia under the Dutch, and Suparman, a former assistant to Professor Thijsse at ITB.[64]

Moochtar, and his successor in *Cipta Karya*, Rachmat Wiradisuria, obtained from the Dutch consultants an approach for planning the Jakarta region that

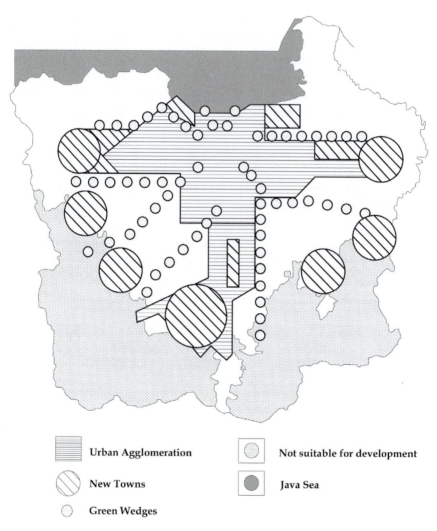

Figure 3.11. Regional Concept with Self-Sufficient New Towns developed for the Jabotabek plan.

sought to manage its tremendous population growth. One prerequisite for an effective regional plan was precise data on the scale and direction of growth of Jakarta's *kampungs*. As Giebels noted, the 'decisive question to be answered before planning concepts for the region could be developed, was to consider the phenomenon of *kampung* settlement, which in Indonesia dominates the urban morphology'.[65] He acknowledged that *kampungs* should not be treated as the sort of temporary slums or shantytowns prevalent in other developing country cities. Instead, they were a more permanent human settlement type that provided a transition for the masses from rural to urban life. The Kampung Improvement

Program, which was introduced and expanded by Sadikin in Jakarta's inner-city neighbourhoods, needed to be broadened from infrastructure improvements to include reconstruction of housing to a more permanent state, that this 'would necessitate "extensification" of the *kampung* in Jakarta'.[66] In the areas beyond the city limits where urbanization was occurring, *kampungs* would emerge as a first step towards constructing a permanent urban settlement. How to accomplish this in an orderly manner was a key concern facing the *Cipta Karya*'s planning team. This 'planned deconcentration' of metropolitan Jakarta was 'the very purpose' of the initial Jabotabek studies.[67]

The structure of Jakarta's planned deconcentration as set forth in the Jabotabek regional plan was 'bundled deconcentration', a concept borrowed from the urbanization scheme being implemented in the Dutch Randstad. The idea was to control 'wild *kampung* development' by forcing growth into a pattern of concentrated clusters, linked together by improved transport. The bundled concentrations could follow a 'linear system', extending like beads eastward towards Bekasi, to the west towards Tanggerang, and southward towards Bogor. Another model, comparable to the concept that guided the Outline Plan, was a concentric ring of clustered settlements, reinforced by radial transport lines extending from the centre of Jakarta. Both the linear and concentric patterns could accommodate variations whereby additional clusters extended from main lines of fringe development. Where the Jabotabek plan differed from the Outline Plan and the Master Plan was its rejection of new towns and satellite cities in favour of growth centres. The planners felt that sufficient open space was not available in the right places to support entire new towns. Moreover, fostering bundled deconcentration in existing towns and villages would reduce the potential for wild *kampung* development. The Dutch consultants observed that the plan prepared by Watts in the 1950s had called for a greenbelt, but that *kampungs* had invaded this green zone because of the lack of controls on development but also because of the inability of the government to build enough new housing in designated town centres.[68] Maintaining some sort of 'green zone' or an area on the periphery where settlements should be excluded remained a concern but also a source of frustration for planners.

An underlying principle in the Jabotabek planning scheme was to use the existing railway lines to determine the development path of these new settlements clusters. As Geibels noted,

preference has been given to public transport above private transport. The railway system has been strongly promoted, next to roads (for buses, bemo, colt and the like).[69]

One of the growth centres along the railway connecting Jakarta to Bogor was the market town of Depok, which had only a few thousand inhabitants in the early 1970s. It was designated in the Jabotabek plans as a growth centre to accommodate the overspill of Jakarta's low- and moderate-income families, with the goal of accommodating 100,000 inhabitants in 15 years. In fact, Depok grew far more rapidly, reaching more than 390,000 in 1990. During the early 1990s its growth exploded and by 2000 had reached 816,000, fostered in part by completion of the new campus of the University of Indonesia.[70]

By advocating deconcentrated settlements, it was expected that these communities would not be 'mono-functional dormitories' but multi-functional urban centres that provided not only housing but also services, employment, and recreation. To accomplish this, given the limited overall industrial development in the Jakarta metropolitan region in the 1970s, it required government investment in new employment and services, such as locating the University of Indonesia in Depok, with its potential to foster considerable new private investment.

An important feature of the Jabotabek plan was its concern to protect landscaped buffers, especially between Bogor and Cibinong, to provide a recharge area for the aquifer that provided water for so much of the region.[71] This was not the greenbelt identified in the earlier Jakarta Outline Plan but rather a proposal to limit urban development in those places which the planners identified as vital to sustaining water resources and where runoff from urban developments contributed to the pollution of the rivers that passed through the region on their way to the coastal plain. The other areas to be protected from new development were some strategic farming areas north of Bekasi on the eastern side of the metropolis and north of Tanggerang to the west, adjacent to the sea and near where a new international airport would be located. Both were recommended as 'permanently reserved for rice production', although it was noted that after 1985, if 'the need for new settlements will exceed the need of rice (or other crops)' then 'the absorption capacity of the west and east wing can be enlarged'.[72] Neither the plan, nor the annual problem of flooding in these lowlands, could stop the march of urbanization across these critical lands.

Giebels prepared a report on a proposed administrative organization to implement the Jabotabek plan, which included establishment of a planning and development body to coordinate the interests of the various government units affected by the planning effort. This brought into a single body the central government, DKI Jakarta and the Province of West Java, the three main government units with a stake in the Jakarta metropolitan region. He also recommended extension of Jakarta's boundaries further into the metropolitan region. Rather than creating a Jabotabek authority with implementation powers, in 1976 the Indonesian government created the much less powerful and advisory Jabotabek Planning Team under a Presidential Instruction (*Instruksi Presiden*, 13/ July 1976). The establishment of a joint secretariat came about through resolutions from DKI Jakarta and the Province of West Java. The Jabotabek Planning Team oversaw preparation of the first Jabotabek Metropolitan Development Plan (JMTD) which was produced in 1980. Beginning in 1976, the World Bank took over funding Jabotabek planning from the United Nations and Dutch consultants.

While the Jabotabek planning concept was being nurtured, Jakarta was in the process of developing a revised master plan (ultimately released in 1984). When the Jabotabek team undertook a revision of their 1980 plan in 1983, they did so with an eye to coordinating with the forthcoming Jakarta Structure Plan, 1985–2005. One of the Jakarta plan's objectives was to reduce the rate of growth of Jakarta's population so as not to exceed 12 million by 2005, since at the prevailing growth rates it would reach that point by 2000. Related to reducing the population growth rate was a commitment to improve land management to accommodate the growth that was going to happen. To reduce land needed for highways, it proposed improved public transport to limit the use of private cars. It also proposed a series of environmental initiatives to improve river water quality, to channel new urban development towards the east and west and to halt growth southwards into prime agricultural areas.[73]

The stated intention of the 1985 structure plan to foster greater reliance on public transport was not matched by specific actions, however. As the 1973 Jabotabek planning study noted, 'the deconcentration model stresses on the use of public transport, since a full private motorization should be avoided anyway'.[74] Except for a brief mention of alternatives such as separate bus lanes on main roads, an approach that would dominate public transport discourse in Jakarta after 1998, the list of specific projects to implement the deconcentration policy was basically a complete set of road projects. These included construction of the Jagorawi highway, doubling the road from Jakarta southwards through Parung to Bogor, the building of a new road to link Jakarta to Bekasi and Tanggerang, several new ring roads south of Jakarta, a new road from Serpong through Ciledug to Jakarta and upgrading an existing roadway between Serpong and Tanggerang. All of these roads would be constructed over the next decade. The only specific projects for public transport involved electrification of the Jakarta-Bogor railway to increase the speed and safety of this one commuter line, and upgrading of the Jakarta and Tanggerang rail line to transport both people and goods.[75] The lip service to improved public transport was typical of plans for large metropolitan areas like Jakarta. What set Jakarta apart was that it had no public transport to begin with, let alone to improve, a situation that made the city heavily reliant on private vehicles. It was evident in both the Jakarta and Jabotabek plans that a vastly expanded highway system was the only serious consideration on how to meet the city's mounting transport needs.

Conclusion

During the first three decades of Indonesian independence, the preparation of plans was a regular feature of urban administration in Jakarta. Beginning with planning for the satellite city of Kebayoran Baru in the early 1950s, Jakarta drew on a combination of the Dutch planning legacy, global ideas concerning the ideal city, and indigenous expectations of what was needed to fashion a viable capital improvement strategy. It would be inappropriate to overstate the importance of the plan-making process in the early years of Indonesian independence, given the persuasive evidence that the political leadership, especially President Sukarno, was not inclined to adhere to plans or to give planners the independence or discretion to implement them. The President was impatient with the planning process, preferring action based on his own judgment rather than being hemmed in by plans. This commitment to action was evident on the ground in the 1950s and early 1960s. During the Sukarno regime, Jakarta's landscape was transformed in many ways. Unfortunately, many projects were undertaken without any assessment of the consequences for the wider urban fabric.

The most powerful planning influences on Jakarta's development were initially provided by foreign consultants, especially in preparation of the various plans. Their role began with the plan for Kebayoran Baru since that project was inherited from the Dutch planners. Foreign consultants were instrumental in preparing the Outline Plan, the 1965 master plan, and the draft (and subsequent) Jabotabek plans of 1973 and 1980. Although foreign consultants played such a key role in formulating the conceptual frameworks for these plans, each drew heavily on local knowledge, traditions, and institutions supplied by the Indonesians who participated in the plan-making projects.

Jakarta's initial efforts at master planning in the post-colonial period represented an attempt to link recommendations to the prevailing international models for urban development. The pace of population growth during the 1950s and 1960s set Jakarta apart from other big cities and made accurate forecasting of the city's needs virtually impossible. Those needs greatly exceeded the city's capacity to meet them, even though as a capital city Jakarta had access to substantial national government resources to assist in providing services and facilities. However, insufficient government resources and an inadequate private real estate development sector precluded any chance of constructing the six satellite cities recommended in the Outline Plan. But new towns would later dominate the metropolitan development approach in Jakarta, a process controlled by the private sector rather than through a structured planning scheme.

Even though implementation of the Outline Plan satellite city concept was not accomplished, there was a certain value in attempting to articulate an overall vision for a metropolis undergoing such rapid change. The master plan of 1965 and the subsequent Jabotabek plans, refined the overall vision initiated in the Outline Plan. The 1965 master plan provided a means not only to see the city as a whole, but also to understand better what was happening in its sub-areas. The 1973 Jabotabek plan recognized the need to confront urbanization challenges not just within the context of Jakarta's administrative boundaries but within the larger contiguous megapolitan region.

The comprehensive plans produced to guide Jakarta's infrastructure investments and to regulate development from the 1960s to the 1980s were state of the art products. The various versions of the Jabotabek plan, such as the 'Proposed Guided Land Development Programme for Greater Jakarta' completed in December 1980, reflected progressive visions of metropolitan development that acknowledged the limits to the carrying capacity of the rapidly growing region, the inadequate level of housing and services, the threats to liveability by continued problems of unregulated development, and the urban area's rapidly growing reliance on automobiles. Planning for the greater Jakarta metropolitan area was guided by a planning team dominated by central government ministries, chaired by the Deputy Minister for Regional and Local Development of the National Development Planning Board (BAPPENAS), a director general from the Ministry of Home Affairs (to whom all local government officials reported under the Indonesian government system), the director general of the Public Works agency responsible for housing, building, planning and urban development, as well as the chairs of the planning agencies of DKI Jakarta and the province of West Java. BAPPENAS, Home Affairs and Public Works also supplied staff to the Technical Advisory Team, with funding for the planning and the infrastructure projects supported by a joint financing arrangement between the government of Indonesia and the World Bank.[76]

The two keys to imposing the Jabotabek plan on the Jakarta landscape were an effective means to control land development in the outer areas and a complementary programme of infrastructure improvements, especially regarding transport, in order to reinforce the desired bundled deconcentration settlement pattern. By 1980, the government had decided on the use of toll roads to help finance the highway network. Three radial toll roads between Jakarta and its hinterland created the anchors of the transport network, including the Jagorawi toll road to connect Jakarta with Ciawi south of Bogor, and at the entrance to the major highway through the Puncak Pass to Bandung, the Jakarta-Merak toll road and the Jakarta-Cikampak toll road. The network also included an inner urban system of toll roads to serve the central business areas, and an outer circumferential toll road from the harbour at Tanjung Priok and then westwards to the interchange with the Jakarta-Merak toll road. The scale of investment needed for this road system, and the limited options suggested to improve public transport, were barriers to implementing the plan. Six separate studies of transport needs in the 1970s fleshed out the problems confronting the metropolis. These included proposals not only for highway improvements but identified the need for rapid rail transport, upgraded services on existing lines, and improved bus transport.[77]

The development of the road network in Jakarta in the 1980s extended the metropolis deep into the periphery. Building the roads was an expensive endeavour but relatively easy to accomplish given the vast areas of undeveloped agricultural land that made up the bulk of the metropolis. It was the reconstruction of the inner areas of Jakarta, especially in the *kampungs*, which posed the greatest challenge, and where the greatest attention of the planners and government was focused in the 1970s and 1980s. It was here that the success or failure of Jakarta's 1965 master plan and the credibility of the Governor Ali Sadikin's regime would be put to the test.

Notes

1.   Needham (1988).
2.   For a discussion of planning in United States cities, and the role of the commercial-civic elite in supporting these efforts, see Brownell (1975), pp. 339–345; Silver (1984).
3.   The best available study of Japanese influences on urban policies in Indonesia focuses on Surabaya. See Frederick (1989), pp. 81–118.
4.   Heiden (1990), pp. 79–81; Schagen (1967), pp. 5–6.
5.   Abeyasekere (1989) p. 157.
6.   JMCG (1996), pp. 25, 27; ROI, MPWP (1953), p. 5
7.   ROI, MPWP (1953), pp. 8, 16, 24–28.
8.   For a discussion of the *Indisch* architecture tradition, which blended elements of European design with traditional Indonesian features, see Kusno (2000), chapter 1; Jessup (1989), pp. 204–301.
9   ROI, MPWP (1953).
10.   See Map 1, Castles (1967), p. 160; Abeyasekere (1989), p. 172.
11.   Giebels (1986), pp. 101–115.
12.   For a diagram of the Concept Plan, see Surjomihardjo (1977), p. 69.
13.   Cowherd (2002), p. 175.
15.   *Ibid.*, p. 405.
16.   JMCG (1996), p. 29.
17.   Heeren (1955), pp. 349–368.
18.   Watts (1960), p. 401; Wirosardjono (1974).
19.   See Sendut (1995).
20.   See discussion of Kebun Kacang in Chapter 4.
21.   Nas and Malo (2000), p. 231.
22.   Nas and Malo (2000), pp. 230–231; PDKIJ (1977), pp. 69–70.
23.   For a discussion of the neighbourhood level administrative system, see Logsdon (1979a), pp. 53–70.
24.   PDKIJ (1977); Nas and Malo (2000), p. 233.
25.   ROI, MFA (1962), p. 6.
26.   Nas and Malo (2000), p. 236.
27.   Anderson (1983), p. 483; Kusno (2000), p. 51; Hughes (1968), pp. 3–16.
28.   Boddy (1983), p. 51; LeClerc (1993), pp. 38-58; MacDonald (1995), pp. 270–293.

29. Kusno (2000), p. 52.
30. Watts (1992), pp. 16–17.
31. For a discussion of the planning for the proposed new capital, Palangka Raya, see Watts (1961), p. 752; Wijanarka (2003), pp. 443–448.
32. ROI (1962), p. 131.
33. *Ibid.*, p. 131.
34. *Ibid.*, p. 131.
35. *Ibid.*, p. 134.
36. *Ibid.*, p. 139.
37 Boddy (1983); Sukarno speech cited in Abeyasekere (1989), p. 168.
38. Nicoletta (2005), p. 7.
39. *Ibid.*, p. 9.
40. Kusno (2000), pp. 60–62.
41. *Ibid.*, p. 61.
42. JMCG (1996), p. 35.
43. Nas and Malo (2000), pp. 102–103.
44. Watts (1960), pp. 401–405; Watts (1961), pp. 785–791.
45. Watts (1961), pp. 787-791.
46. See Watts (1960); Franklin (1964), pp. 229–231
47. See Watts (1961), pp. 750–793; Herbowo, Tisnawinata, Moochtar, and Simonsen (1962*a*).
48. Herbowo *et al.* (1961), p. 1.
49. *Ibid.*, p. 1.
50. Herbowo *et al.* (1961); Herbowo *et al.* (1962).
51. Interview with Tisnawinata (2005).
52. Watts (1961), pp. 785–90.
53. Jakarta, DKI (1966), p. 1.
54. Sostroatmodjo (1977), p. 205.
55. Jakarta, DKI (1966), p. ii.
56. Jakarta, DKI (1966), p. 2. The presidential regulation, 2/1961 established the Special Territory of the Capital-Djakarta, but it was not until 1966 that the autonomous powers of the territory were granted by the Provision Council of People's Representatives (M.P.R.S.) No XXI/M.P.R.S., July 5, concerning 'the granting of the widest autonomy of the territories'.
57. Jakarta, DKI (1966), p. 2.
58. *Ibid.*, pp. 11–13; Interview with Tisnawinata (2005).
59. Sostroatmodjo (1977), pp. 204–30.
60. Interview with Rais (2005).
61. *Ibid.*; Interview with Zhang (2005).
62. Jakarta, DKI (1966), pp. 49–51.
63. *Ibid.*, p. 49.
64. Giebels (1986), pp. 105, 107.
65. *Ibid.*, p. 111.
66. *Ibid.*, p. 111.
67. ROI, MPWP (1973).
68. *Ibid.*, p. 115.
69. Giebels (1986), p. 113.
70. ROI, MPWP (1973), pp. 121–122.
71. Giebels (1986), p. 113; ROI, MPWP (1973), p. 151.
72. ROI, MPWP (1973), p. 149.
73. Soegijoko (1996), pp. 404–406; JRDPB (1985).
74. ROI, MPWP (1973), p. 151.
75. *Ibid.*, p. 147.
76. ROI, MPWP (1980).
77. See JMATS (1972–1974); PCI (March 1979); JICA (March 1978); JTSI (1978); JARDEP (1979).

Chapter Four

Planning for Housing, Neighbourhoods and Urban Revitalization

... houses here are so close together that fresh air is unable to flush out the stale air heavy with shit and gutter gases. This gutter's water, friend, can't flow unless municipal laborers push it along, since every resident throws his trash into it ... in my peaceful *kampung*, with its stink and its condition, people die one after another.

Pramoedya Ananta Toer, 'My Kampung', *Tales from Djakarta*, 1957

[Minister] Ginandjar expects no poor people by the year 2004...

Jakarta Post, 18 October 1996

There was no more fundamental challenge facing Jakarta's leadership in the early years of the Indonesian republic than accommodating in decent shelter the swelling population of the city. As evidenced in the construction of the satellite city of Kebayoran Baru and large residential settlements like Pulo Mas, the Sukarno government was aware of the importance of addressing the housing needs of the city, but principally through a construction programme that added new units at a fraction of the pace of overall metropolitan population growth. No one government agency addressed housing and neighbourhood development needs in Indonesian cities, although by default the Ministry of Public Works filled that role. It was not surprising that this led to a greater emphasis on infrastructure development rather than dwelling units *per se*. Various other ministries and agencies, in particular the military, tried to meet their employees' housing needs to the extent that their meagre budgets allowed. However, their efforts met just a fraction of the housing demand. As a consequence, new housing production in Jakarta in the 1950s and 1960s came about almost exclusively through self-build or spec building by small entrepreneurs. Newly constructed units were wedged into the once relatively spacious native communities scattered along the periphery of the old city. Subdividing the larger homes of former Dutch businessmen and civil servants into multiple apartments was another strategy employed to expand the housing supply.

Whether it was in the peripheral *kampungs* or the former Dutch residential enclaves in the city centre, none of the areas of expanding housing units was adequately provided (if provided at all) with basic infrastructure during the massive population influx. All the immigrant receiving areas were transformed during these two decades from modest working-class enclaves to overcrowded slums teeming with humanity. Sukarno's successor as president, the army general Suharto, in 1967 inherited a capital city with some impressive new facilities, including the Senayan sports complex, a new ring road and other stretches of modern highway, an almost completed national monument, and a score of partially completed modern commercial structures (including the famous Hotel Indonesia). But he also presided over a city plagued by extensive dilapidated neighbourhoods, a substantial homeless population, an economy in shambles, and no obvious strategy in place to fix these glaring urban deficiencies. On the plus side, he inherited an energetic governor for Jakarta, appointed by Sukarno in the waning days of his regime, who brought incredible energy, organizational skills, and a practical understanding to the task of managing a major metropolis.[1]

Ali Sadikin developed quickly the reputation of an activist governor, a builder, and a doer. But he made his mark not by conceiving and constructing grand structures but by paying attention to the needs of a broad segment of the city's population and committing his government to supporting the centre of indigenous community life, the *kampung*. It is remarkable that Jakarta's most famous modern governor forged his enduring reputation on the transformation into models of good planning those crowded, smelly and disease-prone places that Pramoedya Ananta Toer, the famed Indonesian social critic, associated with the worst failings of the nation. Through the *kampung* improvement programme, Jakarta pursued comprehensive housing and neighbourhood improvement during the first two decades of the Suharto's New Order government. This was the foundation for a much more ambitious urban revitalization effort beginning in the late 1980s that ultimately led to the demise of many *kampungs* which had initially been rescued by Sadikin.[2]

Planning Jakarta's *Kampungs*

In October 2004, the World Bank bestowed on the aging former governor of Jakarta, Ali Sadikin a special and unprecedented honour. The 76 year old 'Bang

Ali', unquestionably the most popular and one of the longest serving chief urban executives in modern Indonesia (at least until the current reign of Jakarta Governor Sutiyoso), received an award for his role in removing some of the stench and refuse from Jakarta's sprawling *kampungs* and in the process providing the international donor community with a model that was emulated throughout the developing world.

In 1969, the cash-strapped Sadikin government launched the Kampung Improvement Program (KIP) in Jakarta as a low-cost alternative to full scale urban reconstruction and a counterpoint to the unworkable model of constructing entire new cities as in the case of Kebayoran Baru. It was also an alternative to the indifference of previous regimes to the needs of the city's deteriorated and under serviced neighbourhoods. Jakarta's KIP was officially designated the *Proyek Muhammad Husni Thamrin* (the Mohammed Husni Thamrin Project) in honour of the Betawi city legislator who had so forcefully advocated infrastructure improvements in the native communities throughout the latter years of the Dutch regime.

Sadikin's KIP was an enhanced version of the Dutch colonial scheme introduced in the 1920s to clean up Jakarta's poorer neighbourhoods by addressing health and sanitation conditions and improving key components of the infrastructure without disturbing the essential community fabric. What was different in the 1960s was the scale and intensity of neighbourhood problems. In the colonial era, the objective behind *kampung* improvement measures was to protect nearby European residential enclaves from the spread of disease from nearby *kampungs*. In Sadikin's Jakarta, these areas had been forced to absorb several million new rural migrants without any infrastructure investment. Nearly all *kampungs* lacked the most basic services, typically occupied land routinely subject to flooding, and remained places where public health problems were significant.

However, the *kampung* improvement strategy was not undertaken principally because of the threat they posed to more affluent neighbourhoods as was the case during the Dutch colonial era. The city's leadership recognized *kampungs* as the basic residential environment of the vast majority of Jakarta's residents and so could be not treated as a problem at the margin. Yet while essential to community life for the vast majority of Jakarta residents, the *kampung* also was a major impediment to realizing the goal of transforming Jakarta into a modern, international city. This was a goal that Governor Sadikin shared with the president who appointed him, Sukarno, as well as President Suharto under whom he served for another 12 years before being forcefully removed.

Although Sadikin later became a staunch critic Suharto's the New Order government, his approach to urban management in Jakarta, grounded firmly in his military training, matched closely the style of his new boss, Suharto, focusing government intervention less on show case projects and more on basic infrastructure needs to guide urban development and as a way to win the confidence of the capital city's masses. Sadikin's style of urban leadership was the 'take charge' variety. He was not averse, for example, to hopping onto a city bus or making frequent visits to Jakarta's toughest areas to examine personally the problems of the *kampung* dwellers. Moreover, he sought the counsel of many, borrowed openly and unabashedly from his advisors and, in the spirit of the pragmatist, seemed more concerned with what worked than with adhering strictly to tradition or to following protocol. In the chaotic capital of the early years of Suharto's New Order government, Sadikin's personal energy was a calming element in a city overwhelmed by the uncertainties of a military-led regime change and the lingering misery of Sukarno's failed efforts to bring prosperity to the new nation.[3]

As the centrepiece of the Sadikin governorship, the KIP was more than just the resurrection of a neglected Dutch community reform strategy. It was an urban revitalization effort consistent with a new philosophy guiding community development within international development circles, commonly referred to as the 'sites and services settlement upgrading process'. This approach was sustained by a popular contemporary theory of planning for low-income housing and community development, propagated by American housing reformer, Charles Abrams. The New York-based housing reformer held that low-income self-help in housing and service delivery was more successful than organized government efforts to regulate the process.[4]

In the case of Jakarta, it was a strategy born not just of principle but also of necessity, given the limited resources available to address the infrastructure, housing and service needs of such vast areas of the nation's capital. Sidik Noormohamed's assessment of the Jakarta KIP after a decade of implementation emphasized the cost efficiency of the approach. As he noted, providing even the most modest one-room new housing unit in a sites and services project, as was the case in the Klender project in Jakarta, cost four times more than the upgrading scheme without providing housing. As he said: 'All income groups have benefited from the KIP, including the lowest income decile, whereas no families in the lowest two income deciles have benefited from one-room public housing in Klender'. Abeyakesere observed in the late 1980s (as the KIP was winding down) that 'the Kampung Improvement Programme represents a sensible choice to leave the *kampung* undisturbed and instead try to upgrade the environment'. The Jakarta government's 'decision to improve the *kampungs* seems justified as it is an effective way of helping a large number of the poorest people', Abeyakere concluded.[5]

The urban places that needed upgrading in Jakarta in the late 1960s were very different from the original *kampungs* that the Dutch sought to improve in the

1920s. As Nas has demonstrated, the concept of *kampung* has multiple meanings within Indonesian society which differ by locale and at different historical periods. A *kampung* is not a village (*desa*) although it has many of the attributes of a traditional Indonesian rural enclave. Yet it is not exclusively an urban slum phenomenon either. It is best defined as an area of the city that is 'indigenous, unplanned, with low-rise building', that exhibits 'a lack of infrastructure and services, a high population density, and a generally lower-class but mixed socio-economic composition'. While none of these characteristics alone defined a *kampung*, and some were more pervasive in certain areas, all display a number of these traits.[6]

The multiple meanings of the *kampung* in Jakarta life have been confused by the tendency of some scholars to regard their formation as a manifestation of modern social stratification. Atman contributed to this confusion by linking the *kampung* development process to the start of the industrial revolution in Indonesia in the late nineteenth century. As he asserts, 'faced with the financial problem of

Figure 4.1. A Jakarta *kampung* area (near Jalan Pekojan) with significant environmental deficiencies, 1971. (*Source*: KIT Tropemuseum, Amsterdam)

obtaining a city home, most of the migrants withdrew from the city and built their own shelter on its periphery'.[7] In fact, the *kampung* dwellers surrounding Indonesian cities in the late nineteenth century were not industrial workers but peasants who participated in subsistence agriculture in rural clusters near the city. Moreover, most did not leave the city to relocate in *kampungs* at the edge. The majority of *kampung* dwellers were rural migrants to the city since these areas served as initial receiving areas for those moving to urban areas.

Atman is on more solid ground in describing the step like transition of villages to urban *kampungs*. He identified four stages of *kampung* transformation, from rural *kampung*, to semi-rural *kampung*, then to semi-urban *kampung*, and finally to urban *kampung*. This is what he refers to as the 'rural-urban continuum theory'. As the *kampung* became urban, it was transformed from pseudo-permanent to permanent structures, reflecting the desire of urbanized residents to express their progress in terms of the type of residential structure. Atman also accurately predicted that one of the potential problems in transforming *kampung* structures is that they then become attractive to more affluent urban residents and for the sake of securing a return on a modest investment in land, the original *kampung* inhabitants are lured, or in some cases pushed, out.[8] While Atman's analysis was undertaken in the 1970s during the heyday of Jakarta's *kampung* preservation and upgrading, his notion of *kampungs* being taken over and destroyed because of their locational advantages anticipated accurately the dominant trend in Jakarta during the 1990s and early 2000s in Jakarta.

As a historian of Southeast Asia, Anthony Reid noted the *kampung* had its origins in pre-colonial urban settlements as the space set aside for indigenous workers inside the residential compound of the wealthy (*orangkaya*). This urban compound accommodated both the dwellings of the wealthy property owners and the homes of slaves and other consigned labourers who made up the household unit. Stand alone native neighbourhoods did not exist within colonial Batavia where slavery was widespread. In the late nineteenth century free native labourers began to establish their own self-contained compounds, or *kampungs*, adjacent to agricultural lands surrounding the city.[9] In the case of early twentieth century Batavia, the growing *kampung* population resided outside the corporate boundaries of the city in a rural setting, and was not subject to municipal regulation. Growing up in the shadow of Batavia, the surrounding *kampungs* retained a 'rural ambience because of their spaciousness, the abundance of (fruit) trees and the hordes of small animals'.[10]

In a move to gain some control over *kampung* development and to protect the adjacent European settlements from the public health threat of these densely-settled neighbourhoods, Batavia incorporated many of the adjacent *kampungs* into the city in the 1920s. Once incorporated into the urban fabric, these areas increased in population density and gradually shed some of their rural traits. The standards of residential quality that had been acceptable when the *kampung* was not officially part of Batavia were deemed insufficient for a neighbourhood within the city. The colonial administration formalized the concept of *kampung* improvement through a legal statute in 1934 (*Kampong Verbeeteringsordonnantie*, 1934). As previously noted (Chapter 2), a small but determined band of European housing reformers, and backed by the most esteemed native voice on Batavia's municipal council, M. Husni Thamrin, launched a pioneering but modest *kampung* improvement programme prior to the Japanese occupation of the early 1940s. There is no evidence that the initial KIP in Jakarta met even partially the desires of housing reformers, although construction of government housing units prior to the Japanese invasion was accompanied by some *kampung* upgrading in select areas of the city. A more apparent link between the colonial experiment and the efforts of the 1970s was through Sadikin's direct experience. As he recalled in a recent interview, it was a visit to an uncle living in a *kampung* near Menteng in the late 1960s, that made him aware of the Dutch precedent and at least one successful outcome of their efforts. His uncle resided in a *kampung* whose neat appearance was attributed to the improvement carried out under the original *kampung* programme. Sadikin realized that the *kampung* improvement strategy was the urban revitalization model he needed to tackle Jakarta's biggest problem.

Unlike the 1920s and 1930s, when Batavia's population growth was steady but manageable, the unprecedented explosion of Jakarta's population in the 1950s and early 1960s, demanded a scaled up version of the *kampung* improvement programme. Sadikin confronted a housing crisis of tremendous proportions that seemed to get worse by the day. Moreover, the *kampung* problem exposed the complexity of the indigenous residential enclaves. There were by the 1950s, three distinguishable types: the inner-city *kampung*, with typically the highest residential densities; the peripheral *kampung* which retained some rural traits but was increasingly impacted by expansion of the urbanized area; and the woodland *kampung* which would not be swallowed into the urban fabric until the massive suburbanization of the 1970s and 1980s. Sadikin's initial *kampung* improvement efforts centred on inner-city *kampungs*.[11]

Lea Jellinek's study of one Jakarta inner-city *kampung*, Kebun Kacang, illustrates the implications of the phenomenal population pressures on Jakarta's indigenous neighbourhoods during this period, the human dimension of urban *kampung* life, the relationship of these low-income communities to the broader forces of change in the city, and the complexities of implementing even the simple measures covered by the KIP. Kebun Kacang (literally meaning peanut garden) was located near Jakarta's emerging business district south of Merdeka Square. It had begun as a market village outside of Batavia in the 1920s. By the 1950s, it was a dense inner-city *kampung* near the rapidly expanding commercial corridor, Jalan Thamrin, and this prompted higher land values. By the time Jellinek discovered Kebun Kacang in the 1960s, only a handful with any recollection of their rural origins remained. Migrants to Kebun Kacang who had arrived there in the colonial era had come for waged employment unavailable in the rural village. Most had migrated there either from the Tanggerang area west of the city or from Bogor located about 50 kilometres to the south. Both these rural settlements were within a day's commute of Batavia (and both would later become urban growth centres within the expanding Jakarta megacity).

Unlike older and more densely populated *kampungs* adjacent to the older sections of Batavia, Kebun Kacang (which was located near the European enclave of Menteng) was sparsely populated, providing ample room for the simple but relatively spacious housing, gardens, play areas, and trees for shading and for sustenance that typified the *kampung*. This was not an impoverished urban slum but a simple peasant village brought into the urban orbit, where local residents secured wages by commuting to the harbour far north at Tanjung Priok to work as cargo handlers, or to work as cart drivers on the city streets, or as domestics and labourers in the affluent European households of nearby Menteng. According to Jellinek, '... kampung dwellers felt themselves to be part of a privileged group with easy access to Batavia rather than part of the vast urban mass that they were later to become'.[12] In the view of these long-term residents who remembered how it was in the colonial era, before the Japanese occupation, the subsequent chaos of the independence struggle, and the pressures of poverty and overpopulation in the 1950s and 1960s, Kebun Kacang in the 1930s was an orderly and secure place.

There was stability and security. Money still had value. There was great respect for law and order and more trust amongst people... For whatever reason, kampung dwellers did feel that life under the Dutch compared very favourably with the years that followed.[13]

Compared to conditions in the outlying rural villages during the Japanese occupation, life in Kebun Kacang remained relatively calm. Residents who had worked for the Dutch took great pains to disassociate themselves from their previous employers, fearing that any such association meant death, but otherwise, there were no remembered reprisals. There was an influx of migrants from the countryside to Jakarta's *kampungs* between 1942 and 1944 as conditions deteriorated in rural villages and the prospects of working for the Japanese seemed better than starving in the villages. The exodus of the Japanese in 1945, the return of the Dutch and the ensuing independence struggle, brought instability to Kebun Kacang. According to the *kampung*'s residents, during the attempted Dutch restoration, it was practical to appear as allies of the returning Dutch in Batavia in certain circumstances and adamant about expelling them when interacting with the nationalists who controlled the surrounding countryside; in short they learned to negotiate the fluid political environment. After Independence was finally secured in 1949, Kebun Kacang was one of Jakarta's many *kampungs* to attract a substantial number of new residents.[14]

Even in the economic chaos of the 1950s and early 1960s under the Sukarno government, the *kampung* dwellers were able to turn the situation to their advantage. For residents of this community, jobs were plentiful. As Jellinek notes, during rationing under the early Sukarno regime, *kampung* dwellers earned money standing in line for food provisions on behalf of middle-class recipients, provided repair services to their neighbours in Menteng, and engaged in the seemingly unlimited opportunities for hawking food and other goods along the new modern streets that the president was building to showcase the national capital. One indicator of the *kampung*'s prosperity was that most newcomers in the early 1960s were able to purchase their modest 30 to 60 square metre houses and the land on which they stood. Original settlers who were willing to sell off some of their land benefited from the influx of new residents. The Agrarian Law 5/1960, which brought *kampung* land under government control (and nationalized Dutch companies), provided an opportunity for residents of the *kampungs* to apply for formal land title.[15] While largely indifferent to the confusing national and local political machinations, most Kebun Kacang residents worshipped Sukarno and continued to do so openly until it was politically dangerous to do so under Suharto's New Order government.

One of Sukarno's last acts as president was to appoint Sadikin as the Governor of Jakarta in April 1966. Sadkin assumed his duties during a period of intense political instability and, by his own admission, he knew virtually nothing about conditions in the city. The living conditions in Jakarta in general were at their nadir at this time. The cost of living rose more than 1000 per cent between December 1965 and December 1967.[16] As previously noted (Chapter 3), Sadikin believed in the value of rational approaches to urban problems, and quickly sought to bestow official sanction on the plan for Jakarta's development that had been formulated during the waning days of the Sukarno government. He took on and completed many of the infrastructure projects initiated by Sukarno, most notably construction of the six-lane highway corridor, Jalan Thamrin, that connected Merdeka Square to the roundabout adjacent to the Hotel Indonesia, and which had such a devastating impact on Kebun Kacang in the 1970s. Several of the buildings along Jalan Thamrin were constructed by the city's development authority, *PT. Jaya Pembangunan*, headed by the future kingpin of suburban residential and commercial development, Ciputra.[17]

Sadikin, the builder, was the image portrayed in the media, but his over-whelming urge was to bring order and discipline to an urban area that had been

Figure 4.2. Older building in Kota area adjacent to the Kali Besar. (*Source*: KIT Tropemuseum, Amsterdam)

neglected in terms of service and management. He was particularly concerned with insuring a sufficient revenue base to finance needed public improvements, and made his mark by devising new ways to offer improvements that were accomplished at the least cost. In an official statement of his approach in 1969, it was asserted that,

the principle of efficiency will always be the guiding principle of the municipality government of Djakarta in the utilization of the development budget. The purpose is to optimize the objectives within the constraint of available funds.[18]

He was determined to make good his promise to improve Jakarta's services. Between April 1967 and December 1968, for example, the number of buses operating on the city streets increased from 352 to 554. Accompanying the increasing number of buses, the Sadikin government constructed new bus terminals. He also set ambitious targets for rehabilitation of elementary and *madrasah* (Islamic) schools and, in turn, through this building programme expanded the student population attending school. He also invested in improving major and secondary roads, and increased the supply of drinking water. Sadikin's 3 year rehabilitation plan covered 1967 to 1969 and aimed:

to create the best possible social and physical environment in order to promote incentives for development. The Kebun Kacang residents were among those who benefited from these initiatives.[19]

The Sadikin government, ever conscious of the limited funds available to tackle such enormous service needs, resurrected the Dutch pre-war *kampung* improvement strategy. For the cash-strapped governor, the concept of constructing new flood-proof paths and drainage systems in the *kampung*, in some cases introducing communal toilet and water facilities, and improved solid waste management seemed easier and less costly than trying to construct new centralized systems on a citywide basis. Even this piecemeal approach was daunting, given that *kampungs* covered approximately 60 per cent of the land area of the city and housed about three-quarters of its population.

According to a 1969 assessment of conditions in Jakarta's approximately 500 separate *kampungs*, few had even basic services. Sixty-eight per cent of *kampung* houses had no private toilet; 90 per cent no piped water; 80 per cent no electricity; many were situated along canals into which garbage was thrown; and there were relatively few permanent housing units. Only 24 per cent of the buildings had solid walls, floors and roofs, while nearly 44 per cent were temporary structures made of bamboo and thatched roofs, and another 32 per cent were a combination of temporary and permanent, or semi-permanent as noted in the city survey. The *kampung* improvement programme was not intended to address structural deficiencies in the housing but to focus on the environmental amelioration through minimum infrastructure improvements that would encourage residents to undertake the work necessary to improve their housing. '[P]aved roads and footpaths, drainage ditches, communal water taps, sanitary latrines, garbage bins, and social services such as schools and health clinics' were the tools employed to upgrade these areas but also to forestall the need for relocation and to avoid disruption of community life.[20]

The Jakarta government launched the Kampung Improvement Program (KIP) using city revenues, and only after 1974 did central government and foreign loan funds expand the programme throughout Jakarta and into other Indonesian cities. Between 1969 and 1974, approximately 20 per cent of the urbanized area (or 2,400 hectares) and 1.2 million residents were covered by the first phase of the KIP. By 1974, the KIP concept had drawn the attention of the World Bank, and with its first urban loan to Indonesia financed KIP efforts covering another 1900 hectares. Through a second urban loan, World Bank funding brought the

KIP to the remaining 3000 hectares of Jakarta's *kampungs* between 1976 and 1979. Over the decade, the city constructed 399 kilometres of paved roads and community footpaths, 140 kilometres of feeder drainage canals, 101 kilometres of water supply lines, 71 sanitary units, 394 rubbish bins, and 26 health centres. A total of 89 *kampungs* were upgraded under the initial KIP.[21] After 1979, the KIP team began work in newer fringe area *kampungs* as well as to bring water supply and sanitation to the oldest *kampungs*. In Jakarta, from 1974 to 1981, there was Rp 73,653 million (approximately US$11 million) invested in 310 *kampungs* encompassing 6,816 hectares and affecting 2.3 million people.[22] But by 1979, with Sadikin out of government, Jakarta's KIP no longer had the champion of community infrastructure improvements it had had in the early 1970s.

Sadikin's KIP was comprehensive in scope but modest in its expectations. The fact that it addressed four significant community components, including the physical infrastructure (roadways, neighbourhood pathways, water service and sanitation), social services (health, education and recreation), economic services (job training, credit for micro enterprises and technical assistance) and home improvement programmes (to enable property owners to improve their houses) attests to its comprehensiveness. Its approach was intended to limit disruption to the neighbourhood fabric compared with other strategies that called for total clearance and rebuilding. The other innovation in the KIP was its reliance on maximum participation by residents during implementation. The investment of both time and resources on the part of the community was the required match to the limited government funds. In the long run, it created a sense of ownership of the process among residents that ensured that the investments made would be protected.

The initial phase of the KIP involved those areas in Jakarta with the worst environmental conditions, high population densities, areas prone to flooding and near existing infrastructure and those neighbourhoods with a projected high level of resident participation.[23] The initial KIP budget was a mere US$10 million. In an effort to jump start the programme, various government departments were

Table 4.1. Summary of Jakarta's Kampung Improvement Program,1969–1979.

	Phase 1 1969–1974	Phase 2 1974–1976	Phase 3 1976–1979	Total
Area Improved (ha)	2400	1980	3000	7380
Percentage of 1969 urbanized area (12,000 ha)	20.0%	16.5%	25.0%	61.5%
Population that benefited (000)	1200	890	1200	3290
Average cost per ha (US$)	6500	18,000	24,000	17,000
Average cost per capita (US$)	13	40	60	37

Source: World Bank, cited in Taylor and Williams (1982), p. 242.

involved with different components of it. While this brought additional government expertise to bear on the problems of the *kampungs*, the lack of a single coordinating body hampered operations during the first five-year development plan (*Repelita I*).

To improve coordination of the KIP in Jakarta, the Muhammed Husni Thamrin Project was structured into an independent technical unit under Jakarta's city government in 1974. Sadikin did not relinquish administrative authority, however and all finals approvals of KIP plans remained with the governor.[24]

In the first phase of the KIP, standardized development objectives were applied uniformly on the assumption that all *kampungs* were alike. For example, each KIP received 75 metres of paved roads, 132 metres of paved footpaths per hectare, one public toilet per 11 hectares, and one water pipe for every 4 hectares. Experience in implementation demonstrated the flaws in this method. There was great variation in needs among Jakarta's *kampungs* and the existing one-size-fits-all approach in some cases created duplication of services while in others left vast areas unimproved. Revised standards called for all dwellings in a given *kampung* to be within 100 metres of a roadway serving emergency vehicles and within 20 metres of a paved footpath. For water and sewerage facilities, the revised standard was a water pipe for every twenty to fifty families and one toilet seat for every twelve families. Community health facilities were provided on the basis of different levels of service, with places for first aid, larger facilities for more comprehensive treatment and primary schools based exclusively on serving a fixed population cohort.[25]

There is ample evidence that the KIP had a positive impact on the environmental conditions in Jakarta's extensive *kampung* areas. In a study in the early 1980s, Marcussen determined that the extremely poor conditions found in *kampung* studies undertaken prior to the KIP were only visible 'in small pockets inside the older kampungs' once implementation occurred. His case study of Pademangan, a *kampung* area on the transit route between the old city (Kota) and the harbour of Tanjung Priok in North Jakarta, verified this conclusion. This swampy area that once held fish ponds was originally part of a *landerijen particuliere* (private estate) owned by a Dutchman, Willem van de Groot. It found its way into the hands of Indonesians through a series of smaller plots after 1945. Then subdivided further, this sparsely populated area became a congested urban *kampung* of approximately 68,000 residents by the early 1980s. Although the swampy areas were filled in, the major problem confronting Pademangan remained the regular flooding. The KIP programme brought in fresh water and electricity, new paved roads were constructed and connected to houses by means of paved paths. Drainage ditches were installed to handle runoff. But to prevent flooding, the whole area needed to be raised by 2 metres, which was not possible since the KIP was not intended to clear and rebuild *kampungs* but merely to upgrade what was there.

While Pademangan residents should have benefited from the installation of public toilets, and in the case of more affluent residents the installation of septic tanks, the high groundwater level made this impossible. The continued channelling of latrine waste directly into the nearby swamps and canals undermined the sanitary improvements of the KIP in this area.[26]

Steinberg suggested that the KIP had a limited impact because it was not accompanied by a programme to upgrade the larger urban infrastructure networks, especially the water supply and sewer system, which was not possible at the *kampung* level. Since the KIP was a fully subsidized programme, there was no means of cost recovery. This limited the city's ability to secure development funds to cover the larger infrastructure projects. Further, given the absence in practice of a participatory element including the community residents, this slowed implementation in many cases.[27]

One notable outcome of Jakarta's KIP was that it spurred a revival in interest among scholars to understand the development and function of the *kampung* and housing conditions in Indonesian urban development in the tradition of Tillema and Karsten during the colonial period. Scholarly studies such as Soeboer Boedhisantoso, *Djagakarsa: A Fruit-producing Village near Jakarta* (1967), Gerald Krausse, *The Kampungs of Jakarta, Indonesia* (1975), Bernard Dorléans, *Etude geographique de trois 'kampong' à Djakarta* (1976), Lea Jellinek, Chris Manning and Gavin Jones, *The Life of the Poor in Indonesian Cities* (1977), Adi R. Thahir, *Low Income Settlement within the Jakarta Region* (1982) and Lars Marcussen, *Third World Housing in Social and Spatial Development* (1990) exposed the challenges confronting these distinctive urban enclaves.

Marcussen expanded on the work of Thahir in 1983 through a detailed investigation of three different *kampungs*, and the individual experiences of a host of *kampung* residents. His study found that the worst conditions disclosed in the studies of the 1970s had been alleviated by the KIP, although it was not clear that over the long term that the improvements could be sustained. Marcussen concluded that given the size of Jakarta's informal housing sector, another KIP was unavoidable within the next decade. One way to anticipate future needs was to turn the KIP programme into a proactive rather than a reactive endeavour. Jakarta's planners could designate additional lands for low-income housing and support self-help housing, something which the government had tolerated to meet the needs of low-income residents but had not officially sponsored. Through cooperation with *kelurahan* administrators, who were the city's sub-district-level officials, land for development could be secured from owners and services incrementally added in anticipation of future development. This blended the informal and government sectors into a partnership that could produce sustainable neighbourhood improvement.

Who were the primary beneficiaries of the KIP? The population served by the programme in Jakarta was predominantly immigrants from Java. Based on a 1980 study (which surveyed 300 individuals), the heads of households of nearly 87 per cent of the *kampung* population came from outside the city, with nearly 70 per cent drawn from the nearby Javanese and Sundanese communities. Forty-one per cent of the households were headed by individuals with a primary education, while just 13 per cent had completed high school. According to Amir Karamoy and Gillian Dias, 'this general low level of education among heads of households in Jakarta meant that they do not possess many of the skills that can be used in the formal job market'.[28]

An earlier but more systematic study of urban poverty in Jakarta in 1972 under the direction of Gustav F. Papanek with assistance of Harvard University faculty and students from the Faculty of Economics at the University of Indonesia confirmed the huge dimensions of poverty in Jakarta. The average daily income of 280 rupiah (US$0.60) was supposed to cover food and housing costs that together averaged Rp 570. But, the daily income in Jakarta was approximately double that earned back in the rural village. The averages masked a vast range of incomes among the poor, however. Petty traders were at the top of the hierarchy while cigarette butt collectors were at the bottom. Those at the bottom spent all of their income on food while those at the top had 'a significant margin of income above subsistence'. The Papanek study identified eight occupational groupings in the following order of ranking from the highest to lowest: petty traders; construction labour; bus recruiters; *becak* drivers; kerosene sellers; shoe shiners; wastepaper collectors; and cigarette butt collectors. Women were especially important among the petty traders. Yet in Papanek's survey sample, one-third of the 32 women interviewed earned a living through prostitution. As he noted, 'prostitution seems to have become a significant source of income, and an index of social disorganization in the city'. Virtually all the women were supporting an average of two dependents through prostitution.[29]

Although Jakarta was declared a closed city by Governor Sadikin in a futile attempt to curtail further population growth by denying new residency permits, only 14 per cent of those Papanek surveyed were native Jakartans. Of the 506 respondents, 24 (4 per cent) were from nearby Sumatra and 4 were from outer islands. The remaining 478 were from Jakarta, West Java, Central Java or East Java. Most came from nearby villages in West Java. To obtain a residency card and necessary documentation cost between Rp 3000 and Rp 6000 (US$7.20 to US$14.40) and for workers averaging Rp 250 per day (US$0.60) that was an impossible sum. But as Papanek observed, it was only 'a fraction of the increased income obtainable in the city as compared to rural areas'.[30] Another strategy to discourage migrants was the designation of *becak* free zones within Jakarta, intended not only to modernize the city's appearance but also to reduce the demand for fresh crops of *becak* drivers from the rural villages. This action appeared to cause some reverse migration and a temporary decrease in the rate of population growth in Jakarta. One result was that certain segments of the urban poor, especially the petty traders, benefited from improved economic circumstances while others, like the *becak* drivers, were hurt, leading to growing disparities of some magnitude among Jakarta's poor.

There is little evidence that individuals switched occupations readily to accommodate changing circumstances. Papanek found that between 70 and 90 per cent of those surveyed were doing the same job either 5 or 10 years earlier. North Sumatrans were bus conductors, nearly a quarter of those from Central Java were cigarette butt collectors, but less than 10 per cent collected wastepaper. *Becak* drivers hailed from four neighbouring places on the north coast of West and Central Java (Indramayu, Cirebon, Brebes and Tegal), while petty traders typically came from Bogor and kerosene sellers from nearby Bekasi. There was little evidence of migrants climbing the occupational ladder to a higher status job. Rather, they stuck firmly to the occupation consistent with that of their friends or relatives (often fellow villagers) who recruited them to the city in the first place. Papanek's researchers discerned a high literacy among the youngest cohort in the sample, with only about a quarter of the sample described as illiterate and those being mainly over 34 years old. This was the age cohort that had missed out on expansion of education opportunities since independence.[31]

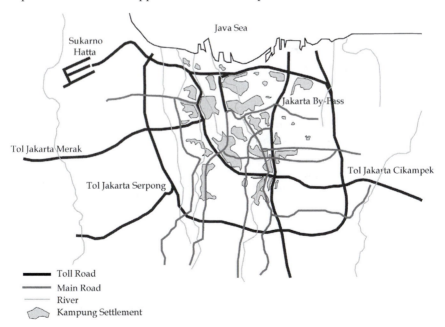

Figure 4.3. Kampung areas in Jakarta as identified in Krausse's seminal study. (Adapted from Krausse, 1975)

The stability evidenced in the occupational structure of Jakarta's poor was matched by stability in residence. Sixty per cent had a permanent place and either owned their own house or squatter hut, while just 30 per cent rented. The housing typically had a bare dirt floor and bamboo walls but usually (79 per cent) a tile roof. Sixty per cent of those who had lived in Jakarta for 10 years or more lived in the same *kampung* in which they had they originally settled. Most respondents indicated that they engaged in neighbourhood programmes, including repairs to the infrastructure and helping those in need through a practice known as *gotong royong*. *Gotong royong* is a traditional participatory model which places the community above the individual, and assumes that the individual is dependent in all aspects of life on others within the community. It involves collective works, such as those needed to implement the KIP but possesses the higher meaning of subservience to the larger good.[32] Given their allegiance to this concept residents appreciated the spirit of the *kampung* improvement programme and regarded it as helpful to the needy. But when the KIP involved widening streets or building a new pathway, and, consequently required taking property from individual residents, it was a perceived as a problem. Some displaced residents were forced, like those in the government's transmigration programme, to move far away from their familiar areas. *Kampung* removal, like transmigration, was a process orchestrated by government to redistribute Indonesia's population from the crowded spaces of Java to under populated distant places.

Papanek's study casts doubt on the popular perception that Jakarta's poor were a desperate group wallowing in the 'culture of poverty'. He put it this way:

While the Jakarta groups were absolutely very poor, migration had substantially increased the income of the migrants. They had been even worse off before moving. Their average income increased by at least half … a majority had some education, and a substantial proportion had secondary schooling. The neighborhoods in which they live appear to be quite stable and well-organized social institutions. They are essentially villages transplanted to an urban environment. Most of the migrant inhabitants have their families in the city and have lived in the same neighborhood since they migrated. Cooperative self-help is nearly universal. The ties to the rural areas are often quite strong, in terms of frequent visits to the premigration home, observance of previous traditions, and entertainment preferences in the city.[33]

By the time Jakarta's KIP reached its conclusion in the late 1980s, and having touched most of the city's *kampungs*, the government had begun to embrace an alternative strategy to meet the increasing demand for a more focused housing initiative. The KIP continued to be funded through the national budget of the 5th Five Year Development Plan (*Repelita V*, 1989–1994) as a poverty alleviation strategy and accounted for a Rp 407 billion (US$24 million) investment nationally (or about 4.7 per cent of the development budget). But in the 1980s it was reconfigured into the Community Infrastructure Program as part of a more comprehensive urban infrastructure improvement programme known as the Integrated Urban Infrastructure Development Program (IUIDP).[34] At the same time, an institutional structure had been created to encourage the private sector to supply additional new low-income housing. Through the national housing agency, *Perusahaan Umum Pembangunan Perumahan Nasional* (PERUMNAS – the National Corporation for the Development of Housing) private developers built small permanent structures on land acquired by the government. Sustaining the improvements of Jakarta's KIP was not a prominent planning concern for the administrators who succeeded Sadikin. The urban development strategy for Jakarta in the 1980s and 1990s focused on new private housing, with PERUMNAS operating mostly in outlying areas where land was less expensive. When necessary, a substantial portion of KIP-improved *kampungs* might be removed in order to construct the new neighbourhoods and expanding commercial areas of the modern metropolis.

New Housing for Urban Neighbourhoods

The strength of the KIP was that it brought infrastructure improvements to large sections of Jakarta, and did so with a relatively modest public investment. The KIP also acknowledged the government's inability to facilitate the supply of new affordable housing or to guide development within the metropolitan area. It was a reactive strategy and did nothing to affect the supply of housing for the surging population of Jakarta. What new publicly-financed housing was built depended on the initiative and resources of individual national government ministries. This approach generated just a handful of new units and these were targeted to the growing civil service corps. For non-civil service workers, there was no new low-cost housing. In the 1950s and up to 1964, housing cooperatives created by local governments provided very few new housing units. While there were 120 separate cooperatives in towns and cities throughout Indonesia, the result was a paltry 1,250 housing units by the time the programme was officially terminated in 1964. Also, the private sector built some speculative units in the 1970s even after the national government passed an Investment Act in 1968/69.[35]

A renewed relationship between Dutch planners and the Indonesian government, which came to fruition in 1970, led to some needed technical assistance in the housing area. The Dutch consultant sent to Jakarta to provide advice on how to address the housing problem was C. Becht, a former mayor of Surabaya and the current chair of the National Board for Peoples' Housing of The Netherlands. He proposed a national housing organization, and made this idea the centrepiece of a workshop that he organized in the Presidential Palace (Bina Graha) in Jakarta in 1972. His recommendations included designation of a minister for housing to improve coordination of the government's housing programmes, creation of a national low-cost housing construction agency, and an institution to provide financing for the housing sector in the form of a national mortgage bank.[36]

In 1974, in conjunction with Indonesia's second five-year plan, PERUMNAS was created to produce new low-cost housing in urban areas throughout the nation's twenty-seven provinces. It was set up in conjunction with the World-Bank-financed Jakarta Urban Development Project which was designed to complement the environmental improvement programme of the KIP. Actually, there were several components to this new national low-cost housing programme, including a National Housing Authority (NHA) established by Presidential Decree in 1974 to set overall housing policy and to coordinate with all relevant ministries. The NHA was, in effect, a committee of ministers chaired by the Minister of Public Works and reporting directly to President Suharto. PERUMNAS was the corporation charged with securing and developing urban lands for construction of low-cost housing on sites that had basic services provided. A national mortgage bank was created in 1975 to provide mortgage financing and later a housing mortgage corporation was initiated to provide mortgage financing at market rates to higher income housing purchasers.

PERUMNAS's scope was narrowed considerably by Presidential Guidelines issued in 1976. This presidential order specified that most of the low-cost units built by the agency would be for government employees (including military) and at least initially these units would be managed by PERUMNAS as rental units (with the possibility of purchasing later on). PERUMNAS built modest 'core' houses ranging between 21 and 36 square metres, largely on the periphery of Jakarta.[37] The high cost of inner-city property prevented it from operating in existing Jakarta *kampungs*. Moreover, there was no mention of integrating these units into neighbourhood or community plans, or to accommodate other residential needs in newly developed areas.

PERUMNAS was a housing production organization intended to meet national targets for new urban units for government workers on the lower rungs of the bureaucracy. By the early 1980s, from a small rented space in Jakarta with a handful of professional staff, PERUMNAS had become a complex government institution employing thousands of architects, engineers and planners, operating a massive headquarters in Jakarta, 7 regional and 13 area offices, 70 estate management offices and another 24 project offices. Its two factories produced prefabricated building materials for its housing projects that by the early 1980s accommodated an estimated three-quarters of a million residents.

PERUMNAS's housing projects in the Jakarta area were large scale. The Klender project started in the late 1970s in East Jakarta, encompassed 200 hectares and involved construction of nearly 10,000 low-income housing units, along with markets, schools, clinics, and recreational fields. It eventually developed into a community of 50,000 inhabitants. An even larger housing project was initiated in the early 1980s in Depok, a satellite city in southern Jakarta, with a planned population of 200,000 when it was completed.[38]

New Housing and Jakarta's *Kampungs*

There was an inner-city housing construction programme that got underway later and on a much smaller scale. In 1981, construction was completed on 960 units in the Tanah Abang area to the west of the national monument and adjacent to an active city centre market. Because of their location, the Tanah Abang units were priced beyond the means of the poorest 80 per cent of Jakarta's population, with a monthly carrying cost of more than Rp 100,000 (or nearly approximately $100) per unit. Yet as the Tanah Abang project filled up with the non-poor, the Minister of Public Works reiterated that housing for the lowest income was a high priority of government. As proof, Kebun Kacang, located just to the south of Tanah Abang, was to be the site of this more affordable housing. The KIP had come late to Kebun Kacang given that this area's conditions were far better than the typical *kampung*. More importantly, most residents of Kebun Kacang were homeowners. The announced government housing project was to be rental units. So the prospect of trading their homes, which cost them relatively little to maintain and nothing to own, for units in a multi-storey building (with perhaps less liveable space) that required a sizeable and regular monthly expenditure, made no sense to the residents. Although less expensive than the Tanah Abang units, it was not better housing that Kebun Kacang residents needed, but rather relief from the daily anguish of earning enough to survive.[39]

Rumours of the Kebun Kacang project, and the importance the government attached to this effort as a demonstration of its commitment to provide affordable housing, were substantiated in August 1981 when a team of planners and government officials announced the Kebun Kacang housing initiative at a community meeting. Those present learned that the existing *kampung* housing would be removed and replaced by new multi-storey structures. To demonstrate how strongly government supported this project, the community meeting was attended by the Minister of Public Works, the Director General of Housing from the Ministry of Public Works, the Mayor of Central Jakarta and lead staff from the city government and PERUMNAS. Residents were assured that this was not 'a demolition programme' but rather 'urban renewal'. In other words, even though all of the houses would be demolished, the fact that replacement housing would be built meant that it was not demolition *per se*.

The key to this distinction between 'demolition' and 'renewal' was how much compensation residents received for relinquishing their houses and land, and whether they would secure improved housing as a result, either in Kebun Kacang or in some appropriate alternative area. Although initially the residents were guaranteed space in another PERUMNAS project, that guarantee was later qualified by a condition that it applied only to those with sufficient resources. The promise of relocation to the nearby Tanah Abang housing development was unrealistic because these units, costing between Rp 5–8 million (US$7,000 to 11,400), were beyond the means of most Kebun Kacang residents. Even though the Kebun Kacang project was intended to serve the lowest income, somehow PERUMNAS officials offered no assurances that displaced residents could be relocated back into their former neighbourhood when it was ready. In fact, when completed, the Kebun Kacang housing ended up serving the same higher income group that occupied the Tanah Abang project. Its location was attractive to white collar workers working in the nearby office towers, and there was no mechanism in place to ensure that the intended target population would get priority for these units.

When the land purchasing process began in September 1981, and residents discovered that the compensation they were to receive precluded any possibility of moving into the nearby PERUMNAS housing project, Kebun Kacang residents protested vehemently. It seemed that the project site had been selected not on the basis of any understanding of the neighbourhood composition (including the high rate of resident ownership of land there) but simply because it looked poor and was adjacent to a prime commercial area. Not until late October did any officials from PERUMNAS take a close look at the place they intended to destroy. The PERUMNAS project planner, Duddy Soegoto, discovered on a belated tour of the area that Kebun Kacang was a more established neighbourhood than had been previously assumed, that the housing generally was in good condition (even if most lacked basic infrastructure) and that much of it served simultaneously as a work place. As a result, demolition of the housing not only would displace people but also would have a significant impact on the local economy.

As Soegoto belatedly became more familiar with local conditions, he assumed, unofficially, the role of neighbourhood advocate and expressed doubts about proceeding with the project as originally designed. But it was too late to derail it; there was too much government prestige on the line to abort or even to modify the plan. The President, the Minister of Public Works, and the Minister of Housing were all wedded to the project, and were intent on showcasing Indonesia's aggressive urban redevelopment efforts. So the Kebun Kacang project moved forward without modification. What Soegoto was able to accomplish on behalf of displaced residents was free rent in temporary structures until they could be relocated into new housing, and additional compensation for those who owned land in the *kampung*.[40] However, the additional compensation did not all go to those displaced. The local headmen used the project as an opportunity to extract payments from land owners in order to have their property purchased at the higher rates from PERUMNAS, so the property owners had to relinquish some of their profit in order to be allowed into the deal.

The Kebun Kacang project was the first, and most publicly visible, case of *kampung* removal to accommodate expanding commercial development along Jalan Thamrin and Jalan Sudirman. The series of *kampung* removals that followed eliminated much of affordable housing in inner-city locations closest to potential jobs. According to data from Jakarta's housing agency, the city had 1,433,539 housing units, consisting of 629,754 permanent houses, 522,165 semi-permanent structures, and 281,620 make-shift dwellings. With 60 per cent of the population living in *kampungs*, many located along river banks, near railway tracks, and under power lines, the need for replacement housing to eliminate the worst conditions remained substantial despite more than two decades of clearance of substandard housing to make way for new commercial development. Because land costs rose so dramatically, Jakarta's policy was that all new low-cost housing built within the city was in multi-storey housing estates. Between 1985 and 1995, the city added just 7,163 low-cost apartments, ranging from the smallest units of 18 square metres to some of 54 square metres. The pace of low-income housing construction picked up after 1995, with approximately 1,200 added to the housing stock in one year. Projects were underway in Jati Bunder, Karet Tengsin, Bendungan Hilir, and Tebet. In 1996, projects were under construction in four of Jakarta's five mayoralities (except South Jakarta) for low-income occupants. Between 1995 and 2000, Jakarta set a target of 15,750 new low-cost apartments. By 1997, just as the nation's fiscal crisis shut down the government's housing construction programme, only about 5,200 new units had been added through these public efforts.[41] This was far short of the annual demand of approximately 10,500 units.

Adding to the crisis, housing prices for existing units rose rapidly, making it prohibitive for all but a small segment of the working poor to afford even modest 21 square metre units. The purchase price of these rose from 4.5 million to over 5 million rupiah (US$1,800 to 2,100), putting them well beyond over 30 per cent of Jakarta's population who made less than 50,000 rupiah (US$21) per month. The average annual income of 600,000 rupiah (US$250) for the working poor represented less than 15 per cent of the purchase price, and without any means of long-term financing (which did not exist in Jakarta's housing sector for most buyers), these modest dwellings were really only affordable for the 17 per cent who made over Rp 200,000 (US$80) per month. As a result, the only alternative was crowding into under-serviced and dilapidated units in older *kampungs*, or

Figure 4.4. Four-storey apartment block built by PERUMNAS between Kemayoran and Pulo Mas. (*Photo*: author)

perhaps finding or building more affordable dwellings in urban villages in the peripheral areas of Jakarta.[42]

The diminishing supply of affordable housing in the inner city faced other threats. In January 1996, fire swept through the Muara Baru neighbourhood in North Jakarta, resulting in the instantaneous loss of 2,000 housing units in that crowded slum, and the displacement of 5,000 residents. Frequent tragedies like the Muara Baru fire simply compounded the wider housing shortage, given that there were so few new subsidized units being created, and given the size of Jakarta and its housing needs. There were widely varying figures on how much housing the city administration added. According to Thamrin Djamain, President of the city-owned development firm, *PT Pembangunan Sarana Jaya*, between 1987 and 1994, 8,734 housing units were built and from 1994 through 1995, another 2,687 housing units were added. The city's ambitious, but unattainable, goal was to add another 27,568 units between 1996 and 2,000. The fiscal crisis beginning in 1997 undermined that plan.[43]

The city adopted a cross subsidy programme to link the growing number of high end houses to provision of more low-cost units. The cross subsidy law,

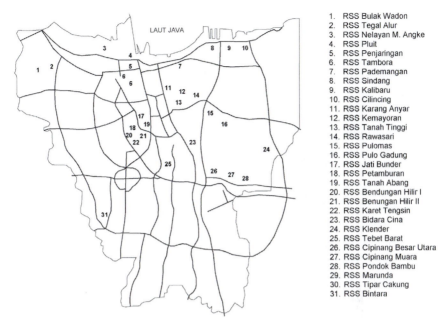

1. RSS Bulak Wadon
2. RSS Tegal Alur
3. RSS Nelayan M. Angke
4. RSS Pluit
5. RSS Penjaringan
6. RSS Tambora
7. RSS Pademangan
8. RSS Sindang
9. RSS Kalibaru
10. RSS Cilincing
11. RSS Karang Anyar
12. RSS Kemayoran
13. RSS Tanah Tinggi
14. RSS Rawasari
15. RSS Pulomas
16. RSS Pulo Gadung
17. RSS Jati Bunder
18. RSS Petamburan
19. RSS Tanah Abang
20. RSS Bendungan Hilir I
21. RSS Benungan Hilir II
22. RSS Karet Tengsin
23. RSS Bidara Cina
24. RSS Klender
25. RSS Tebet Barat
26. RSS Cipinang Besar Utara
27. RSS Cipinang Muara
28. RSS Pondok Bambu
29. RSS Marunda
30. RSS Tipar Cakung
31. RSS Bintara

Figure 4.5. Government supported multi-storey housing in Jakarta. (*Source*: Jakarta, DKI, 2005)

commonly referred to as '1-3-6', required developers of luxury housing to add three medium and six low-cost residences for every high end house they built. Enforcement of this regulation was difficult since it was commonplace (and allowable) for the low-income units to be built after the more costly structures were completed. The developers of a luxury waterfront community in North Jakarta, known as Pantai Indah Kapuk, constructed 1,100 luxury and middle-class housing units before they even began work on their pledged low-cost apartments. They intended to construct a complex of sixty five-storey apartment blocks to accommodate 1,920 families. Delays in starting these units, coupled with the onset of the fiscal crisis, got the developer off the hook.[44]

Just as the fiscal crisis was heating up late in 1997, Jakarta's Governor Sutiyoso announced his intention aggressively to eliminate slums and illegal buildings along Jakarta's rivers, especially along the Ciliwung River, the largest of the thirteen that ran through the city. He couched the removal efforts in terms of returning Jakarta's waterways to their natural state. But at the heart of the strategy was elimination of slums, particularly those prone to flooding along the rivers. Although he assured those who would be displaced that they would be moved to new low-cost apartments, this was a promise he could not keep, given the sluggishness of the low-income housing programme. Sutiyoso's assault on the temporary housing along the rivers was also tied to a previously prepared plan to build a series of multi-storey housing complexes through Jakarta that would be less impacted by the annual flooding and also consume far less land. The city's housing agency proposed construction of 238 high rise housing structures which would add a total of 19,793 units. Over a third of the units (7,250) were to be built in Central Jakarta, with the rest divided equally between West Jakarta, East Jakarta, and North Jakarta. South Jakarta was to get only 520 units largely because private development was handling housing construction effectively there.[45]

Another factor feeding into the low-income housing crisis in Jakarta in the 1990s was that the KIP was winding down. A detailed assessment of the impact of the programme on improving urban areas in Indonesia was prepared by the World Bank in 1995, as work under the fourth (and final) urban development loan concluded. Overall, Bank urban development projects had resulted in an investment of US$438.3 million in the KIP and much of this in Jakarta. The study reconfirmed findings in earlier studies that the KIP had 'induced housing and environmental improvements for low-income urban households in Indonesia at a low cost of investment'. This included improved footpaths, lighting, education and health facilities, more and better living space, improved access to clean and safe drinking water, access to sanitation, and a reduction in the threats of flooding. The report noted lingering problems such as new roadways built under the KIP that increased flooding in some neighbourhoods. But the most serious problem facing Jakarta's KIP neighbourhoods was that the ground on which they stood was being drawn into the overheated urban land market. The result was that large swaths of these areas were being razed for new development. There was minimal compensation to the existing occupants because the KIP process had overlooked the matter of securing property rights for *kampung* inhabitants.[46] Throughout the 1990s, the displacement underway in Jakarta's *kampungs* in the face of development pressures fundamentally transformed the face and the social composition of both the inner and outer areas of the city.

The options available to the displaced were limited. Jakarta did not have a substantial supply of housing that could be rented by the low-income population. According to a study conducted in the late 1980s, rental housing for low-income Jakartans represented a small proportion of the overall housing stock. Just 27 per cent of all households in Jakarta were house renters (that is renting both the house and the land) and another 3 per cent rented a room from someone else. While the 30 per cent renter households in Jakarta was higher than that of all Indonesian cities, it was significantly less than other comparably-sized and situated cities in the world. The provision of new rental housing came not through public programmes but through the initiative of small-scale developers building three units or less, and quite often on available land adjacent to their own residence. These units tended to be self-built by the property owner as a way to secure additional income, and came online only when the property owner had enough extra cash to pay for building materials.[47] This was not an effective way to provide sufficient housing within the city to compensate for the losses sustained by the intense development pressures on its *kampungs*. As a result, the only viable alternative for many was to look outside the city to the peri-urban settlements that still had space to accommodate new low-income residents.

Conclusion

There was no more critical and challenging issue facing planners and administrators in Jakarta from the 1960s to the 1990s than improving the supply and the quality of housing for the great mass of residents. The government created institutions to address housing and neighbourhood needs but these came late in the process and were not funded to the level necessary to have a noticeable impact. The lead organization designed to expand the supply of government financed housing, PERUMNAS, ended up serving largely the emerging middle class because the unit cost of its housing exceeded the financial capacity of the very poor and working poor. These Jakarta residents had been served by the KIP, which provided Jakarta's expansive tracts of *kampungs* access to basic services previously unavailable. Under the pressure of continuous mass migration into Jakarta from rural areas, anything other than the provision of a base level of service was both impractical and unaffordable. Many of these *kampungs* would persist as permanent enclaves for the poor, the working class, and an emerging middle class within Jakarta. But a great many occupied land ripe with opportunities to clear away the temporary facilities and to build on that space the modern metropolis. To do that required a mass relocation of traditional urban residential functions to the periphery of Jakarta.

Suburbanization in Jakarta began intensively in the 1980s (which will be discussed in detail in Chapter 5) and was dominated by efforts to construct new forms of residential and commercial settlement, aimed largely at the more affluent side of the market. But at the same time, there was a dispersal of Jakarta's low-income population to the urban periphery. Large complexes of simple houses built by developers with support from PERUMNAS added a new feature to the suburban landscape. Some of the dispersal of the working class accompanied the development of new towns, especially those that were intended to support industrial and commercial functions. The implications of the decentralization of Jakarta's working-class communities went far beyond the changing social spatial structure of the city. It impacted the demand and location of public transit, the need for infrastructure improvements, and the availability of jobs to support the population. It was also tied directly to a fundamental transformation of the form and function of the inner core of Jakarta. When examined from the macro scale, the socio-spatial composition of Jakarta in the 1990s resembled that of the colonial city, with the more affluent occupying the core (with some pockets of affluence in the select spots in the outer city) but with the overwhelming majority of the city's population, of much more modest means, squeezed out of the city and spreading over the periphery. The planning process for transportation infrastructure and for new residential settlements in Jakarta that helped to fashion the commuter-oriented, neo-colonial city during the 1980s and 1990s, is the story to which we turn next.

Notes

1. Kusno (2000).
2. Interview with Sadikin 4 January 2005.
3. Interview with Sadikin 4 January 2005.
4. See Abrams (1964), pp. 4–5.
5. Noormohamed (1980), p. 504; Abeyasekere (1989), p. 215.
6. Nas *et al.* (2005), p. 2.
7. Atman (1975), p. 216.
8. *Ibid.*, pp. 218–220.
9. See Reid (1980), pp 235–250.
10. Nas *et al.* (2005), p. 1.
11. See Krausse (1975).
12. Jellinek (1991), p. 6.
13. *Ibid.*, pp. 1–7.
14. *Ibid.*, pp. 7–10
15. Silas (1984), p. 73.
16. Abeyasekere (1989), p. 215.
17. Born Tjie Siem Hoan in Parigi, Central Sulawesi in 1931. Ciputra is an architect by training.
18. Jakarta, DKI (1969), p. 10.
19. *Ibid.*, p. 8, figures 8, 11, 13, 17, 18.
20. See Taylor (1982), pp. 240; 1968–1969 Jakarta Survey.
21. Taylor (1982), pp. 242–244.
22. Silas (1984), p. 87, note 5.
23. Patton and Subanu (1988), pp. 181–185.
24. World Bank (1969), p. 220.
25, *Ibid.*, pp. 219–220.
26. Marcussen (1990), pp. 126–132.
27. Steinberg (1992), p. 370.
28. Karamoy and Dias cited in Marcussen (1990), pp. 185–192, 196.
29. Papanek (1975), pp. 7–8.
30. *Ibid.*, pp. 10, 16 Table 8. The US dollar equivalents are based upon official exchange rates of Rp 415 per dollar that were in effect from August 23, 1971 through 1973. The rupiah depreciated to 625 per dollar in 1978 and fell further to 970 per dollar by 1983.
31. *Ibid.*, pp. 14–15.
32. See Koentjaraningrat (1977).
33. Papanek (1975), p. 25.
34. See Steinberg (1992), p. 372, note 11.
35. Silas (1984), p. 70.
36. Giebels (1986), pp. 103–104.

37. Jellinek (1991), p. 128.
38. Rosser (1983), pp. 136–40, 142–3, 146.
39. Jellinek (1991), pp. 130–3.
40. *Ibid.*, pp. 134–7.
41. *JP*, 26 June 1997; 29 June 1995.
42. *JP*, 16 June 1996.
43. *JP*, 21 August 1995.
44. *JP*, 17 July 1995.
45. *JP*, 3, 5, 20, November 1997; Jakarta, DKI (2005).
46. World Bank (1995), p. 6.
47. Hoffman *et al.* (1991), pp.183–185, 192.

Chapter Five

Expansion, Revitalization and the Restructuring of Metropolitan Jakarta: the 1970s to the early 1990s

In 1976, Indonesia's President Suharto issued an official order concerning the future development of the capital city. That executive act set in motion a process of expansion in Jakarta that would radically revamp both the form and quality of the urban environment over the next three decades. Presidential Instruction No 13/1976 (*Inpres* 13/1976) specified that the regional city of Bogor, located approximately 60 kilometres to the south of Jakarta, along with the smaller administrative cities of Tanggerang to the west, and Bekasi to the east, would be designated as the nodes of development in the capital city area connected by the emerging modern highway system.[1] This presidential directive formally sanctioned the new planning strategy referred to as 'bundled deconcentration', an approach prescribed for the Jakarta region in 1973 by the Dutch consultant team headed by Lambert Giebels.

Yet where the Dutch planners saw an opportunity to implement a managed system of spatial decentralization through investment in a mass transit system linking the centre city to these designated suburban development centres, the Indonesian government and the real estate development community saw a rationale for encouraging fringe area development that did not have to wait for such expensive transport infrastructure. Adding to the highway system started by Sukarno in the early 1960s seemed a much more feasible approach, especially since there was an opportunity for the toll roads to generate revenue as well as to lure in private investment. A modern highway system offered a more flexible transport network that could more easily serve the ten identified business groups that were poised to expand the urbanized area into the periphery. So with promulgation of *Inpres* 13/1976, it was the automobile, the bus and the truck that triumphed over transit in delivering a modern public transport system to Jakarta.

Moving the Masses

Studies of possible mass transit systems continued to be commissioned by the government, but it was the network of limited access circumferential highways, modelled on the system ubiquitous in major United States cities, that became the core of Jakarta's transport infrastructure. As quickly as the pavement was laid down, new residential, commercial and industrial developments crowded along the edges of these highway corridors. The planning and development of this highway system in the 1980s and early 1990s was the key factor in transforming the basic structure of the capital city into an auto-dominated metropolis.

The stage had been set for the emergence of the auto metropolis in the early years of the republic. As previously noted, President Sukarno had ordered the electric trams removed from Jakarta's streets in the 1950s, a move intended to free the city of what he regarded as an unnecessary relic of the late nineteenth century. Sukarno's removal of the trams was swift and thorough. In 1954, Indonesia nationalized the Dutch electric tram company, the *Bataviasche Electrische Tramweg Mij*, under the *Perusahaan Pengangkutan Djakarta* (PPD) and, with support from the Australian government, replaced the trams with 250 Leyland buses.[2] But the conversion from tram service to buses did not happen smoothly. Although by the mid-1960s PPD had increased the fleet to 370 buses, there were not enough vehicles to meet the transport demands of Jakarta. With virtually no programme of bus maintenance, the actual capacity was considerably lower than the number of vehicles. Typically only forty of these buses ran at any one time. To fill the void created by the ineffective bus system, thousands of mini vehicles, such as the *bemos* and *opelets*, operated by private vendors, appeared on Jakarta's streets.[3]

With substantial support from the national government and the international donor community, the Sadikin administration improved management and added hundreds of new vehicles to Jakarta's system. In Indonesia's first five year plan (1969–1974), new buses and terminals were added and a vigorous rehabilitation of older vehicles was undertaken by PPD, with nearly 1,800 buses in operation in Jakarta by 1974. Through a loan from the United States, Jakarta acquired another 2,000 Dodge buses under the second five year plan (1974–1979), but with the stipulation that these would not be operated by PPD but given to ten new private companies with set routes. By the end of the 1970s, eight of these private firms were unable to meet the payments on their loans.[4] As a result, the private bus companies were absorbed by PPD and the state enterprise for land transport, *PN Damri*, and these two firms supplied Jakarta's public transport (with *PN Damri* also running buses in other Indonesian cities).

Besides modernizing the fleet, another transport innovation was smaller buses to serve places where the large Mercedes-Benz and Dodge vehicles could not manoeuvre. The creation of *PT Metro Mini* in 1976 put under a single public regulated corporation a fleet of approximately 700 vehicles that had been in operation since the 1962 Asian Games. This aging fleet was replaced by new Toyota buses in 1980, and these bright red vehicles became the backbone of the inexpensive, no frills Metro Mini fleet that continues to ply Jakarta streets providing cheap fares on vehicles now as battered as the original fleet.

For low-income Jakartans, the three-wheeled pedicab, the *becak*, appeared in the 1950s and met a need that the poorly maintained and inadequate supply of motorized vehicles could not. While commonly and mistakenly associated with the colonial era rickshaw pulled by humans, the *becak* was a rickshaw-like cart pulled along by a bicycle rig that was an invention of necessity for transport and employment in the post-independence city. As Soegijoko notes,

Becaks as urban public transportation gained popularity in the 1960s at the time when the buses were faltering and minibuses had not yet been introduced.[5]

But in 1973, the Jakarta government enacted a local regulation that stipulated that by 1979, the city would shift its neighbourhood transport system from the

Figure 5.1. *Bajajs* in Jakarta neighbourhood. (*Photo:* author)

non-motorized *becaks* to the motorized version, known as the *bajaj*, named from a company in India which exported these three-wheeled chariots.

By 1979, there were six components making up Jakarta's transit system (not including the discredited *becaks*), led by buses with 2,400 vehicles serving approximately 1.5 million passengers per day. The minibuses handled another half million customers, while the *opelets*, *bemos*, taxis and *bajajs* accounted for another 700,000 daily trips. The three-wheeled motorized *bajajs* that replaced many of the human powered *becaks* already numbered more than 10,000 and were by far the most visible component in the system. Not only did they provide an important neighbourhood service but quickly became a major source of employment. The other means of public transport was the railway system (as distinguished from the intra-city trams) operated under the State Railways Company (*Perusahaan Jasa Kereta Api*, or PJKA). Trains provided access to select suburban areas along routes extending east, west and south from the city. Government regulations kept fares low on all modes, except for the *bajajs* which operated under informal sector bargaining. Writing in the late 1970s, transport analyst Howard Dick claimed that through price controls the public had reasserted its authority in the transport sector. He contended that 'The planners have indeed established their ascendancy',[6] an ascendancy premised on use of an expanded and modernized road vehicular fleet rather than resurrecting a rail transit system.

It was the city administration's vigorous campaign to remove the *becaks* from Jakarta's streets (and several other large Indonesian cities) which began in the 1970s (and continued into the 1990s) that proved to be the most controversial component of the transport modernization efforts. One argument against the *becak* was that it slowed traffic. 'In the view of many consultants and transport planners', Dick noted, 'the replacement of jitneys and *becaks* by buses and *bajaj* [are] justified on the sole grounds of relieving traffic congestion'. But there was also the view that the *becak* drivers were an exploited group, that *becak* driving was 'socially unacceptable' and 'incompatible with human dignity'. Yet from the standpoint of the neighbourhood service, as well as the increasing unskilled and semi-skilled labour pool in Jakarta, the *becak* was a vital labour source and a means for entry into the workforce for newcomers, including many who were drivers in the smaller towns and cities from which they migrated.[7]

Highway Planning

There was no concern when it came to increased automobile usage, and to building the new road network to accommodate the growing number of vehicles. The first leg of the metropolitan highway system, the Jagorawi toll road was completed in 1978. It extended from Sukarno's inner ring road south to the Bogor district, and opened a vast undeveloped agricultural area south of Jakarta to urban development. The second highway, the Jakarta to Tanggerang toll road completed in 1984, opened up the western periphery to development. The inner ring road continued to be constructed around the centre city shadowing the route of Sukarno's road, and included a separate spur to serve the new Sukarno-Hatta international airport under construction along the north-east coast of Jakarta. The central government pushed this project to completion by the early 1990s. And concurrently work began on a new circumferential, the outer ring road, to serve developments that had already been started in the areas between the highway axis formed by the north-south and east-west toll roads.

Car ownership in Jakarta still was under 200,000 when the Jagorawi toll road opened in the late 1970s but rose rapidly during the 1980s, reaching 600,000 registered vehicles by 1987. The million car mark was achieved some time in 1995. In the meantime, the ambitious rail development schemes set out in the original Jabotabek plan of the late 1970s were 'deferred until after the road network had been built-out and sufficient population densities had been attained to justify it'.[8] Yet those densities were unlikely to occur given the relatively dispersed and low-density pattern of residential, commercial and industrial development in Jakarta's periphery. What eventually made an expanded transit system a critical need were

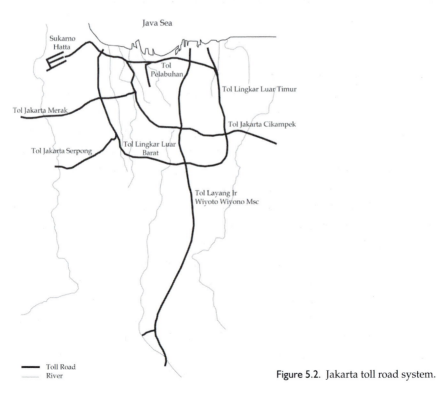

Figure 5.2. Jakarta toll road system.

the choked roads in the city centre caused by too many car owners from these new suburban areas trying to funnel into concentrated centres of employment in central Jakarta.

In anticipation of the opening of Jakarta's expanded toll road system, there was a surge in requests for real estate development permits in the Tanggerang regency in 1983. According to data from the National Land Agency, the built-up area of the Tanggerang district in 1980 was approximately 11 per cent of the land area. It increased to 24 per cent by 1985 and to approximately 34 per cent by 1994. Within 2 years of completion of the western toll road, development of Bumi Serpong Damai (BSD), Jakarta's most ambitious new town since the creation of Kebayoran Baru in the 1950s, was started on a 6,000 hectare tract in Tanggerang. Adjacent to BSD two other massive residential developments were coming online: Cikarang new town built on a 5,900 hectare site and Tigoraksa new town on a 3,000 hectare site in 1987.[9]

Bogor, located 65 kilometres south of Jakarta, also anticipated improved highway access and grew even more intensively than either Bekasi or Tanggerang during the 1970s. New developments in and near Bogor consumed an area equal to the entire built-up area of Jakarta in 1970. By 1988, the built-up areas of Tanggerang, Bekasi and Bogor combined amounted to approximately 110,000 hectares, more than three times the size of the developed areas within Jakarta proper. By the late 1980s, nearly two-thirds of the Jakarta metropolitan area was built-up with another 500,000 hectares in the peripheral communities being brought online for development. Jakarta's growth was racing to the periphery and there seemed to be no physical limits to how far it could spread.

The suburban population concentrations that accompanied the developments in Jakarta's peri-urban areas in the 1980s and early 1990s seemed to confirm that the desired 'bundled deconcentration' had been achieved. Between 1980 and 1995, Tanggerang grew from 1.5 million inhabitants dispersed through a spacious rural district into a highly concentrated urbanized area with nearly 3.5 million residents. Bekasi's growth was nearly as impressive. The city of Bogor more than doubled in population during this period, from 247,409 to 647.665, but it was the adjacent rural district of Bogor (as distinct from the city) which experienced the greatest population increase, soaring to approximately 1.2 million by the early 1990s.[10]

The lands on which the new towns and residential settlements popped up like mushrooms in Jakarta's periphery were still in agricultural use, supporting rice production, mixed garden produce (fruit and vegetables), plantation products (such as palm oil and tea) and forested areas. From 1980 to 1994, approximately 66,000 hectares surrounding the city of Jakarta were converted from agricultural to residential, industrial and commercial uses, an area equal to four times the built up area in 1971. Driving the growth in the peripheral areas was the relatively affordable price of the land. Land prices in central Jakarta reached 6.5 million rupiah (US$3,000) per square metre by the 1990s, compared to undeveloped land in the outlying areas (between 15 to 30 kilometres from the city centre) which cost just 200,000 rupiah (US$80) per square metre. At these prices, private developers eagerly scooped up land through a land permit system that granted exclusive rights in anticipation of rising values once the highway system was in place

Highway construction was all but a certainty given the track record of both the Sukarno and Suharto regimes to place road construction at the top of the public works agenda.[11] Cowherd suggests that it was Sukarno's 'inner ring road, with its monumental *Semanggi* cloverleaf interchange', coupled with the Jagorawi highway which connected the city centre to the president's weekend retreat in Bogor, that 'established the framework within which the next several decades of [urban] development was to occur' under the Suharto government.[12]

Although conceived in the 1960s, the inner ring road built in the 1980s proved to be 'an enormously successful stimulus to private sector property development … around the dense core of Jakarta into the 1980s and 1990s'.[13] The inner ring was still incomplete when construction started on a second 'outer' ring road which ran through South Jakarta on an approximately 12 kilometre radius from the Monas. The 1993 Jabotabek plan endorsed the ring-radial model, which revived the ring road scheme originally set forth in the 1973 plan. This proposed outer ring was a 63 kilometre limited access highway with a cost of Rp 5 trillion (US$526.3 million). An 'outer-outer' ring road was also on the highway planners' drawing board to serve the Bekasi-Depok-Parung-Tanggerang Development corridor, and to connect with another north-south toll road which linked Bumi Serpong Damai to Bogor. What was unique was that the outer-outer ring road created a direct link between two sections of suburban Jakarta that completely bypassed the inner city. It implied a functional life of the expanding suburban areas disconnected from the heart of Jakarta. Yet the main concern expressed regarding these last two legs of the Jakarta highway network was not what they implied about the changing structure of the metropolis but that they would invade the environmentally important open space preservation lands known as the Serpong-Depok Aquifer Recharge Zone in direct conflict with all planning efforts.

Yet in 1997, with only 40 per cent of the second ring finished, construction halted on all Jakarta's roads. Indonesia's fiscal crisis, followed by allegations of corruption on the part of highway contractors, led to twenty-four toll road construction projects throughout Indonesia being cancelled. Despite the temporary setback, Jakarta retained its commitment to development via the ring road model. Even after work on the second ring road had been suspended, a 1999 transport plan prepared by the Ministry of Settlement and Regional Infrastructure proposed a third concentric ring (the 'outer-outer' ring) of 150 kilometres located 35 kilometres from the city centre to connect the satellite cities of Cilewungsi, Depok, Parung, Tanggerang and Serpong. Suprisingly, the 1999 plan failed to embrace the environmental sensibilities of the previous plan. It dropped the idea of protecting environmentally sensitive coastal areas in North Jakarta and expressed support for a major land reclamation and development project.[14]

President Megawati Soekarnoputri, the daughter of Sukarno who was elevated from the vice presidency when the sitting president Wahid was censured and removed in 2001, was a keen proponent of highway generated development. Eager to jump start the economy, she used her presidential authority to reactivate twenty-one toll road projects in October 2002, including the 52 kilometre outer ring project. She had wanted to do this sooner, but was delayed by legal challenges against the government. These suits focused on the government's policy of excluding from the toll road projects firms that had connections to the former Suharto government, including PT Citra Marga Nusapala Persada, the company owned by Suharto's daughter Siti Hardiyanto Rukmana ('Tutut') who had been a major beneficiary of the toll road projects in the 1980s and 1990s. Even as Megawati was allowing toll road work to resume in Jakarta, there was a new and growing chorus of voices suggesting that the toll road transport strategy was inadequate for the needs of the metropolis.[15] One reason for the growing criticism was that the strategy seemed to exacerbate the problem it was supposed to alleviate, namely vehicular congestion. The number of cars plying Jakarta's streets had mushroomed to 4 million and cars accounted for roughly a half of the more than 21 million daily trips in the capital.

Some favoured resuscitating a proposal announced in 1994 to build a subway line from the Kota area in North Jakarta to Blok M in South Jakarta. This project, initially estimated to cost US$1.5 billion, was to be financed through a consortium of private investors from Japan, Europe and Indonesia. Throughout the 1990s (as discussed more fully in the next chapter), efforts to develop a mass transit system competed with the ongoing toll road development for precious development funds. Jakarta Governor Sutiyoso revived discussions of the subway project late in 2001 but there was far less enthusiasm for such an expensive solution to the transport needs of Jakarta than was the case in the mid-1990s. The University of Indonesia's transport expert, Djamester Simarmata, urged pushing ahead with one of the mass transit projects developed in the 1990s prior to the financial crisis, but the financial climate was no longer conducive to a purely private venture. As the head of Jakarta's Land Transport Agency, Rustam Effendy, maintained central government financing was necessary for whatever system was implemented in the capital. As he noted, the plans already existed, and all that was needed was the finance. But there were sharply divided opinions about exactly what kind of system would best serve Jakarta. A local community activist, Azas Tigor

Nainggolan, from the Jakarta Residents Forum, regarded the subway as far too expensive and favoured improving the existing surface electric trains.[16]

Jakarta's limited public transit system had been in crisis throughout the 1980s and 1990s. Available information, not to mention the daily experiences of commuters, suggested that it was little better than it had been in the 1970s when actions to deal with traffic congestion first became a priority. The heart of the system in 2003 was a fleet of 4,530 large and 4,978 medium-sized buses, but it

Figure 5.3. Traffic on Jalan Thamrin. (*Photo*: author)

was estimated that only 60 per cent of these were operational at any given time. The buses were extremely crowded, and offered slow service for commutes that were getting longer as the population concentrations moved further away from job centres. The dominant transit vehicles, which served both local and regional needs, was a fleet of 11,848 public minivans, over 25,000 taxis and an even greater (but undetermined) number of motorcycles, *bajajs* and *bemos* patronized by the majority of the less affluent population.[17]

While discussions of various mass transit schemes were widespread by 2003, the focus was on what was known as the 'busway' scheme, an approach modelled after the highly successful experiment in the Latin American city of Curitiba. The busway scheme involved a dedicated lane in both directions on major roadways for a continuous flow of buses operating on a fast-paced schedule. Buses would be accessed through specially constructed walkways and stations that would eliminate pedestrian obstructions to traffic flow, and would provide a service not unlike a surface fixed-rail transit system. A line would link the train station in Kota with the Blok M commercial zone in South Jakarta, exactly following the route initially suggested for a subway, and serving the dominant business corridor in Jakarta along Jalan Thamrin and Jalan Sudirman. At a cost of Rp 90 billion, this initial busway line would be a mere fraction of the cost of the subway project, although its hourly capacity of between 10,000 and 27,000 passengers was roughly half that of the subway.[18] To serve a metropolitan-wide system, additional feeder lines would need to connect to both the eastern and western areas where steady population growth had occurred over the previous decades. Critics of the busway project tended to emphasize its limited carrying capacity (compared to a subway or a fixed rail transit) and on how it would consume two precious lanes of surface roadway, thereby reducing further the space available for the growing number of private vehicles. Jakarta's clogged main thoroughfares required some immediate relief especially since the pressures from additional commuters grew as new towns sprang up around the core city.

Land Development

While completing the toll road construction programme was a critical ingredient of Jakarta's suburbanization process, planning for alternative models of urban communities was underway long before the pavement dried. According to Michael Leaf,

the two important areas which have been instrumental in fostering the suburbanization of Jakarta ... [are] ... a massive programme of subsidized housing finance ... and a municipal permit system for land development created specifically to feed urban lands into the corporate development sector.[19]

And these, he said, were supported by 'government-sponsored provision of trunk infrastructure'. Dick noted that even before large-scale suburban development occurred the artificially low fares charged on the public transit system, subsidized fuel prices for car owners, and the aggressive development of a highway network to support this transport system discouraged high density development. 'In effect', he observed, 'the government is subsidizing urban sprawl, a trend which has been most evident in Jakarta over the past decade [1970s] but which can be found in most other large Indonesian cities'.[20]

The generosity of Indonesia's National Land Agency in issuing permits to allow development of more than 80,000 hectares of land on the fringes of Jakarta between 1985 and 1999 hastened the sprawling decentralized pattern of development.[21] Although only 40 per cent of the permitted land was actually built on prior to the economic crisis of 1997, the net effect of the wholesale granting of development authorizations was to encourage developers to favour peripheral locations over those more centrally located. This was a repetition of a process of land conversion that had first occurred with government encouragement during the third national development plan 1978–1983 (*Repelita III*). During that 5 year period, agricultural areas immediately adjacent to the city, including Pasar Minggu, Jati Padang, Warung Buncit, Pejaten, Pondok Labu, Klender, Ciputat, Cilenduk and Depok were drawn into the urban settlement system. All these communities were located along Jakarta's southern edge, and all were linked spatially and functionally to the only satellite city, Kebayoran Baru. Both the Jakarta to Bogor highway, as well as expanded radial roadways emanating from the inner ring highway, provided ready access to these areas.[22]

Given the scale of new housing, commercial, and industrial development at the edges of metropolitan Jakarta from the late 1970s to the 1990s, it would be reasonable to expect that this would have been accompanied by equally dramatic population losses and commercial decline in the inner city. Even when abundant lands were made available for new development at the edges, this did not dampen demand for land in the city. According to a study of land speculation in the Jakarta region, land prices in strategic areas of central Jakarta rose rapidly during the 1980s and 1990s. In Jakarta's so-called 'Golden Triangle', a new commercial zone framed by Jalan Sudirman, Jalan Gotot Subroto, and Jalan Rasuna Said, the land price per square metre rose from Rp 2500 in 1970 to Rp 700,000 by 1988 (US$7 to 438). But this was just the start. By the early 1990s, land prices in this area averaged Rp 5 million per square metre but in some transactions were known to go as high as Rp 12 million (or US$4,800) per square metre. These inflated prices made it extremely attractive to transform the remaining residential, manufacturing and trade properties to new uses to capture the land value. No wonder that the locus of Jakarta's office boom shifted to the Golden Triangle area. According to the

Table 5.1. Development of built-up areas in Jakarta Metropolitan Region.

Jakarta	1971	1977	1982	1988	1994
Built-up	17,878 ha	32,914 ha	37,021 ha	39,734 ha	54,505 ha
	31.4%	42.0%	57.3%	61.5%	82.1%
Non-built	39,063 ha	33,027 ha	27,632 ha	24,919 ha	11,927 ha
	68.6%	58.0%	42.7%	38.5%	17.9%
Total area	56,941 ha	56,941 ha	64,653 ha	64,653 ha	66,432 ha
Tanggerang		1980	1985	1989	1992
Built-up		14,033 ha	30,773 ha	34,162 ha	44,214 ha
		10.9%	24.0%	27.0%	34.5%
Non-built		114,147 ha	97,407 ha	93,568 ha	83,966 ha
		88.1%	76.0%	73.0%	65.5%
Total area		128,180 ha	128,180 ha	127,730 ha	128,180 ha
Bogor		1974	1980	1987	1994
Built-up		33,150 ha	36,569 ha	60,659 ha	64,672 ha
		14.7%	13.1%	17.7%	19.0%
Non-built		191,978 ha	243,679 ha	282,861 ha	276,434 ha
		85.3%	86.9%	82.3%	81.0%
Total area		225,128 ha	280,248 ha	343, 310 ha	341,266 ha
Bekasi	1973	1980	1988	1991	1993
Built-up	2,578 ha	14,310 ha	15,905 ha	23,486 ha	27,378 ha
	2.0%	10.0%	10.7%	15.8%	18.4%
Non-built	134,025 ha	134,130 ha	132,535 ha	134,954 ha	121,062 ha
	98%	90.0%	89.3%	84.2%	81.6%
Total	136,603 ha	148,440 ha	148,440 ha	148,440 ha	148,440 ha

Sources: National Land Agency; Jakarta Census Bureau of Statistics, Spatial Plan of Bogor, Tanggerang and Bekasi – cited in Winarso and Kombiatan (1997), p. 4.

best available data, from 1980 to 1992, there were 600 new buildings constructed in Jakarta, with a total value of US$3 billion,[23] the greatest proportion in or adjacent to the Golden Triangle. Escalating land prices in central Jakarta led to

the changing function of the core area, from being a center of manufacturing activities to … a center for finance and services… Slum areas are being converted into a business zone, with shopping centers, hotels, offices, condominiums and the like.[24]

The physical transformation and consequent displacement of previous functions in so many areas of central Jakarta, especially near strategic commercial zones, was profound. Yet available population data suggest that population growth in Jakarta's inner areas remained robust in the face of such massive development outside its boundaries, at least through the early 1990s. Only one of Jakarta's five administrative areas, Jakarta Pusat (Central Jakarta), experienced a population loss in the wake of explosive commercial development, but that loss was relatively modest – from 1,182,393 to 1,001,000 (15 per cent) between 1984 and 1994. At the same time, the other four administrative areas increased in population between

Figure 5.4. The commercial towers along Jalan Sudirman heading toward South Jakarta (top) and the high-rise commercial and residential structures surging upward in the area of the World Trade Center in North Jakarta (below) evidence the extent of development from the early 1990s to 2006, despite the interruption of the economic crisis. (*Photos:* author)

37 per cent and 77 per cent. In other words, development in Jakarta's suburban periphery and the dramatic restructuring of older sections of the inner city did not produce the abandonment of the city centre that was so typical of Western cities also experiencing rapid decentralization.

In Jakarta, there was a steady outflow of inner-city residents to new developments along the periphery. A study of who was populating Jakarta's expanding fringe found that migrants moved there from central Jakarta in order to obtain affordable housing.[25] Whether pushed out because their housing was cleared for new development, or facing the pressures of escalating rents (or the chance to make some money by letting a city centre house at an inflated rate while renting something for much less but further out), inner-city neighbourhoods fed the emerging suburbs with a steady flow of new residents. The continuous influx of new migrants from outside the Jakarta region replenished inner urban areas and more than offset the population losses due to out-migration. What is remarkable is that the residential density of Jakarta actually increased from an average of 99.7 persons per hectare in 1980 to 135.7 persons per hectare in 1994.[26]

The increased population density in the inner city, coupled with a continuous process of land-use conversion and rapid development of peripheral areas, constituted a unique urban dynamic that confounded the prevailing planning model devised to manage change.

The transition process in Jakarta's inner and outer cities during the 1980s and 1990s had a disruptive effect, especially in low-income neighbourhoods. Displacement of virtually all the remaining pockets of affordable residential neighbourhoods adjacent to the Jalan Sudirman, Jalan Thamrin and Jalan Rasuna Said commercial areas forced many to crowd into residential areas not directly in the path of the business boom or to join the exodus to the urban fringe. Almost all the replacement housing built in or near the Golden Triangle was geared to an upper-income market. Throughout the 1980s and early 1990s, *kampung* residents in the path of inner-city commercial development tried to resist displacement or at least hold out for improved compensation, but in most cases, residents were forced to move with little compensation. One exception was redevelopment of the abandoned Kemayoran airport in Central Jarkarta. The project displaced 5,200 families in three adjacent sub-districts (*kelurahan*). While the centrepiece of the Kemayoran project was a new international trade centre, it included new replacement low-income apartments. The project plan called for displaced

Table 5.2. Central city population increases, Jakarta, 1984 to 1994.

	1984	1994	Change
South Jakarta	1,476,201	2,023,300	+37%
East Jakarta	1,395,877	2,337,200	+67%
Central Jakarta	1,182,393	1,001,000	−15%
West Jakarta	1,260,818	2,097,700	+66%
North Jakarta	869,553	1,539,400	+77%
Total	6,184,842	8,998,600	+46%

Sources: Statistik Wilayah Tahun (1984); Proyeksi Penduduk DKI Jakarta (1990).

families to have first priority for occupancy in these units. Not all accepted the new housing because it was more expensive than their previous shelter (costing between Rp 30,000 (US$24) and 115,000 (US$52) per month. Others did not like apartment living (it seemed like living in a 'bird cage') and chose to take the compensation for their land and moved to a cheaper area.[27] What was most significant in the case of the Kemayoran redevelopment plan was the introduction of an explicit commitment to replacement housing for low-income families. Although the final dispensation of the project did not work exactly as planned, it is significant that Jakarta's planners recognized that the displacement factor of centre city restructuring was a matter to be addressed.

Suburban New Towns

With a presidential instruction embracing the concept of bundled decentralization of new development in the Jakarta region, an aggressive and politically well-placed group of land developers built more than 1000 separate housing and commercial estates on the periphery of Jakarta in the 1980s and 1990s. Some of these were intended to function as self-sufficient communities in line with an urban planning objective set out in the Fourth National Development Plan, 1984–1989 (*Repelita IV*). As specified in *Repelita IV*,

to solve the problems of large cities and rural areas, it is essential to promote and create new large-scale settlements integrated with improvement in the undeveloped region, to enable the improvement of the welfare and quality of living environment in the surrounding areas.[28]

Bumi Serpong Damai (BSD), Tigaraksa New Town, Lippo Karawaci (LK), Kajuh Naga, Bintaro Jaya, Citra Raya New Town, Puri Jaya City, and Citra Grand City were all built along the western edge of Jakarta and each consumed at least 1,000 hectares of former agricultural land. BSD and Kajuh Naga were the biggest projects, each planned to fill 8,000 hectares with new urban development. A group of similar new towns was built directly to the east of central Jakarta, including Bekasi New Town, Cikwang Baru New Town, Bekasi 2000 New Town, Lippo Cikarang, Legend New City and Bekasi New City. Each was at least 1000 hectares in area. Because of the tight clustering of these individual private developments, they had the effect of creating urban level concentrations in areas that a decade earlier were sparsely settled rural communities.

These new towns were intended to accommodate a mixed-income population. A 1974 national government decree stipulated that in new developments greater than 200 hectares for every luxury house constructed, there must be three small houses, and six very small houses added to the housing inventory by the developer. This cross-subsidy programme was intended to ensure that some of the benefits to the private sector from government permission to build would be used to address the pressing housing needs of the expanding urban population. 'Small houses' were those in the 22–36 square metre range (roughly 237–288 square feet) while the 'very small houses' were just 21 square metres (226 square feet) of living space and had a market cost of just a few hundred dollars.

By 1990, it was claimed that the 1:3:6 regulation had succeeded in greatly expanding the amount of new housing for low income people, although in fact relatively little of this housing was built in conjunction with the new towns. Most of the units for the low-income population were built on cheaper land in less desirable areas, but this was accepted by the government as satisfying the requirements of the 1:3:6 policy. A 1980s decree by the government of West Java allowed developers to contribute Rp 1.6 million (roughly US$1,000) per required unit to the Governor's 'Lovely Houses Foundation' (*Sawang Kadulah*) in lieu of actually constructing the housing, and through this foundation new housing would be built within the province where it was needed. This allowed worker housing to be built in remote locations. Yet in the early 1990s, one local leader, the *bupati* of Tanggerang, Syafullah Abdurachman (1993–1998) strictly enforced the 1:3:6 requirement in his district. As a result, Lippo Karwaci built neighbourhoods within their otherwise exclusive suburban enclave that included *rumah sederhana* (RS), which was a modest house, and *rumah sangat sederhana* (RSS) which was the smaller 'very modest house'.[29]

Other than a few exceptions (including BSD), Jakarta's suburban new towns served a combination of the existing wealthy and the growing middle class. Bumi Serpong Damai was the first and most ambitious of these new suburban communities, initiated in 1984 by one of Jakarta's leading developers, Ciputra, head of *PT Jaya Pembangunan*. This development corporation was the prime mover in the creation of the waterfront amusement area of Ancol in North Jakarta. Ciputra went on to set up his own development company, first to build offices in downtown Jakarta but later branching out into the suburban residential development. His first major suburban residential project was the posh golf community of Pondok Indah in South Jakarta. The Salim Group, headed by Sudono Salim (also known as Liem Sioe Liong), who was Indonesia's wealthiest individual and a close friend of President Suharto, provided the financial backing that enabled Ciputra to undertake so many large projects. Ciputra consolidated his leadership over the suburban development field through creation of Real Estate Indonesia (REI) in 1972. Membership of this group, which included 25 charter members, was a prerequisite to securing government permits to build in Jakarta's suburbs. Ciputra's development of Pondok Indah was followed in 1981 by a larger planned community, Bintaro Jaya, which eventually encompassed

1780 hectares. Ciputra simultaneously had two further large residential projects under construction, confirming Salim's original hunch that he had identified an aggressive and visionary developer who would ensure that his real estate investments brought substantial returns.[30]

BSD brought together two of the most powerful business groups in Indonesia under Ciputra's leadership. According to Ciputra's version of the story, Eka Tjipta Widjaya, who headed the powerful *Sinar Mas Group*, asked the developer/ architect to view some land that he was assembling. Accompanying Ciputra and Widjaya was Salim's son, Anthony, who had become involved with suburban real estate development through property acquisition activities for Ciputra in Pondok Indah. On this noon time excursion, Ciputra claimed to have fallen into a deep sleep (allegedly triggered by a solar eclipse) and dreamed of a new city within the Jakarta suburbs but completely self-sufficient. Shortly afterwards, plans for the new city of Bumi Serpong Damai (BSD) were announced, supported by ten corporations but controlled by the three who had made that fateful noon visit. It is noteworthy that the consortium of investors in BSD appointed as its Chief Executive Advisor, Sudwikatmono, cousin of President Suharto. The challenge of assembling such a substantial site, 6,000 hectares (23 square miles), required more than just the financial backing of two of Indonesia's largest conglomerates. It needed a direct link to government since it was expected that the project would take at least 20 years to complete, and would require significant new infrastructure to make it accessible and attractive.[31]

Ciputra relied on a combination of indigenous and foreign assistance in planning BSD. The overseas assistance first came from the Baltimore-based Design Development Group, but Ciputra later brought in the Athens-based Doxiadis Associates to help refine the master plan and John Portman Associates of Atlanta, the developers of the famed Peachtree Plaza in that city, to provide specific advice on the business district plan. This later concern was significant, since it was Ciputra's intention to establish a commercial base in BSD significant enough to stand alone and provide BSD residents with the option of working as well as living in the community. Over the next 20 years, implementing the commercial district component of the BSD plan proved to be the toughest challenge. Building and selling luxury houses was the easy part.

What distinguished BSD from so many other developments in the greater Jakarta area was that from the outset it was intended to be a self-contained 'new city', not a typical suburban residential settlement. As a new city which was part of the suddenly mushrooming district capital of Tanggerang city, BDS offered a mix of residential, commercial and industrial development spaces. As BSD public relations director, Johannes Tulung, observed in mid-1995, other real estate developments relied on local government to provide services, such as road improvements, water, and waste management. BSD relieved Tanggerang of that burden. The number and range of housing types constructed enabled BSD to meet the government requirement of providing housing in a mix of price and size ranges according to the '1:3:6' formula. Construction of lakes covering 30 hectares not only created sites for 'waterfront' housing and recreation but more importantly a catchment area to reduce the dangers of flooding.[32]

Between the January 1989 project launch and 2004, nearly 15,000 houses were built, slightly more than a tenth of the proposed total of 140,000 when BSD was completed. These accommodated only a fraction of the anticipated final population of 600,000 residents. From the outset, the varying house types were arranged by price and style in separate neighbourhoods. The centrepiece of the community was the Pete Dye designed golf course, which was opened early on in the development process. The community plan included a business incubator facility, the Center for Science and Technology Development (funded by the German overseas aid programme) which was intended to support the employment base for residents. BSD's central business district developed more slowly, however. Not until 1998 was the 8-storey German Center for Industry and Trade, a 15,000 square metre office building, completed. Its opening coincided with the chaos of President Suharto's resignation, uncertainty about the political future of Indonesia, and a devastated economy that was shutting down most projects within the metropolitan region. In one sense, the chaos that seemed to be highly focused in central Jakarta worked to the advantage of this suburban development. Because European-based firms preferred the security of BSD's distance from the ongoing violence in central Jakarta, the centre's director, Jochen Sautter, predicted in July 1999 that the building would be fully occupied soon, and largely by foreign investors.[33]

Although the original business district plan by Portman and Associates called for a large grouping of high-rise offices, only the German Center and the 11-storey *Graha Telekomunikasi* building had been erected by 2005. A pollution free industrial park, Taman Techno (with fifteen local and foreign businesses), two shopping centres with most of the 2,000 retail stores serving the community, several nearby auto dealerships, and the Swiss German University (established in 2000) rounded out the business district.[34] By 2005, BSD Public Service General Manager, Dhony Rahajoe, claimed that approximately 30 per cent of BSD residents found employment locally and that most of the business owners in the two shopping centres were residents. Even with a brisk real estate market returning by 2005 and houses selling in a range from Rp 160 million (US$17,700) to Rp 2 billion (US$222,300), the city management revised its projected completion date from 2014 to 2020.[35]

With fourteen elementary schools, eight junior high schools, eight senior high schools, four universities, four health clinics and a hospital, thirteen mosques, two churches, and seventeen banks, BSD had become a complex and self-contained, if not fully self-sufficient, small city by 2005. It was so much more than the exclusive golfing community that it appeared when it first took shape in the early 1990s. Yet because so many of its residents continued to rely on jobs in Jakarta, the community retained important economic ties to Jakarta's inner city.

To assist those residents who commuted to central Jakarta for employment, there were options besides the private car. BSD provides three shuttle buses daily between the community and major office centres in central Jakarta, including Ratu Plaza in South Jakarta, Pasar Baru in Central Jakarta and Mangga Dua in North Jakarta at a fare of Rp 8000 (US$.82) per trip in 2005.[36] BSD also is served by a commuter train. As a further indication of the desire to foster BSD's growing sense of independence from Jakarta, the newly elected Tanggerang district head announced in 2003 his intention to find investors to construct a sports complex on BSD land as 'an alternative to the Gelora Bung Karno Sports Complex at Senayan, South Jakarta … [to] host various national and international sports events'.[37]

Another major new town built in Tanggerang by a Ciputra competitor, the Lippo Group (headed by banker James Riady) was Lippo Karawaci (LK), a community that shared many of BSD's features. Like Ciputra, Riady borrowed heavily from overseas community designs, not just those provided by the hired United States planning consultants, but also based on his own experiences of living in Southern California while pursuing a graduate business degree. He greatly admired the golf centred, gated communities there, and used that model to design his signature development at LK. As in BSD, Riady placed the golf course at the centre and surrounded it with luxury homes. Riady personally determined who was allowed to purchase property in the Taman Imperial neighbourhood adjacent to the golf course where he built his own house. Higher priced homes were located closer to the centre, prices decreasing with increasing distance from the centre. What set LK apart from BSD, and characterized a number of Jakarta's suburban new towns and planned communities, was the attempt to project an international rather than an Indonesian image. LK could be said to be marketed as a large theme park. For example, it had a Japanese-inspired neighbourhood – Taman Osaka (Osaka Garden); an American-style enclave – Taman Boston (Boston Garden); a collection of pseudo-Dutch homes – Taman Hollandia (Holland Garden); a French motif in Taman Paris (Paris Garden), and a more generic southern European theme in Taman Mediterranean (Mediterranean Garden).

LK's population appeared to be generally more affluent than that of BSD, owing to higher land costs that raised the housing prices. With its own private university, LK needed to provide housing for students in its two more affordable neighbourhoods. Compared to BSD, where a substantial percentage of the residents were government employees, LK residents tended to be drawn predominantly from the private sector. Another difference between LK and BSD was that few LK residents worked locally. Virtually all had to commute to areas outside LK for work, making it largely a commuter suburb and with no intention to become a self-sufficient city. One other discernible difference was the low percentage of Muslims living in LK. It was largely a Christian community, with only the university students contributing any degree of religious diversity. On the other hand, with its thirteen mosques and just two churches, BSD was more representative of the religious make-up of Jakarta's population. Harold Leisch, who assessed whether new towns like BSD and LK were serving the diverse needs of Jakarta's rapidly expanding population, stated both were generating 'a clear social polarization in the agglomeration of Jabotabek … [since] only middle- and upper-class people can afford to live there'.[38]

The largest of the self-sufficient city projects was unveiled in late 1996, and indicated that the Indonesian first family was intent on entering this business venture as well. President Suharto approved his son Bambang's plan to build a new city near Bogor, south of Jakarta on a plot of 30,000 hectares. If this project had been built as originally conceived, it would have consumed an area equal to nearly a half that of the whole of Jakarta. The Jonggol plan called for half the area to be developed for residential uses, an administrative centre, an industrial estate and some other urban service facilities, while the other half would be protected areas for rice fields, tourist sites and a reservoir. One of the major criticisms of the Jonggol project was its location in an environmentally sensitive zone, an area where planners had strongly urged no new development whatsoever since it was the primary aquifer recharge area for the metropolis. Jonggol's development required removing a 3,100 hectare forest preserve managed by the Ministry of Forestry, although the plan called for it to be replaced with new forested areas elsewhere in the region. Even more controversial than the imposition of the Jonggol city project on a protected environment was the suggestion that major components of the national government move their offices to its proposed administrative centre, a first step towards moving the capital out of central Jakarta to the Bogor district.[39]

Some university-based and non-government organizations questioned the wisdom of using land development to sustain economic growth of the metropolitan area, as in the case of the Jonggol project as it elevated land costs making it unavailable for other uses such as schools or low-cost housing. A Bandung-based non-government organization, *Akatiga*, suggested that the commodification of land in Jakarta was at the core of the continuous conflicts over land that routinely derailed planning processes and gave inordinate influence to private developers. None of the new town private developments had been subject to any sort of public hearings to determine their impact beyond stimulating economic growth.

Urban planning professor Djoko Sujarto, of the Bandung Institute of Technology observed that Jakarta's 'planners do not know what public aspirations are in the absence of public hearings'.[40]

Although in October 1996 the National Land Agency instructed its offices in West Java to cease issuing new permits for housing complexes in Bogor, Tanggerang, and Bekasi, this was not intended to countermand the permits already issued, or necessarily to put a stop to illegal projects currently underway. Indeed, President Suharto gave approval to his son's mega development project just one month later. Already permits for 92,298 hectares of housing (which was one and a half times the space of the entire special district of Jakarta) had been issued, so the real effect of the order was minimal. Accompanying the announcement of this administrative action was a statement from a Ministry of Public Works official, Siswoko, indicating that the cessation of new land permits was not intended to be a ban on development but rather an opportunity to reconsider how to create new developments that included sufficient catchment areas to ensure that ground water supplies were replenished. There was also a desire to control development of land adjacent to Jakarta's main river, the Ciliwung, to ensure that it did not receive excessive runoff which would lead to greater flooding downstream.[41]

What ended the rush to control the development of Jakarta's periphery, at least temporarily, was not an effective public planning process or enforcement of government regulations but the dampening effects of massive economic and political crises in the late 1990s.

Preserving and Revitalizing the Core

Aggressive pursuit of economic development, which was a defining trait of Suharto's New Order government until its demise in the late 1990s, created a whole new set of pressures on all parts of the metropolis, although initially most intensive development pressures were felt in the periphery. Yet it was under the New Order government that increasing attention also was given to revitalizing older sections of what had been the heart of the colonial capital. This occurred through new developments but also through rehabilitation and preservation of existing built environment. The motivations for preservation in the urban core were not unlike the guiding motivations behind the New Order's penchant for economic development. James Cobban's assessment of Jakarta's first major restoration project in the Kota section of North Jakarta in the 1970s identified three factors underlying the preservation movement. The New Order government undertook a number of museum construction and rehabilitation projects in order to foster a stronger sense of national identity. The centrepiece of the 1970s historic district plan was the Dutch *stadhuis* (city hall) which was transformed into a museum of Jakarta's history and culture. It was flanked by several other museums devoted to Indonesian culture. These were not educational projects based on meticulous research and careful presentation but rather eclectic expressions of national accomplishments.[42]

Preservation in Jakarta was also a means to address unemployment among the large informal sector population. As a tourist attraction, the city's historic district could 'serve as an outlet for native handicrafts and generate jobs in the accompanying hotels and support services. History- and culture-based tourism would be touted as the sort of economic development that could rescue Indonesia from such heavy reliance on oil for overseas capital. But without historical attractions on a scale comparable to the temples of Yogjakarta and Bali, Jakarta would not be able to capture its share of the increase in tourism. Creating an identifiable historic district was central to Jakarta's strategy to become a tourist destination rather than merely a stopover.

Finally, there was an increasing desire to provide a counterpoint to the modernist design trend in Jakarta's built environment. Although the office and residential development boom occurred in the 1990s, the modernist motif was already dominant in the 1980s. Proponents of preservation maintained that new commercial structures were effacing the distinctive traits of the capital city. In a July 1990 seminar on historical preservation held in Jakarta, Martono Yuwono, Chair of

Figure 5.5. Kali Besar (the big river) cannelized by the Dutch in the heart of the Kota area, and a key component of the historic preservation efforts. (*Photo*: author)

the Foundation for the Preservation of National Culture, described preservation as an 'alternative approach to city development' and that city authorities should integrate preservation with the construction of modern facilities. Also adding his voice to the preservation movement was Abdulrachman Wahid, leader of a major Islamic organization and a future president of Indonesia. He presented a paper at the seminar entitled 'Historical Vision of a Metropolitan City: A Case Study of Development Activities in Jakarta'. Wahid argued that the preservation and restoration of historic buildings was essential to address the social needs of a complex metropolis.[43]

To what extent did the modernizing capital city of Indonesia retain and use the urban constructs of the Europeans who had dominated city life over the previous three centuries? Was the preservation movement in central Jakarta, as Cobban described it in the 1980s, an 'ephemeral' phenomenon in planning the megacity, or did Jakarta embrace an approach to integrating the old and the new that assumed a more central place in metropolitan development? To understand the role of urban preservation in Jakarta's planning for the megacity, it is necessary to examine briefly the precedents established in the colonial era.

The legal foundation of Jakarta's modern preservation movement dated from the 1920s. In the New City Plan for Batavia prepared in 1923 by Berlage, there were several initiatives proposed to restore important sections of the nineteenth-century city, including the town hall square and the commercial areas along the main canal, Kali Besar. Gill noted that there was an aggressive building drive in Batavia in the 1920s, much like that of the 1980s and early 1990s, that threatened to wipe out much of the traditional city. Although Berlage's plan was not implemented, an Ordinance on Monuments (No. 238/1931) was passed in 1931 to protect significant historical structures. Even with this legal protection in place, it took an aggressive stand by the Old Batavia Foundation in 1937 to prevent city authorities from dismantling the old Dutch double wooden lift bridge (Hoenderpasar bridge) over Kali Besar.[44]

The Japanese occupation of the early 1940s, the traumas of the early nation-building era, and the absence of development pressures diverted attention from preservation issues. The beginning of construction in Jakarta's 1970s boom period generated a series of gubernatorial regulations that broadened the scope of preservation activities by recognizing those districts that would be the focus of preservation planning in the 1980s and 1990s. These included Fatahillah Square, the site of the eighteenth-century city hall (Reg. CD. 3/1/70); Pasar Ikan or the Fish Market, next to the traditional harbour of Sunda Kelapa (Reg. No D III-b11/4/54/73); Menteng, the early twentieth-century suburban neighbourhood (Reg. D. IV-6098/d/33/1975); Tugu in North Jakarta (Reg. CB.11/2/8/70); the Chinese area known as Glodok (Reg. D.III-b.11/4/56/1973); and several agricultural areas in which Betawi culture continued and on the islands (Pulau Seribu) in Jakarta Bay. In two separate regulations (Reg. CB.II/1/12/1972 and Reg. D.IV-5492a/13/1974), the Jakarta government affirmed that all historic buildings should be protected and that there was a 'prohibition against the destruction of any buildings in the old areas of … Jakarta'. In 1990, there was an additional gubernatorial decree that stipulated a special permit to construct any new building in the Sunda Kelapa area. Based on a 1972 survey, there were approximately 700 'old buildings' in the city, but only 224 were classified as historic buildings and protected by the gubernatorial decree. Of these, just eighteen were protected by the Ministry of Education and Culture. As the director of Jakarta's City Museum Agency pointed out in 1995, a ministerial decree has much more weight than one from the governor and 'would make it easier to protect the buildings because the [central] government will also be involved in their preservation'.[45]

Enforcement of these regulations was, however, more challenging than their promulgation. In 1985, the finest example of Empire style architecture, the colonial club facility known as *Harmonie* commissioned in 1810 by Governor Dandaels and opened by Raffles in 1814, was torn down for a street widening.[46] Five years later in April 1990, four historic structures were pulled down in the Senen Triangle area of central Jakarta in order to construct a parking garage for a new Senen shopping centre. Since the buildings were not included on the city's list of historic structures, and there was no decree specifically related to the Senen area, the developers removed the structures despite a request from Jakarta Governor Wiyogo Atmodarminto to preserve the buildings. While the city-owned development company, *PT Pembangunan Sarana Jaya*, claimed that it was preserving four of the 570 buildings by keeping the materials and rebuilding them on another site, one critic noted that 'the reconstruction of the buildings cannot return their historical values'.[47]

According to James Cobban, the catalyst for preservation planning in the 1970s was a proposal by city planners to construct two new roads linking Kota to the emerging suburb of Tanggerang and the new airport, both located west of the city. The plans for the new roads were abandoned temporarily, although one existing street was widened to accommodate the traffic that choked this section of the city. The northern expressway would eventually be built through this area in the 1990s as part of Jakarta beltway connecting the Sukarno-Hatta Airport with the container port at Tanjung Priok. Preservationists sought support from the city's administration to revitalize the area using restoration rather than rebuilding, and with the backing of the Vice Governor and the Mayor of West Jakarta, persuaded seven government agencies (Public Works, Planning, Sanitation, Parks, Traffic, Tourism and Industry) to incorporate into their budgets funds to carry out restoration. The sort of preservation that was envisioned was to unclutter the historic areas to make them more accessible and attractive to tourists, but also to maintain Kota's functional connections to the city.[48]

The three-phase preservation work began in the Fatahillah Square area. It included restoration of the eighteenth-century city hall (*Stadhuis*), which was converted into the Jakarta History Museum, and similar upgrades to surrounding structures, dating from the seventeenth to the nineteenth centuries, into museums and new commercial uses. To restore the Fatahillah Square area involved relocating the mayor of West Jakarta's office so as to eliminate parking on the square. Also, a bus terminal at the north end of the square, which served the nearby *kampungs*, was moved several blocks north along Kali Besar. The *Stadhuis*, built between 1707 and 1710, had also doubled as a prison during one phase of its life, holding such famous enemies of the state as the nineteenth-century freedom fighter Diponegoro. The adjacent nineteenth-century Justice building facing the square from the east was rehabilitated as an art museum. Although the restoration plan for Fatahillah Square failed to address diverting the intense commercial traffic that flowed by its east and west flanks, the removal of parking and transport facilities, the restoration of the buildings, and landscaping of the square 'contributed to the objective of beautification and aesthetic appeal'. It gave Jakarta an identifiable historic district which would serve it well in the future.

Figure 5.6. The old city hall (*Stadhuis*) located in Fatahillah Square, Kota area. (*Photo*: author)

The second phase of the historic district development focused on restoration of a Dutch warehouse near the fish market (Pasar Ikan) as a maritime museum, as well as some upgrading of the fishing village and beautification of the Luar Batang mosque adjacent to the historic, but still functioning, Sunda Kelapa harbour. Restoration of the fishing village did not involve any land-use changes but simply removing the mounds of debris that had accumulated along the shore. As in the case of the city museum on Fatahillah Square, Jakarta's preservationists believed that enhancing the appeal of the waterfront required creating a museum, not only to bring an active use to one of the historic warehouse buildings, but also to lure tourists to the site of the city's birth. At Pasar Ikan as well as along Kali Besar, the planners wanted to clean up the foul black waters that made these areas so unattractive to tourists. One plan called for placing model ships along a beautified waterfront adjacent to the still active wooden ships docked at Sunda Kelapa. This included a replica of an East Indies Company ship, a Portugese schooner from the sixteenth century, and a Chinese junk. The ship display never materialized except for miniatures within the maritime museum which opened in 1977 in a VOC spice warehouse. Adjacent to the maritime museum was the restored Lookout Tower which marked the original shoreline of the city (and the site of the seventeenth-century customs house) but which was inland when the tower was built in the nineteenth century on reclaimed land from the Bay of Jakarta.

The third and final phase of the preservation plan involved restoration of buildings and streetscapes in the Chinese commercial areas extending from Kali Besar south to Glodok. This was the slowest and least coordinated phase as it involved working with multiple private property owners rather than restoring publicly owned buildings. In the meantime in Glodok, new commercial facilities were replacing older buildings faster than preservations could respond. There was some streetscape planning for Kali Besar but only minor tree planting and removal of temporary structures occurred. Most buildings remained unrenovated, weeds and foul water choked the river, and by the late 1980s there was no sign of any commercial investment related to attracting tourism. In the early 1990s, a new hotel appeared on the west side of Kali Besar, the wooden bridge was restored and streetscape work progressed. But in the busy Chinese commercial centre of Glodok to the south of the historic district, although preservationists had identified significant structures to save, the area remained virtually 'untouched by historic preservation'.[49] While the 1970s and 1980s saw the restoration of several landmark structures and upgrading in Fatahillah and the fishing village, the historic districts of Kota remained inaccessible to pedestrians because of intensive traffic and the deleterious effects of nearby industrial and warehouse activities.

Despite limited success in implementing the full plan, a discernible historic district was created and this had the effect of focusing attention on Kota as an unrealized urban asset. What had been achieved also helped to redirect the city's planning towards an approach that included a more explicit preservationist component. This was evident in a bold scheme prepared in 1992 by city planners in cooperation with the Indonesian National Heritage Trust for what they called the 'Jayakarta Heritage Park' which encompassed a vast area including Fatahillah Square, Sunda Kelapa, Kali Besar and Pasar Ikan. It called for the transformation of the 1970s and 1980s 'district concept' into an integrated restoration scheme, with substantial new construction as a catalyst for increased tourism and to give metropolitan Jakarta an identifiable historical identity. The envisioned 'theme park' created out of the fabric of Kota depended on a combination of new construction and rehabilitation to create an environment attractive to tourists in what still was a traffic congested, decaying and polluted area along the North Jakarta coast. Preservation efforts focused on the Luar Benteng *kampung*, where the Kampung Improvement Program (KIP) and other community development initiatives would be used to modernize this low-income community. Part of the Bugis fishing village would be retained to showcase the distinctive South Sulawesi culture, but much of it would be cleared and replaced by new houses with modern amenities. The plan also called for a network of footpaths linking all parts of the historic area as far south as Fatahillah Square. The Al Aidrus Mosque would be renovated as would the fish market. The significant new construction to support expanded tourism included a waterfront festival market place, a reconstructed fisherman's wharf, new waterfront houses, a new Jayakarta Quay with *phinisi* boats for tourists to view and with shops and restaurants to serve them, a Jayakarta Art and Craft Market, open spaces for cultural events, and several statues and monuments to commemorate historical figures associated with the area.

While preservation was obviously a centrepiece of this scheme, critics pointed to the amount of clearance and redevelopment necessary to create the theme park. Unlike the historic district approach, critics contended that the Jayakarta Heritage Park sought to disconnect the historic area and tourist facilities from the everyday life of the city. The plan creators had obtained many of their ideas from successful tourism/restoration projects in United States cities where the theme park approach had worked so well. The plan included elements drawn from Baltimore's Harbor Place (with its Festival Market Place), from Williamsburg's use of carefully controlled restoration of a sample of indigenous buildings (as applied to Jakarta's Bugis fishing village) and from those urban attractions that relied on improved facilities for tourist access. But before the Jayakarta Heritage Park scheme received consideration by local planners and private interests, it was superseded by a more ambitious revitalization programme that placed the historic district within a much grander new waterfront city.

The North Jakarta Area Revitalization and Waterfront Reclamation Project,

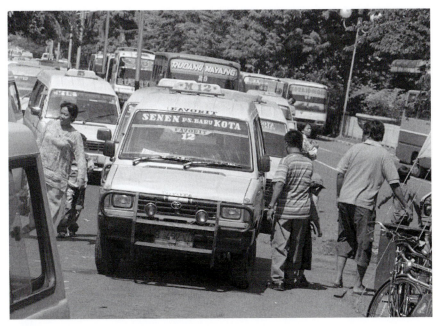

Figure 5.7. *Becak*s have been banned from Jakarta but can still be found in small pockets of the older North Jakarta neighbourhoods competing with mini vans. (*Photo*: author)

unveiled in 1995, was an anticipated 20-year public/private redevelopment project to create an entirely new waterfront city along Jakarta's northern coast. The project's goal was to revitalize the historic North Jakarta waterfront area into a prime commercial/industrial/residential area extending 32 kilometres from the port at Tanjung Priok to the international airport to the west. Besides supporting commercial and industrial interests, the plan called for construction of more than 1200 hectares of new low- and high-density housing by reclaiming 2700 hectares of land from the Bay of Jakarta.[50] The expressway that had been proposed in the 1970s to link the ship port and the international airport, as well as North Jakarta to the expressways that had been built around the southern edge of the metropolis, was completed shortly after the government unveiled the waterfront plan. A related project to construct a subway system beginning in Kota and extending southward to the Block M commercial/transport hub in Kebayoran Baru was also announced in conjunction with the waterfront city plan. The US$2.2 billion subway project was regarded as a key component of the plan to link the congested Kota and central Jakarta areas to expanding southern suburbs without building additional highways. A presidential decree in 1995 (*Kepres* 52/1995) gave authority to the Governor of Jakarta to establish the Jakarta Waterfront Implementation Board (JWIB) and a separate development corporation to facilitate the land reclamation project. As late as March 1997 (just before the onset of the financial crisis) there was

Figure 5.8. Waterfront city plan.

no official go ahead on the subway project since financial commitments remained too loose to proceed.[51] But the planning and design work on the waterfront city had already been underway for several years.

In addition to providing new land for housing, commercial and industrial uses in conjunction with the container port at Tanjung Priok, to support increased tourism JWIB would coordinate restoration of the historic areas near the old city hall and the wooden boat harbour at Sunda Kelapa. The waterfront city plan called for a complete new water and sewerage system to serve both existing and new developments, and for removal of pollution from the canals and rivers that pass through this area into Jakarta Bay. The waterfront city was to have its own central business district, thereby contributing another commercial cluster to the emerging polycentric form of Jakarta. The rendering presented at the unveiling of the concept plan showed a cluster of high-rise commercial towers very much like the new commercial hub of Pudong in central Shanghai being developed at that time also by reclaiming land. Although the financial crisis slowed implementation of the waterfront development plan (and temporarily scuttled the subway project), construction of new housing and commercial settlements along the north shore proceeded in conformity with the general redevelopment plan.

By focusing attention on the historic areas of northern and central Jakarta areas, the waterfront city project plan renewed interest in preservation planning. An editorial in the *Jakarta Post* in June 1995 bemoaned the sorry state of the city's museums. The Head of the City Museum Office, Dirman Surachmat, pointed out that the city planners did not include museum preservation in the planning budget. However, the planners were looking closely at this area, especially the historic warehouses that were part of the plan to provide for new uses in order 'to revitalize the area and transform it into a tourist attraction by modifying the old buildings'. As a demonstration of the government's interest in adaptive reuse, owners of historic warehouse buildings were ordered by the West Jakarta mayor to relocate their operations from the Kota area, and a team of Dutch specialists arrived to consult with government planners on how similar warehouses in Amsterdam had been converted to apartments, hotels, shops, offices, restaurants and theatres. The waterfront reclamation plan also called for substantial clearance in order to accommodate new uses. It was estimated that more than 15,000 fishermen living along the northern shoreline would be displaced by the project.

The ineffectiveness of the grand revitalization schemes of the 1980s and 1990s that attempted to use historic preservation for economic development in Jakarta should not be regarded as the final word on the impact of preservation efforts in the city. A continuous process of incremental restoration and adaptive reuse preserved historic structures and places as part of the contemporary urban fabric. Merdeka Square was a case of partial and incremental preservation. While dominated visually by two of Sukarno's celebrated monuments, the Monas obelisk and nearby national mosque, the four boulevard's that framed the city's most celebrated public space contained some of the most significant structures from nineteenth-century Batavia which were restored and reused as government facilities, including the president's and vice-president's offices, museums, and other public uses. Several of Jakarta's most distinguished old churches also were located in this area. Despite the intense traffic that continuously circumnavigated and crisscrossed Merdeka Square (until it was closed to cars and pedestrians in the late 1990s), it is actually one of the most pedestrian intensive places in Jakarta, and considerably more accessible to tourists than the Kota area.[52]

To the south of Merdeka Square in the residential neighbourhood of Menteng, incremental preservation, offset by considerable new development on lots where the original structures were cleared, occurred during the 1980s and 1990s. Despite rapid decentralization of Jakarta's residential areas in the 1970s and 1980s, Menteng retained its attraction as a residential area for the city's elite. This was not only because of its fine houses and well-landscaped streets, but also because it remained close to the capital's centre of power. President Suharto's main residence was in Menteng, along with the official residence of the Vice-President adjacent to the National Development Planning Board (BAPPENAS). Moreover, many foreign embassies converted some of the large mansions along its principal streets into offices and residences in order to be close to Indonesia's government offices as well as Jakarta's power elite.

As urban historian Susan Abeyasekere noted in the conclusion to her detailed biography of Jakarta,

the growth of the city in recent years has been so rapid that the old buildings and streets have often been swept away or dwarfed by new construction. Yet the determined observer can find large areas which have survived remarkably well.[53]

Not only in the sections of Kota where the historic preservation efforts were focused, but throughout central Jakarta, eighteenth- and nineteenth-century buildings have clung on to life, as much from neglect as from conscious efforts at preservation. Although Jakarta's revitalization efforts over the past three decades failed to produce the sort of tourist-oriented historic district envisioned in various plans, the antipathy towards structural symbols of the city's colonial past that marked the early national period has dissipated as the city's leadership gained an appreciation of the value of linking the vestiges of the historic city to the modern metropolis. From the monumentalism and anti-colonialism of the Sukarno regime through the authoritarianism of Suharto in which many of the cultural vestiges of everyday life gave way to a relentless march toward modernism, key elements of the beauty, grandeur and order of the colonial capital survived. The 350 years of Jakarta's history prior to independence still had the potential to guide future planning of the capital as Indonesia came to grips with the full impact of the modern megacity and, as more recent events revealed, the making of a democratic society.[54]

Notes

1.   See Indonesia Property Report (1995), p. 12; Tjahjono (1997).
2.   See Arndt (1972), pp. 54–61.
3.   See Dick (1981b), pp. 72–88.
4.   Soegijoko (1986), p. 155.
5.   *Ibid.*, p. 155–157.
6.   Dick (1981a), pp. 74–77.
7.   *Ibid.*, p. 87.
8.   Cowherd (2002), pp.171–172, 190.
9.   Winarso and Kombiatan (1997), pp. 4–5.
10. Jakarta DKI (1999), Table 2.2.
11. Winarso and Kombiatan (1997), p. 9.
12. Cowherd (2002), pp. 190–191.
13. *Ibid.*, p. 193.
14. *JP*, 4 September, 2002.
15. *JP*, 22 October, 2002; 19 October, 2001.
16. *JP*, 15 February, 2002; *JP*, 11 September, 2001.
17. *JP*, 2 January, 2003.
18. *Ibid.*
19. Leaf (1994), pp. 344, 353.
20. Dick (1981b), p. 87.
21. Firman (1997a), p. 10.
22. Surjomihardjo (1977), pp. 61–63.
23. Dorléans (1994), p. 51.
24. Firman (1996), p. 109.
25. See Browder, Bohland, and Scarpaci (1995), pp. 310–326.
26. See Marcussen (1990).
27. Malo and Nas (1996), pp. 126–129.
28. Sujarto (2002), p. 83.
29. Cowherd (2002), pp. 225–230.

30. This portrait of Ciputra is drawn from Cowherd (2002), pp. 86–88; Leaf (1991), pp. 225, 239–244; Schwartz (1999), p. 110.
31. Cowherd (2002), p. 89, note 70.
32. *JP*, 7 July, 1995; 9 December, 1994.
33. *JP*, 7 July, 1999.
34. *JP*, October 14, 2005.
35. *JP*, 4 August, 2005.
36. *JP*, 20 July, 2005.
37. *JP*, 16 April, 2003.
38. Leich (2000), p. 99.
39. *JP*, 18. 20 November, 1996; 19 December, 1996.
40. *JP*, 20 November, 1996.
41. *JP*, 12 October, 1996.
42. See Cobban (1985), pp. 300–318.
43. *JP*, 17 July, 1990.
44. Gill (1995), p. 82.
45. *JP*, 1 June, 1995.
46. Heuken (1982, 1989), pp. 183, 186–187.
47. *JP*, 24 March, 4 April, 1990.
48. Jakarta, DKI (nd*a*).
49. Cobban (1985), p. 317.
50. See Jakarta, DKI (1995*a*); Jakarta, DKI (1995*b*).
51. *JP*, 6 March 6, 1997; JWIB (1997).
52. *JP*, 27 April; 5, 17 June; 21 July 21, 1995.
53. Abeyasekere (1989), p. 257.
54. See Forrester and May (1999).

Chapter Six

Urban Village to World City: Re-planning Jakarta in the 1990s

Indonesia had achieved the status of an Asian 'tiger economy' by the 1990s, not quite on par with Singapore and Hong Kong, but because of its size and the wealth of its natural resources, potentially more dynamic if economic growth trends of the previous decade persisted. The World Bank's country report for Indonesia in 1997 identified the growing privatization of Indonesia's infrastructure over the previous decade, in telecommunications, power generation, road construction and port development, as keys to its economic success. On the basis of annual economic growth rates of between 5 and 7.5 per cent during the decade, the World Bank offered the heady prediction that by 2005 the nation's per capita income would rise to $2,300, elevating it to one of the world's twenty largest economies. The Bank's report predicted that Greater Jakarta would reach a population of between 25 and 30 million and that the overall urbanization rate for Indonesia would soon reach 50 per cent.[1]

The Suharto family was directly involved in many of the enterprises that contributed to the tremendous expansion of the Indonesian economy – and benefited handsomely from them. All six Suharto children had a hand in Indonesian business conglomerates. The eldest son Sigit Hardjojudanto controlled the Arseto Group; daughter Siti Hardijanti Hastutit Rukmana chaired the Citra Lamtoro Gung Groups, son Bambang Trihatmodjo controlled the Bimantara Group, daughter Siti Hedijati Herijadi Prabowo chaired the Datam Group, son Hotomo Mandala ('Tommy') Putra ran the Humpuss Group and the youngest daughter Siti Hutami Endang Adiningsih Pratikto owned plantations and agricultural processing plants. And the President seemed well placed to remain in power until at least 2003, given that he was the sole candidate for president in 1998, as had been the case in six previous contests (in 1968, 1973, 1978, 1983, 1988 and 1993). His election in 1993 was by acclamation of the 1,000 members

People's Consultative Assembly. It was expected that Indonesia would need a strong president like Suharto for years to come since, as supporters of his New Order government contended, the country seemed unprepared for a democracy for at least another generation. Another tacitly accepted condition of Indonesian politics was that involvement of the military in support of a strong government remained essential to ensure national stability. According to Franz Magnis Suseno, a former Indonesian ambassador, Indonesia needed 'a strong government and a strong President. We need a government which can't be easily toppled. We need a government which can carry out its plans and programs'.[2]

Jakarta was intended to be a showcase for the Indonesian development miracle made possible through the forceful leadership of the Suharto's New Order government. To give credence to the expectation of Jakarta becoming a 'world city', the early 1990s witnessed the beginning of changes in the city's landscape more rapid and more dramatic than in any decade in its more than three centuries of growth and development. While not limited to any one area of the city, the physical transformation was most in evidence along the commercial spine created by Jalan Thamrin and Jalan Sudirman, extending from Merdeka Square southward to the Blok M market area. Between 1990 and 1995, for example, no less than thirty high-rise office towers were squeezed into every available space between the handful of high-rises that had appeared over the previous three decades. One discrete component of this office construction boom was the Jakarta Stock Exchange complex located just south of Sukarno's famous highway cloverleaf, the Semanggi interchange, and across from the sprawling and lushly landscaped grounds of the Jakarta Hilton Hotel and Convention Center complex. Ironically, this area would become a battleground in the 1998 political struggle that changed the nation and its capital city. Student protesters were demanding that Suharto's authoritarian regime recognize their right to an open and democratic political process. Fired on by the military, the students who died in the Semanggi massacre triggered a nationwide civil protest that resulted in Suharto's resignation in May 1998. His decision to resign was the first crucial step in a national political revolution that would take place over the next 6 years. But in the early 1990s when the New Order government was at the peak of its power and prestige, Jakarta's marble-walled Stock Exchange and adjacent office complex symbolized the role that global capitalism played in transforming Indonesia from an underdeveloped nation into a global player.

Expanding Commercial Centre

Eight years before the Semanaggi incident, Jakarta took a small but highly symbolic step towards its goal of being acknowledged as a world city. In 1990, with central government support, Jakarta acquired its first overseas department store, the luxury Japanese chain Sogo, which anchored the city's first legitimate upscale downtown shopping centre, Plaza Indonesia. Positioned on the roundabout at the junction of Jalan Thamrin and Jalan Sudirman, and adjacent to Sukarno's landmark Hotel Indonesia (HI), Plaza Indonesia contrasted sharply in architectural style with neighbouring 1960s buildings, but shared a common purpose. Like Sukarno's HI, Suharto's Plaza Indonesia was intended to project the city, and through the city's architecture the nation, onto the international stage. While Merdeka Square celebrated national independence, the HI roundabout ensemble of commercial structures demonstrated Jakarta's global interconnectedness. The familiar 'welcome statue' created in the early 1960s in conjunction with the Asian Games, now announced entry to the massing of commercial towers that was becoming Jakarta's international business centre. The extensive commercial expansion along the Thamrin-Sudirman corridor had given another identifying characteristic to this area, namely the most recognized traffic bottleneck in a metropolis. Trying to mitigate the traffic congestion along this corridor connecting central Jakarta to booming South Jakarta would be a consuming concern of the city's planning staff throughout the 1990s and into the twenty-first century.

By the early 1990s the Hotel Indonesia had become a shabby and dated remnant of Sukarno's quest to modernize the capital city. In marked contrast, the

Figure 6.1. Hotel Indonesia and Welcome Statue at the intersection of Jalan Thamrin and Jalan Sudirman. (*Photo*: author)

glittering upscale Plaza Indonesia, anchored not only by Sogo but also by the five-star Grand Hyatt Hotel, offered foreign visitors and affluent Indonesians access to the top line fashion, food and accessory stores before only found by travelling to Singapore. With another five-star hotel, the Mandarin Oriental on the eastern side of the circle and a Westin Hotel being built literally in the backyard of the HI, the refurbished and intensified commercial role of one of the city's most treasured spaces took on a new role in supporting Jakarta's aspirations to be a global city. As Abidin Kusno contends, the transformation evident in the HI area was from a space dictated by the aspirations of the state to Sukarno's vision of a place where the city and the state were served by

investors and professionals whose common interest was the most profitable development of particular yet large scale activities such as the construction of modern skyscraper offices, elevated highways and luxury housing.[3]

These private interests worked hand in glove with the government (indeed it was a necessary precondition to gaining access to the system) and therefore supported state aspirations. But unlike the Sukarno quest for national pride and national respect, the new goal was sustainable profit through support from the state. The symbiosis of public and private was at it peak in the early 1990s and it was not just about modernizing the HI space; this partnership set out to reconstruct the basic fabric of Jakarta.

There were many important ingredients in the New Order's urban vision that required far more than filling in undeveloped commercial spaces or sprucing up the HI square. The centrepiece of the 1985–2005 plan for Jakarta was the creation of an entirely new central business district in an area commonly referred to as the Golden Triangle. This area had undergone piecemeal redevelopment for a decade, with the privately developed office towers along Jalan Sudirman representing the first leg of this triangle. The segment of Sukarno's ring road from the Semanngi interchange, known as Jalan Gatot Subroto, formed the base of the commercial triangle. The third leg ran northwards along Jalan Rusuna Said on a diagonal to where it nearly connected with Jalan Sudirman (just south of Menteng and adjacent to Jakarta's lone waste water treatment facility). These three major local roadways outlined the Golden Triangle area.

Jakarta's planners faced no small undertaking in trying to manage the many actors involved in realizing the world city vision. Beyond the enormous challenge of sustaining the commercial boom necessary to meet the economic development aspirations of the government and private sector, there was the equally daunting task of redeveloping the space designated as the Golden Triangle since it was still a densely populated collection of traditional *kampungs*, many having grown up in the period of mass in-migration from the 1950s to the 1970s. In addition to *kampungs*, there were also affluent neighbourhoods within the area, with a considerable amount of the land still in the hands of old *Betawi* families. Jakarta Governor Ali Sadikin had taken the first steps in transforming the area in the early 1970s when he secured enough land to carve out the Jalan Rasuna Said corridor to connect South Jakarta with Menteng. By the early 1990s, much of the land along Jalan Rasuna Said had already been developed as offices, some government buildings, and a number of embassies that had relocated from temporary quarters near Merkeda Square into modern and more spacious facilities along this busy commercial boulevard. Yet to create a spatially coherent new central business district rather than just a string of offices and facilities along the major thoroughfares required massive surgery in those interior neighbourhoods.[4]

Transport for a Megacity

This massive urban redevelopment enterprise, coupled with the more piecemeal changes along the adjacent roads, underscored the urgency of creating a modern high-capacity transport system to support the new commercial concentration. Jalan Thamrin, Jalan Surdirman, Jalan Rasuna Said, and Jalan Gatot Subrot, the major access points to the central Jakarta area, were plagued almost daily by gridlock that reduced speeds to a crawl for large portions of the day. New commercial construction along these already choked routes compounded the terrible traffic problem. The initial strategy focused on traffic management, especially along the Thamrin-Sudirman corridor. The enactment of a mandatory three persons per vehicle policy (the so-called 'three-in-one system') during rush hour (except for the thousands of taxi cabs), the removal of mini vehicles, the requirement for motor cycles and local buses to stay on the adjacent service roads that provided access to buildings, and the willingness of the police to let drivers turn the three lanes into four or five lanes by squeezing cars into every available bit of the paved space were all used to move more vehicles efficiently. Given that the city continued to allow the construction of more high-rise commercial buildings along this corridor (which, of course, added more traffic demand) and took no steps to control off-peak automobile use, better traffic management had little impact.

A modern mass transit system, either a surface system utilizing buses or fixed rails, or a subway system, became the focus of transport planning in the early 1990s and remained the most contested planning issue in Jakarta for the next 15 years. As previously discussed (in Chapter 5), Jakarta enthusiastically embraced toll road construction as a transport strategy, especially to serve the growing settlements on the periphery. It was at this time that the ring road, started under Sukarno's government in the 1960s and which surrounded the central areas of Jakarta, opened to commuters.[5] Using the inner loop highway and paying the toll, it was now possible to circumnavigate central Jakarta, literally travelling above the road congestion on the adjacent streets that was an everyday problem in the urban core. Widening existing streets or carving up the inner city with additional toll roads was not an option, given the existing configuration of the new commercial buildings which were so close to the edge of the corridor. What Jakarta needed was a mass transport system comparable to that of urban rivals such as Singapore, Taiwan, and Kuala Lumpur. The idea of a subway located beneath the major north-south transport route in Jakarta, had been considered by transport planners since the 1980s. It resurfaced in 1994 as the answer to Jakarta's perpetual transport crisis, expensive but necessary infrastructure if the goal of a global city was to be realized.

Discussions of the mass transit needs for the city during the 1980s had included both grand plans such as a subway but also more easily implemented strategies, such as elevating the ground level tracks of the busy commuter rail and interurban trains running from the station in Kota through central Jakarta. Work on this approach began in 1988 and continued intermittently into the early 1990s. The project took considerably longer than planned because funding from international donors was irregular. Yet when completed, the elimination of surface rail crossings significantly improved the traffic flow through core areas of the city but had no impact on the Thamrin-Sudirman corridor.[6] Another short-term and relatively inexpensive strategy was the addition of a dedicated bus lane along several major streets, but it was stymied by the continued increase in numbers of private automobiles that clogged the pick-up points and demanded a major share of paved road space.[7]

To meet the need for improved and inexpensive transport for residential areas not served by buses, the city introduced two different three-wheeled motorized vehicles, the *bemo* and the *bajaj*. These were the alternative to the illegal bicycle vehicle, the *becak*, which had traditionally provided not only cheap transport but also employment for many living in *kampungs*. The Director General for Land Transport in the Ministry of Transportation had decreed in 1984 that all three-wheeled vehicles be banished from the city, but the transport needs of Jakarta's expanding low-income residential areas prevented this from being fully implemented. During the Muslim festival of *Idul Fitri* in 1990, Governor Wiyogo suspended the ban on *becak* drivers, but after the holidays resumed what had become routine sweeps of neighbourhoods by the police to confiscate *becaks*. Seized vehicles were dumped into the waters of Jakarta harbour to ensure that they did not get back onto the streets.[8]

A study prepared with support from the Japan International Cooperation Agency (JICA), offered a more comprehensive approach to the transport crisis. It suggested that Jakarta's planners tackle transport improvement in three stages.

The first stage was to improve bus services through re-routing and station improvements. The second step was to implement a rapid bus system through dedicated lanes and new vehicles. This could be accomplished relatively quickly and cheaply and would serve city needs up to 2005. And then as the final stage, the bus systems would be replaced, or at least supplemented, with a new mass rapid transit system.[9]

Jakarta appeared poised to jump directly into the third stage. In July 1995, a memorandum of understanding involving a consortium of investors from Indonesia, Japan and Europe, signalled the beginning of design work on the boldest transport scheme ever floated, a subway line running 14.5 kilometres from the Kota area in North Jakarta southwards to the Blok M market area in Kebayoran Baru. The estimated cost of the project was $1.3 billion and it was to be a public-private partnership, although heavily relying on private investors to make it work. As with so many of the toll road ventures in Jakarta, one of the initial Indonesian partners was the company owned by President Suharto's oldest daughter, Siti Hardiyanti Rukmana. But the subway project ultimately attracted a broad base

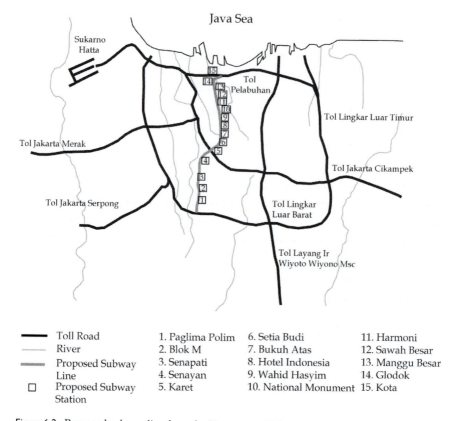

Figure 6.2. Proposed subway line from the Kota area to Kebayoran Baru.

of financial support, led by financial titan Aburizal Bakrie's company, *PT Bakrie Investindo*, but also Ciputra's *PT Pembangunan Jaya*, the banking powerhouse the Lippo Group, PT Bukaka Corporindo, a local taxi company, *PT Steady Safe*, and two components of Bambang's Bimantara group, *PT Krisnatara* and *PT Investasi Kusuma Arta*, as well as private firms from France, Canada, Japan and the United States.[10]

The public announcement of the subway project met with mixed reactions, partly because of its enormous cost, and partly because it seemed likely to serve only a limited portion of Jakarta, albeit the corridor where the vast majority of the businesses were located and with a density likely to support such an expensive undertaking. But a further reason for the mixed reaction was the support for a less expensive surface transit system, which included upgrading both the rail and bus services. To complicate the debate, several groups of investors immediately proposed alternative and potentially conflicting schemes.

One alternative to the subway, known as the Manggarai project because it involved expanding the existing rail station at Manggarai, proposed the transformation of the existing station into a four-storey facility served by twenty-two tracks, four for underground express lines, and space to accommodate surface buses, minibuses and taxis. In addition, the 124 hectare site would include a commercial centre and apartments. Another scheme, the so-called three-tier transit system, involved construction of a new elevated railway, a toll road and an arterial road, all stacked into a single right-of-way, to link the city centre with Cinere and Kebayoran Lama in South Jakarta. What complicated the situation more was that Siti, through her company, *PT Citra Lamtoro Gung Persada*, had backed out of the subway deal and became the sole backer of the Mangarrai project while also heading a consortium for the three-level system, a consortium which also included the powerful suburban land developer, Ciputra. Jakarta's leading suburban developer was obviously an interested party as his property holdings would benefit directly from the three-level system. As specified in the initial plan, it would connect his massive residential planned community at Bintaro to the city centre.[11]

The political intrigue around the transit debate stepped up a notch when it was announced early on that the Mangarrai project would be constructed solely by Siti's company, *PT Citra Lamtoro Gung Persada*, whereas the subway project developer would be determined through a tender process. To counter the negative publicity around the Suharto family links to the Mangarrai project, backers of the three-level scheme created a new joint venture company, *PT Citramoda Margakencana Persaida*, which consisted not just of Siti's firm but also the state-owned railway company *Permuka* and the state-owned highway corporation, *PT Jasa Marga*, as well as several lesser investors. The toll road and light rail components of the three-tier scheme would link Bintaro, through Kebayoran Lama and Blok M to Kota, covering a distance of more than 23 kilometres. One of the biggest concerns with the surface transit proposals, both the three-tier and the Manggarai transit station projects, was anticipated protests from land owners required to sell land to create the right-of-way. By the time a detailed plan for the three-tiered transit system was ready for presentation to the city's spatial planning agency in 1997, the cost had been determined as in excess of $2.5 billion, making it nearly twice as expensive as the original subway scheme.[12]

Suharto had given tentative approval to the Minister of Transportation in February 1996 to push ahead with both projects, but the necessary official presidential order was withheld. Moreover, the Jakarta government's official position was that both projects needed to be incorporated into the city's spatial plan to make them legal before a final decision could be made on how to proceed. Deputy Governor for Economic and Development Affairs, Th. M. Rais insisted that a project of the magnitude of the Manggarai transit facilities needed to be assessed with regard to its economic, social and environmental impacts on the city, especially as it ran counter to the existing provision of the Jakarta plan to move intercity bus facilities to the outskirts of the city. The potential displacement of approximately 4,000 residents living near the existing station was one of these impacts, since the state-owned railway only controlled 72 hectares of the proposed site, meaning that an additional 54 hectares would need to be appropriated from the residents who lived there.[13]

In May 1997, the subway project (now with a price tag of $2.3 billion, but still slightly less expensive than the three-tier system) and the North Jakarta land reclamation project were added to the revised 1997–2010 spatial plan for Jakarta. By August, the city Development Planning Board was ready to recommend that the three-tier transit and the Manggarai terminal expansion be included in the revised spatial plan. But neither made it into the final revision of the plan, although the city government continued to allow their backers to proceed with preparations for development.[14] The subway project got a timely political boost when, in late April 1997, Suharto's son, Bambang Trihatmodjo signed a memorandum of understanding at a ceremony hosted by mayor Surjadi Soedirdja at city hall to be officially added as an investor. This came just four days after the joint venture for the three-level transit system was acknowledged officially in a ceremony also held at city hall.[15] So there were suddenly two very different and very expensive proposals to improve Jakarta's transport. Whether the investment community and the government coffers could handle both simultaneously was a key question, although there was also a lively debate in the media concerning which was likely to make the most impact on the city's crippled transport system.

According to Professor Budhy Tjahjati S. Soegijoko of the Institute of

Technology, Bandung and head of the Jakarta-based Urban Regional Development Institute (URDI), revisions to Jakarta's spatial plan in the mid-1990s failed to give attention to the overall transport needs of the megacity. She noted in 1997 that a plan previously announced to create a transport authority integrating various transport providers into a single agency had not been followed up. Coupled with poor control of land-use planning and the issuing of building permits, the lack of coordinated transport planning undermined urban management efforts. She contended that the three proposed projects, the three-tier system, the subway, and the Manggaria transit terminal, were proposed independently rather than related to a single overall plan. Since 'Jakarta faced rising competition from megacities in the Asia-Pacific region', Soegjijoko noted, it needed development to be based on an integrated transport plan. The transport project proponents were about to carve up the heart of Jakarta, but there was no overall public vision of what would be created once this was done.[16]

It was the private investors who had a plan to integrate the three schemes, and to provide a way for the city and the national government to embrace all three. Aburizal Bakrie, who headed the subway consortium, announced a change in the route, beginning it at the National Monument on Merdeka Square, rather than extending the additional 5 kilometres northwards into the Kota area. This area would be served by the three-tier transit system, and thus subway users could switch to the elevated railway to access the downtown Kota area. Also by moving the southern terminus to a new location owned by the state-owned railway company, *PT Permuka*, development costs would be further reduced. Bakrie insisted that this made the project more feasible although he could not indicate when it would start.[17]

However what ultimately undermined all three schemes in 1997 was not the lack of a plan, but the beginning of the economic collapse, marked by the free fall of the rupiah in the second half of 1997. Backers of the subway project contended that the rupiah crisis was not a danger to their project since it had been developed on the basis of dollar costs, and actually might cost less if local labour and materials were used. But as early as January 1997, even before there were indications of a looming economic crisis, the *Jakarta Post* took the position that Jakarta could not afford both the subway and the three-tier system simultaneously. In its style of challenging government policy without crossing into the danger zone of openly criticizing the Suharto family, it noted that throughout 1996 it was a certainty that the subway would be the priority project, pending an executive ruling by Suharto. But when Siti's Citra Group announced in early January 1997 that it planned to build the three-level system without government approval, based on a determination of the ministers of Public Works and Transportation that the 1993 Train Law allowed *Perumka* to operate the proposed light rail without an executive ruling, it was evident that politics rather than planning were determining how Jakarta would meet its transport needs. 'For most of us', the editors noted, "the behind-the-scenes battle is too complex to grasp … Jakarta cannot sustain both projects, when the city administration is not even clear how it intends to pay back the huge capital outlay for the [subway] project…'. 'What system the city chooses', they concluded, 'it had better make up its mind quickly because the cost seems to be escalating with the delay'.[18]

When the retired three-star general Sutiyoso took office as Jakarta's governor in October 1997, he was confronted with a stalemate on the mass transit front, and the failure of traffic management to make a dent in the problem. The *Jakarta Post* greeted his tenure with the pronouncement that 'Jakarta's traffic woes are perhaps the worst in the world, and tomorrow does not hold any promise for better conditions because the number of cars here increases daily'. Sutiyoso took on the challenge of Jakarta's transport crisis during what became a contentious two-term governorship under five different Indonesian presidents.[19]

Contributing to the demand for improved transport was a proliferation of auto-oriented shopping malls both within the urban core and in the rapidly expanding suburban areas. Plaza Senanyan, near the sports complex built by Sukarno, Plaza Senin, close to a traditional market in the Merdeka Square area, several new shopping centres in the Blok M area, and one of the most ambitious projects, a megamall, Taman Anggrek, in north-west Jakarta near the newly opened toll road leading to the international airport, all sprung up during the 1990s. Taman Anggrek was a massive mixed-use development. The 6-storey mall was capped by eight high-rise residential towers, jutting up from the roof of the mall and the parking deck like huge candles on a cake. 'It is a gated community where living, shopping and recreation are combined', noted Peter Nas and Pratiwo. Inside the mall area there are theatres, an ice rink, and corridors, 'which are furnished like streets with booths and kiosks, making one feel as if one were in the city'. While offering many of the amenities of the city, it also offered a sanitized and safe environment. Its clientele was drawn from the minority of affluent in Jakarta and there were no beggars as on the streets. 'It is a place of refuge in a hostile city.' Yet it was also intended to support the requirements of the affluent to reside close to the core: recreational amenities such as swimming pools; gardens unfettered by vehicular and unwanted human traffic; well designed housing units; and all the benefits of living close to one of the biggest shopping compounds in the entire metropolis.[20]

The $100 million Megamall Pluit in North Jakarta, touted as one of the largest in Southeast Asia, had let nearly all its 142,000 square metres before it opened in early 1996. Pluit Megamall was intended to give a better balance to the location of new shopping facilities in North Jakarta, most of which had been concentrated so heavily in South Jakarta (37.4 per cent of facilities compared to North Jakarta's 8.7 per cent; while West Jakarta, Central Jakarta and East Jakarta accounted for 21.2 per cent, 17.7 per cent and 15 per cent respectively). Through the development of inner-city shopping malls like Pluit, the developers sought to capture an underserved portion of the urban market. In turn, the city benefited from a better locational balance of commercial facilities. Given the absence of an efficient public transport system, the pattern of new facilities scattered throughout the metropolitan area was an appropriate planning strategy.[21]

Jakarta's Shifting Population

Another major commercial and residential complex, also intended to restructure the inner city, was planned and developed beginning in the early 1990s on the grounds of the city's original airport, Kemayoran in north-eastern Jakarta (as briefly discussed in Chapter 5). The 450 hectare public project was officially launched in July 1990 by Governor Wiyogo under a corporation created by the central government and the Jakarta International Trade Fair Corporation and involving five Japanese firms and several private Indonesian firms. The project was intended to support commercial revitalization in the north of Jakarta, with its easy access to the international airport. It was planned to re-institute the trade fair function, including the popular art market for indigenous cultural products previously held on the fairgrounds at Konigsplein, popularly known as 'Pasar Gambir'.[22] Shifting the fairgrounds to the defunct airport site provided an opportunity to remove all the remaining commercial uses from the space around the Monas, including the Taman Ria recreation park and some restaurants, so creating as the *Jakarta Post* put it, a 'vast and beautiful city park which can function as the city's lungs, bringing clean air right into the heart of the capital'.[23]

A group of local investors later proposed including in the Kemayoran project the construction of the world's third tallest building 'as a monument to the success of the New Order government'. The proposal drew strong criticism from social activists who thought that the wealthy business leaders should contribute their funds to poverty alleviation rather than building another office tower. The outspoken populist Mubyarto, assistant to the minister at the National Development Planning Board, and architect of the nation's major programme to channel government development funds to poor villages, suggested that 'the government should not let the conglomerates fund a "tower of social inequality"' when there was still so much poverty to deal with.[24]

Underlying all the major planning in Jakarta was continuing concern over sustained population growth and the widening gap between the vast majority of poor and the affluent. Indonesia's national family planning programme, initiated in the mid-1970s, had been successful in reducing overall population growth to an annual rate of 1.66 per cent by 1995. But the increasing population size and density of Java and Sumatra, which were the primary sources of migrants to Jakarta, ensured large numbers of immigrants continued to arrive. In 1990, nearly two decades after Governor Sadikin's unsuccessful campaign to declare Jakarta a closed city, the speaker of the City Council, Suparno Wiryosoebroto, called for a new public agency to curb the population in-migration, which was estimated to add 300,000 to the city each year. Several strategies were floated, such as requiring city residents returning to their hometowns during *Idul Fitri* to obtain a travel permit (that would be needed to return to Jakarta), and a crackdown on peddlers and *becak* drivers to discourage new migrants. While these were under consideration, Suparno felt that the most effective mechanism would be to stop unauthorized housing construction within the city and to institute better distribution of new units outside of Jakarta.[25]

As long as the construction economy remained hot, as it did until late 1997, there were ample opportunities for migrants to find a place to live and a job. Many migrants arrived in the city without identification cards or the necessary documents from their village heads and so were illegal. Periodic sweeps by the Jakarta authorities to find individuals without proper documents revealed some of the illegal migrants, and those caught were sent back to their villages. Governor Surjadi Soedirdja ordered his 265 sub-district heads to identify illegal newcomers and to enforce the regulations against their being in the city without proper approval. However, the City Population Office had been issuing an average of 75,000 new Jakarta citizenship cards a year since 1989, thereby ensuring, without taking into account the illegal immigrants, Jakarta's population was expanding by nearly 800,000 per decade.[26]

Ungreening Jakarta

To accommodate the swelling population and the demands of new commercial development, every bit of land was used to its maximum. The disappearance of open spaces accompanied the transition of Jakarta from a big village to a megacity. Although the removal of commercial activities in the Monas area had, by the early 1990s, added a large downtown park, the simultaneous expansion of office towers and residential complexes absorbed large swatches of open space throughout the centre that had previously given Jakarta such a village-like atmosphere. Until the 1990s, stands of banana trees still lined Jalan Sudirman, but given the huge value of land on which they grew, it was inevitable that the trees would soon disappear.

Further loss of open space came about through the conversion of government owned parks to other uses, such as schools, mosques, parking lots and commercial facilities. The City Population and Environmental Agency studied the open space issue in 1990 and determined that the rate of loss over the previous two decades suggested that there would be none left within the next two decades unless the government stepped in. The major focus of Jakarta's environmentalists was on cleaning up rivers and stopping new development in the aquifer recharge areas south of Jakarta. But within the city itself, the reduction of open green spaces was an equally critical problem. In the 1970s, open and undeveloped green spaces represented between 40 and 50 per cent of Jakarta's surface area of 64,120 hectares. In the meantime, not only privately held lands but also public parks gave way to development. The City Population and Environmental Agency's 1990 study found that 246 of the city's 412 public parks had been converted to some other function. In violation of the master plan, a police station was built in the Taman Puring Park in South Jakarta in the late 1980s. The addition of roof gardens to the high-rises along Jalan Sudirman was one way to compensate for the loss of green spaces on the ground,[27] but few in Jakarta knew this was happening and even fewer benefited in any way from it.

Megadevelopments and Plan Revisions

As the value of the Indonesian rupiah tumbled in Fall 1997, Jakarta's premier developer, Ciputra, announced a massive commercial project for Central Jakarta. The US $3.7 billion project, initially known as Ciputra City, called for development of the 'Koridor Satrio' into a pedestrian-focused commercial complex consisting of a massive 125,000 square metre shopping centre and two large hotels. While some local legislators bristled at the idea of another massive development carrying the name of the developer, the biggest concern was that it would continue to fragment the metropolis along both spatial and class lines. City councillor Lukman Mokoginta felt that 'the administration should not allow private developers to build small cities within Jakarta because the capital is already burdened by the growth of satellite cities around Jakarta'. He also said that were Ciputra City built, it would increase the gap between the poor and the rich.[28]

On an even larger scale than Ciputra City was the plan for a new waterfront city through development of the North Jakarta coastal area together with a further 2,700 hectares reclaimed from the Jakarta Bay. The Jakarta waterfront project was really a national undertaking, although the 1995 decree (Presidential Decree No. 52/1995) placed responsibility for it within the Governor's office. It involved the creation of an entirely new city of high-rises, including renovation of the historic areas in North Jakarta and expansion of the recreational facilities along the coast. It was intended to employ state of the art infrastructure technology to provide Jakarta's affluent residents with facilities comparable to those found in Singapore.[29]

The plan for the 2,700 hectares was to use nearly half of the land (1,222 hectares) for residential development, 514 hectares for commercial and industrial uses, 136 hectares to expand the port facilities, 371 hectares for general facilities, and 457 hectares for green areas, including creation of a mangrove forest to safeguard the area against erosion. The rationale for north coast reclamation was the scarcity of land near the urban core, although work was already progressing on BSD nearly 30 kilometres to the west, and the Jonggol project 50 kilometres from Jakarta was ready to get underway. But critics, drawn largely from Jakarta's environmental interest groups, expressed concern that the proposed north coast land reclamation would exacerbate the problems of flooding in the city unless additional funds for flood control by the Jakarta government were included in the project. Work on the North Jakarta land reclamation began in 1996, with the project divided among several local developers, one being Suharto's youngest daughter, Siti Hutami Endang Adiningsih. She was given control of a 500 hectare area east of the Ancol amusement complex in concert with the state-owned port management company, *PT Pelindo II.* An affiliate of the Salim Group, headed by one of Suharto's close business associates, received exclusive control of the Kapuk Naga project which involved reclamation of 674 hectares.[30] The North Jakarta project was to provide a vast windfall for the Suharto family and its business allies.

One of the constant concerns among those observing the potential impact of these privately-financed mega developments in Jakarta in the 1990s was that 'serious planning' for public needs was not a part of the process. The city's 1985–2005 spatial plan drawn up in the early 1980s was so out of line with the developments that had occurred or that were planned and approved, that Governor Sjurjadi Soedirdja, under the leadership of his deputy governor of economic and development affairs, Tb. M Rais, was busily preparing a revised plan in the final months of his governorship in 1997. The revised master plan was to take Jakarta through to 2010 and was to reconsider some of the basic assumptions of the 1985 plan, for example the strict separation of uses and lack of consideration of existing population density when planning new developments.[31]

Challenges facing the Poor in Jakarta

In the midst of Jakarta's booming real estate market, another side of the city was slipping further behind. Impoverished areas in Jakarta were less numerous as new developments squeezed out *kampungs* in the centre city. But those that remained were often even more dilapidated, crowded and impoverished than they had been before the boom. The national government's anti-poverty programme, the *Inpres Desa Tertinggal* (IDT), provided financial assistance to the poorest urban and rural villages in the form of small grants (roughly $8,400) to the village heads to disperse in the form of loans to assist small village enterprises. The poverty line for urban villagers was a maximum monthly income of Rp 38,246 (or $15.90). According to government figures, in 1996 there were 22.5 million Indonesians (about 11 per cent) living below the poverty level, one-third (7.2 million) living in cities. This was cited as a significant improvement over conditions in the 1970s, when roughly 60 per cent of Indonesians were considered poor.

But the new approach to poverty in Jakarta was no longer the holistic approach to community revitalization embedded in the successful Kampung Improvement Program. The lack of substantial investment in infrastructure in the poorest areas of the city was probably because it was thought that these areas, especially in targeted development sites, would not remain low-income areas for very much longer. For example, a feature story in the *Jakarta Post* concerning poverty alleviation in the North Jakarta fishing village of Kamal Muara indicated that what that village most needed was 'a lot more wells and public toilets as well as other public facilities', services that were not a part of the newly established IDT programme.[32] Kamal Muara residents were helped by an antipoverty programme jointly administered by the Jakarta city government and staff from the University of Indonesia's Demographic Institute, who provided emergency assistance with food, rebuilt housing destroyed by flooding, and gave support to residents when specific needs were identified. But much of Kamal Muara was slated for removal as part of the waterfront city project. So why reinvest there for the existing residents if they were soon to be displaced?

Not only in the poorest neighbourhoods in Jakarta but among a larger segment of the low-income population, the housing crisis which had so plagued the city during the 1950s and 1960s, returned with a vengeance in the 1990s. While growth in the overall size of the poor population remained one contributing factor, more significant were the rising costs of housing even before the financial crisis in 1997 totally shut down housing construction in Jakarta and throughout the nation.[33]

Jakarta military commander Sutiyoso replaced Surjadi Soedirja as the eighth governor of Jakarta in October 1997. In attendance were five previous governors, Ali Sadikin, Cokropranolo, Soeprapto, Wiyogo Atmodarminto and his predecessor Surjadi. The presence of so many ex-governors, all of whom had served under Suharto, demonstrated the degree of continuity and political predictability that characterized national leadership. Yet the circumstances in Jakarta that Sutiyoso stepped into in late 1997 were highly unstable and, except for the experiences of Ali Sadikin in the mid-1960s following the overthrow of Sukarno's government, were unlike anything that his predecessors had confronted. Sutiyoso inherited a wide array of major projects that had been introduced during Surjadi's administration but which were either still in the planning stages or were just beginning to be implemented. The subway project, the waterfront city in North Jakarta, the international trade centre at Kemayoran as well as mega-commercial projects throughout the metropolis needed to be managed. Solving the longstanding transport problems in Jakarta, balancing new development with the problems of unemployment and what many saw as a growing gap between Jakarta's wealthy and the poor, were the challenges he said that he planned to address. He instituted a military style training regime for new civil servants to underscore his commitment to nurturing clean government. To help reduce the amount of traffic, he planned to create five new bus terminals outside the urban core to facilitate transport of Jakarta's 70,000 civil servants.[34]

Yet one his first actions, under direct orders from President Suharto, was to clear make-shift housing from the capital's riverbanks[35] and to continue the systematic removal of slum areas from the city centre. Building low-income housing outside the city had been started under the Surjadi administration, with support from the national government's housing programme. In the Parung Panjang housing complex located in Bogor south of Jakarta, 95 per cent of the occupants of its 35,000 low-cost houses commuted to Jakarta. The resettlement plan which Surjadi and Sutiyoso implemented in Jakarta was really a part of a national plan prepared by the State Minister of Public Housing, Akbar Tangjung. As Tanjung noted, land prices in Jakarta were too expensive for low-income housing, which was 'why we have no choice but to move human settlements around Jakarta to areas where the price is much cheaper, and at the same time provide them with transport facilities'. The Parung housing complex was connected by train to Central Jakarta, the journey taking about an hour. The available low-cost housing in central Jakarta was too expensive for most of those displaced from slum areas; typically those displaced who were eligible for the housing units transferred the rights to middle-class people who could afford them. In the Benhil section of Central Jakarta, most of the 373 residents displaced by a fire in 1995 had to sell their rights to new apartments because they could not afford the down payment and monthly instalments. It was common for victims of fires to rebuild on the same land, despite city government efforts to stop reconstruction of the make-shift structures in those areas, and to replace low-rise units with a high-rise structures.[36]

It was not just the inability of low-income residents to afford low-cost housing, but a similar price squeeze affected the middle class in the 1990s. The middle class seeking housing closer to work (rather than enduring the long commute from the periphery) purchased low-cost apartments (in violation of rules prohibiting sale until after 5 years) because with the 50 per cent subsidy provided by the city these units were significantly less expensive than comparable housing built by the private sector. The price of the government-supported housing in 1996 was Rp 4.9 million (US $2,100) for a 21 square metre structure and Rp 6.9 million ($2,960) for a 36 square metre unit. In the private sector, without the city's subsidy, a 36 square metre structure sold for approximately Rp 45 million ($19,200). City developers were supposed to allocate 20 per cent of their land for housing in this size according to a 1992 rule, which later was modified to the 1-3-6 formula. Also to reduce the migration of workers to Jakarta, a group of sixteen developers planned to build thousands of simple houses in the West Java district of Maja (near Tanggerang) in the 21 and 36 square metre range, at a cost of between Rp 4.6

Figure 6.3. Within the Kota area rehabilitation of the heritage sites is underway, including the Bank of Indonesia building (top) as well as other privately owned structures along the area's historic waterway, Kali Besar (below). (*Source*: URDI)

million and Rp 15 million over the next 5 year period. This area was connected by train to the Central Jakarta station at Tanah Abang.[37]

In the Bendungan Hilir community in Central Jakarta, where 400 houses were lost to a fire in 1994, the initial plan to build apartments on the site was vehemently opposed by the residents. In early 1995, a riot broke out, fuelled by a rumour that a private developer was going to be given the residents' land. The city enforced a ban on residents rebuilding their own houses on the site but it also fulfilled a pledge to rebuild housing for the displaced. In June 1996, a 10-storey, 614 unit apartment complex consisting of three towers, was officially inaugurated, with at least some of the former Bendungan Hilir residents returning to take up the modest-sized units. In this case, the city was providing one-half the cost of the units which sold for Rp. 20 million to Rp 30 million. While pleased at being able to re-establish their community, concerns about making the monthly payments, which ranged between Rp 88,000 and Rp 191,000, coupled with a service charge of Rp 39,000, challenged those who did not have a steady source of income, especially if that income came from small enterprises run out of their homes but which were not as easily run from an apartment building.[38]

In 1996, the city administered nine low-cost apartment complexes in the city: Penjaringan Satu, Penjaringan Dua, Cengkareng, Pondok Kelapa, Cipinang, Pondok Bambu, Jatirawasari, Tambora and Karang Anyar. These provided units rented by the day, with fees ranging from Rp. 800 per day for a 14 square metre apartment to Rp 5,000 per day for a 54 square metre apartment. Plans were to add seven more apartment blocks by 1997. The city also intended to appropriate land for additional apartments in five other areas These were to replace 2,016 hectares of slum which had accommodated as many as 891,880 slum dwellers. The new units would accommodate only a fraction of that number.[39]

Converting slum areas to new housing and business activities was consistent with the city's plan to restructure North Jakarta. The city's development firm, *PD Sarana Jaya*, announced plans in late 1996 to clear and rebuild the Pademangan area along the same lines as projects in Mangga Dua and Kemayoran areas. The company director, Kemal Basa, indicated that the 72,000 families in Pademangan would be resettled in nearby apartments, and thus should not consider the redevelopment of the 190 hectare area as a forced removal. It was planned to take between 5 and 7 years to complete, and in the end would 'integrate middle and working class accommodation so that residents can conveniently get to their offices and shops without having to travel far'.[40] In the beginning, at least, the emphasis was on new middle-class housing to support Jakarta's expanding white collar labour force. Working-class housing would come later. Yet if history was a guide to the city's behaviour, it was unlikely that affordable housing for low-income residents would actually be built.

Master Plan for a Global Megacity

The master plan prepared in the early 1980s and intended to guide decisions about redevelopment and development over the next two decades had not anticipated nor sufficiently guided the massive restructuring of the city that was underway. In 1995, as part of a routine reassessment, Jakarta's planners discovered that so many changes had occurred, or were approved for implementation, that the 1985–2005 plan was obsolete already. Not only did the unanticipated new developments alter the spatial patterns of the city in fundamental ways, but the 1985 plan was premised on several flawed assumptions. One was inflated projections of population growth based on trends from the 1970s, and these projections skewed the allocation of space for residential uses. Although Jakarta's population continued to grow steadily through in-migration, natural increases, and a lowered mortality rate, the annual growth rate was not nearly as high as it had been in the past. This was not because Jakarta had become a less attractive destination (indeed, growth in the number of unregistered and unemployed rural migrants remained a serious issue) but to a related, flawed assumption that migration patterns affecting Jakarta were a one-way process, that is, people moving into the metropolis from outside. In fact, Jakarta was confronted by the additional challenge of managing continuous out-migration from the core to the periphery.

What Jakarta's planners discovered in the early 1990s was that those who made up its modest but growing 'middle class' were moving outside the corporate boundaries in larger than expected numbers. Land prices and housing costs in the city had risen so high that the cost of commuting from the fringe areas where more affordable housing was available was worth it. In an effort to try to curb the exodus of the middle class from the city, new strategies for affordable housing needed to be incorporated into the plan.

At the same time, a new spatial planning law in 1992 made some of the provisions of the 1985 plan insufficient to address new criteria for regulating land uses. The new spatial planning law required Jakarta to be more inclusive in its spatial planning, taking into account conserving and developing green areas, identifying priority areas for new development, supplying and managing infrastructure to support the anticipated population, and identifying all major land use functions such as residential use, forestry, mining, industry, commerce and tourism. In the process of revising the master plan, the fiscal crisis that had crippled the Indonesian economy in 1997 and 1998, coupled with the subsequent political revolution, injected new elements of uncertainty and unpredictability into the planning processes. Throughout the crisis, Jakarta's planners continued the master plan revision process and completed the work in 1999. What had begun as a process of modifying the 1985 plan ended with the presentation of a fundamentally different vision for Jakarta. The 1985–1995 plan became the *Jakarta 2010 Plan*, the most up-to-date strategic vision of the megacity.[41]

The 2010 plan provided a fresh approach grounded in the rhetoric of sustainability and with greater attention to social concerns, especially affordable housing and environmental improvements. This was captured in the plan's central theme, 'growth through equality'. The plan was intended to guide the spatial transformation of Jakarta in 'an integrated, harmonious, coordinated, balanced, efficient, effective, civilized and sustainable manner'. It divided DKI Jakarta into three development zones so as to conceptualize the broader development patterns that would be spelled out in greater detail through 43 district level plans. The North Development Zone consisted of the Thousand Island Development Zone in Jakarta Bay and the North Coast Development Zone, thus taking in the older seashore areas which included the port facilities and fishermen settlements, and the new seashore area which was both physically and functionally separate from the old seashore. It did not specify the new waterfront city *per se*, but continued to call for 'developing a reclamation program' that included 'international commercial facilities, upscale housing, and recreation port and tourist facilities'.[42]

The Central Development Zone was subdivided into three areas, one being the Mid-Central Development Zone which encompassed the highest concentration of government and commercial offices, supplemented by high-density housing, with a complementary development zone to the west which had its own business centre (referred to as the 'New West Primary Center') but which was predominantly residential, and a zone to the east which handled industrial and warehousing functions along with housing and its own 'primary centre'. The South Development Zone was predominantly residential, with high spatial intensity in the portion adjacent to the Central Development Zone, and lower densities in the southern part of the zone (the Southern-South Development Zone). It was explicitly stated in the plan that the lower density development, 'with low floor area ratio' was intended to preserve this area 'as a water recharging area'.[43] The 2010 plan reinforced the concept that DKI Jakarta would support a multiple business centre configuration, and that it was the intention of government to foster new primary commercial centres in the East, West and North areas. It called for the use of mixed-use areas throughout the metropolis, reinforced the Taman Medan Merdeka area for public buildings and government functions, endorsed the new waterfront city on the North Coast, and the need for a mass transport system 'as a main transportation mode between activities centers and between city's regions'. Also, it devoted far more attention than previous plans to the goal of upgrading the city environment by cleaning up the thirteen rivers and other water bodies in DKI Jakarta and expanding green spaces in all five of Jakarta's municipalities.[44]

The five key elements of the 2010 plan involved urban housing, green areas,

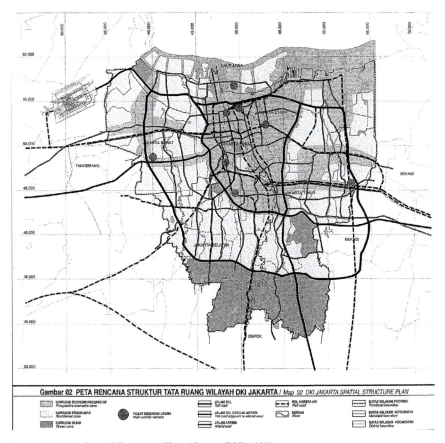

Gambar 02 PETA RENCANA STRUKTUR TATA RUANG WILAYAH DKI JAKARTA / Map 02 DKI JAKARTA SPATIAL STRUCTURE PLAN

Figure 6.4. 2010 Spatial Structure Plan. (*Source*: DKI, 1999).

economic prospective areas, activities centres, and upgrading to infrastructure and utilities (which included the need for improved transport). One of the targets was to increase the proportion of the city's land kept as green space from the current 9 per cent to approximately 13 per cent. To do this, the plan suggested that land acquisition in slum areas be converted from residential use to parks. It proposed 'impact fees' on developers of large projects whereby 20 per cent of the land be dedicated to public facilities such as schools, parks, churches, or mosques.

The idea behind the revised policy towards the thirteen rivers that flowed through Jakarta was to transform them from polluted places hidden as the 'back yard of the built environment' into scenic avenues located in the 'front yard'. This involved clearing the riverbanks of illegal and temporary structures, and then building roadways alongside the rivers (so called 'Jalan Inspecsi') so that they could be seen and, when cleaned up, admired. This was a logical extension of the 'Clean River Program' (*Program Kali Bersih*) that had been spearheaded by the

University of Indonesia economist, Emil Salim, when he served as minister of the environment in the early 1990s. The environmental movement in Jakarta had been kept alive by a band of persistent environmental non-governmental organizations. The 2010 plan made river clean-up and reconstruction a centrepiece of the city's vision, and tied it to the Waterfront City plan that remained an ongoing goal even though the economic crisis and the defeat of the New Order government had altered the timing and configuration of that project. Moreover, there was continuing tension between strengthening environmental protection and accommodating growth. Major protests later surfaced when Governor Sutiyoso ordered trees to be cut down along the routes of his controversial busway project in 2004.

Environmental improvements also related to the ongoing problems of improved drainage to reduce the flooding that annually plagued the city. Clearing rivers was one measure to reduce the incidence of flooding, but even more important were additions to the flood canal system. The West Flood Canal, constructed during the Dutch era, needed to be supplemented with an East Flood Canal, a project which was being studied with support from the Japanese, but was an expense that Jakarta's government found difficult to absorb at that time. Also, the 2010 plan offered no specific plans to deal with the massive increase in solid waste. A study by the Japan International Cooperation Agency (JICA) identified two sites outside Jakarta, one in Tanggerang and one in Bogor. The site in Tanggerang was eliminated when the Tanggerang's planners revised their spatial plan and eliminated that area for use as a solid waste facility. Bogor was taking some of Jakarta's waste, but when in late 2004 residents near the Bojong waste site discovered they were taking Jakarta's solid waste , they staged a public protest against the plan. A new plan for solid waste, funded by the World Bank, suggested that disposal should take place within DKI Jakarta's borders by using an area in North Jakarta.

The 2010 Plan also specifically addressed the issue of the role of the public sector in providing an adequate supply of affordable housing. The DKI Jakarta Housing Agency (*Dinas Perumahan*) was the lead agency for 'social housing' which involved units in the 21 square metres to 36 square metres range. To create space for new social housing, slum clearance would continue within the Central Jakarta municipality, although there remained a substantial portion of the DKI Jakarta low-cost housing in parts of West Jakarta closest to the centre (such as in Tambora). Use of high-rise ('vertical') housing to accommodate low-income families in the Central Jakarta district was a distinct change from the long-standing policy of accommodating low income-families through self-built housing clustered into the *kampungs*. Yet as the *kampungs* were torn down, the politicization of the displaced residents began with profound implications for the city and the nation.

Jakarta and the May 1998 Revolution

The re-election of President Suharto in March 1998 was a foregone conclusion long before the official start of his seventh term. The election of the Peoples' Consultative Assembly in late 1997 was dominated by Suharto's Golkar party and his allies in the military and as it was this body that elected the President and Vice President, Suharto was unopposed. That he would step down two months later, on 21 May, was the great surprise. There had been rumours in Indonesian political circles that the 76 year old Suharto, who suffered from nagging health problems, might not complete another full term in office, but this seemed more wishful thinking on the part of his opponents given how easily his Golkar political party had engineered one of the most lopsided victories in the polls in 1997. But there were deeper problems confronting Suharto than his state of health.

The biggest problem he confronted was the miserable condition of the economy. In July 1997, the Indonesian rupiah had begun a freefall, and over the next 6 months foreign capital fled the country, projects shut down and, consequently, unemployment rose, prices rose, supplies of everything dwindled, and protest mounted. In early 1998, as reported by Human Rights Watch Asia, there were ongoing demonstrations, riots, bomb threats and bombings throughout Java, many taking place in Jakarta. A lot of these exhibited an overtly anti-Chinese tone, and there was no doubt that many were orchestrated with the intent of shifting blame for the economic mess from government to Indonesia's Chinese community.[45]

When in March Suharto appointed to his cabinet his golfing partner and business friend, Bob Hasan, and his daughter Tutut to head the Ministry for Social Welfare, as well as placing his son-in-law, Prabowo, in command of the military's special forces, new grievances were added to the growing disenchantment with the New Order government. The words cronyism and nepotism, which had never before been openly mentioned with regard to the first family, became part of the public outcry and call for political reform. It was not the novelty of Suharto's favouritism so much as his blatant disregard for widespread public disapproval of the individuals involved that so thoroughly undermined his position.[46]

What emerged over the next two months was full blown political insurgency, led by student protests throughout Indonesia's cities, which initially focused on the corruption of the Suharto government and called for *reformasi*, but that soon grew into calls for a new democratic system. On 12 May, with Suharto out of the country attending a conference in Cairo, students from Trisakti University staged a protest. The goal was to march on the National Parliament building near the Semanggi highway cloverleaf close to the Hilton Hotel and the Stock Exchange, but the protesters were fired on by the police before they reached their destination, resulting in six students being shot, four fatally. The following morning, as family and friends attended a memorial service for the dead students, rioting broke out in the Tomang district of Jakarta, and quickly spread towards Glodok and the Chinese business community. Troops which had been deployed in the city to confront the student protesters shifted their focus to protecting the presidential palace, government buildings and select luxury hotels, while the rioting masses seemed intent on finding and destroying all the Chinese businesses in the city. For three days, many parts of Jakarta, but especially those identified with the Chinese, were on fire and under a constant assault from roving bands of rioters which, unrestrained by either the police or the military, looted, raped, murdered, and destroyed property.

Internal conflicts within the military accounted, at least in part, for their inaction in stopping the rioters. Later assessments suggested that they might have been complicit in allowing the rioting in the Chinese community. Only when Suharto returned on 15 May did the tanks and troops take control of the streets, and were the fires that still burned dealt with by firemen supported by troops. At that point, more than 1,000 people had died, with many more seriously injured and, according to official statistics, 2,479 Chinese shop-houses, another 1,026 ordinary houses, 1,604 retail shops, 383 private offices, 65 banks, 45 workshops, 24 restaurants, 12 hotels and 40 shopping malls, not to mention several thousand vehicles had been destroyed.[47]

The next six days were free of rioting but dominated by calls from various quarters for Suharto's resignation. A mass protest scheduled for 20 May, which might have reactivated the street violence, was called off by Amien Rais, the leader of the large Muhammadiyah organization and outspoken critic of Suharto, and Abdurrahman Wahid 'Gus Dur') leader of the even larger Moslem organization, Nahdlatul Utama. Meanwhile, armed forces commander, General Wiranto allowed a small group of demonstrators to occupy the National Parliament building, while a large group of Suharto's cabinet officials indicated that they would no longer serve unless he resigned and Vice-President Habibie took his place. Although without any popular base of support, and little support from the military, Habibie had been one of Suharto's key links to the international business community, and one of the architects of the modernization part of the New Order regime. Suharto resigned on 21 May, Habibie was sworn in, and the embattled former president retreated to his compound in Menteng.

Jakarta had been paralysed by the trauma of the rioting, and the ongoing economic crisis in the aftermath of those violent two weeks in May perpetuated a state of lifelessness throughout the metropolis. A mass exodus of foreigners and Chinese Indonesians in May had stripped the city of a key economic ingredient. As the Habibie government searched for a strategy to address the national crisis, Jakarta Governor Sutiyoso confronted the challenge of restoring some level of confidence in a city with large sections gutted, an unemployment problem exacerbated by the sudden departure of some of its biggest spenders, and filled with the remains of large urban development projects that had been stopped because the flow of overseas capital had been shut off. The global city had been stopped in its tracks by the combined impacts of political chaos, economic crisis, and a society ripped apart by racial, religious and ethnic conflicts. But the sudden departure of the Suharto government, even with one of his most loyal lieutenants in charge of Jakarta, had created an opportunity for change that seemed little more than a remote future possibility just a short time before. Jakarta was about to become the capital city of the largest emerging democracy in Southeast Asia. A new political system and a new way of planning was carved out of the chaos of the late 1990s.

Notes

1.   *JP*, 23 June, 1997; World Bank (1997).
2.   *JP*, 30 June, 1997; 2 October, 27 November, 1995.
3.   Kusno (2000), p. 122.
4.   Information on Ali Sadikin's strategy to acquire land for development from Betawi families was provided by Zhang interview, 14 January, 2005.
5.   *JP*, 9 November, 1989.
6.   *JP*, 12 February, 16 June, 1990.
7.   *JP*, 27 December, 1989; 13 June, 16 July, 1990.
8.   *JP*, 1 and 5 May, 1990.
9.   *JP*, 12 February, 1990.
10. *JP*, 2 August, 1995; 9 and 12 September, 1996.
11. *JP*, 23 August, 1997.
12. *JP*, 2 and 20 May, 1997.
13. *JP*, 29 June, 1995; 2 and 3 September, 1996.
14. *JP*, 23 August, 1997.
15. *JP*, 24 and 30 April, 1997.
16. *JP*, 28 May, 1997.
17. *JP*, September 12, 1997.
18. *JP*, 16 and 18 January, 1997.
19. *JP*, 22 April, 1995; 15 October, 1997.
20. Nas and Pratiwo (2003), p. 292.
21. *JP*, 22 May, 1995.
22. *JP*, 11 July, 1990.
23. *JP*, 14 July, 1990.
24. *JP*, 19 September, 1995.
25. *JP*, 21 June, 1990; 19 June, 1995.
26. *JP*, 23 February, 18 March, 1996.
27. *JP*, 9 July, 1990; 11 January, 1997.
28. *JP*, 30 September, 1997.
29. *JP*, 18 October, 1997.
30. *JP*, 9 February, 1996; 29 July, 1997.
31. *JP*, 12 June, 1997.
32. Although the IDT programme was largely aimed at rural villages, the Kamal Muara was a prime example of the worst slum areas in Jakarta that received a modest level of support in the post-Kampung Improvement Program era.

33. *JP*, 18 October, 1997.
34. *JP*, 7 and 14 October, 1997.
35. *JP*, 20 November, 1997.
36. *JP*, 3 November, 1997; 29 and 30 April, 1996.
37. *JP*, 20 August, 1996; 3 and 31 December, 1996.
38. *JP*, 1 June, 1996.
39   *JP*, 22 March, 1996.
40. *JP*, 19 November, 1996.
41. Interview with Vera Revina Sari, 3 January, 2005.
42. Jakarta, DKI (1999), Chapter 3, p. 5.
43. *Ibid.*, Part Two, pp. 6–7.
44. *Ibid.*, Part Three, Article 9, p. 7.
45. Friend (2003), pp. 314–315.
46. *Ibid.*, p. 325.
47. *Ibid.*, pp. 328–329.

Chapter Seven

Planning in the New Democratic Megacity

Jakarta today is a very different place from the city I first encountered 18 years ago. This period has been one of constant change and one of the most formative in the city's history. In terms of the city's physical form and outward appearance, the transformation can only be described as catastrophic. What took place between 1990 and 2007 was a near doubling of Jakarta's urban area. Through a relentless process of removal and reconstruction, the loosely knit network of urban villages has become a more formalized, multi-centred urban conglomeration.

This transformation was an outcome of the economic stimuli provided by Suharto's pro-development New Order government from the 1970s to the 1990s. Indonesia's economic collapse in the late 1990s, which hit Jakarta hard, temporarily derailed the growth machine and destabilized the previously unshakable government. What began in mid-1997 as a crisis of confidence in the Indonesian currency rapidly escalated into economic meltdown. Factories closed, there was a rapid and sizable outflow of foreign investment accompanied by soaring unemployment, and a sharp upward spiral in the cost of basic goods. For the first time in its recent history, the Indonesian government could not meet its debt payments.

This crisis called into question the New Order government's approach to modernization in Indonesia and brought into the open how it had relied on corruption, collusion and nepotism to sustain economic success. The level of corruption, which involved the whole of the Suharto network, was no longer shielded from exposure by fear of retribution. What began as demands for an effective government response to the economic crisis escalated into calls for a new government based on political reform. Indonesia's collapse into economic, political and social chaos in 1997 and 1998 not only accounts for the widespread suffering endured for the following 4 years (and for many until the present day) but it also brought fundamental changes to political processes.[1]

The political revolution that swept through Indonesia in the wake of the economic crisis affected the methods and objectives of planning at both national and local level. This assault on the highly centralized and top down system of the New Order regime led ultimately to a more open, participatory and more contested system of local governance and planning, but it did not fundamentally alter the ability of the powerful development community to dictate the basic pattern of urban development.

The capital city recovered economically well beyond the expectations of its planners, its political leadership, and probably the vast majority of its citizens who initially believed that the demise of the New Order government foreshadowed the end of the 'economic miracle'. The broad based movement clamouring for an open, democratic political process did not, as some feared and predicted, lead to a collapse of Indonesia's social order.

The relatively smooth transition from an authoritarian regime to more democratic political practices at the national level fostered new planning values and approaches in local affairs, including in Jakarta. This was not surprising since the city's planners had always been more likely than other local officials to embrace progressive development approaches even when the New Order government was in power. The ascendancy of the reformers and the backing of newly empowered civic organizations encouraged local planners to set a very different urban agenda. Even the rhetoric of Jakarta's planners changed, echoing that of planners elsewhere in the world. No longer were they consumed with meeting government development targets set out in the nation's 5 year plans. Jakarta's planning documents focused on values such as sustainability, inclusiveness, equity and environmentalism. These new values tempered but did not wholly displace the tradition of equating urban progress with economic growth and showcase additions to the hardscape of the city. Ironically, the return of more favourable economic conditions in Jakarta by late 2003, coupled with a more open and tolerant political environment, spurred a development rush that made sustainability and preservation of environmental amenities even more difficult to realize. Thus, one must understand not only the changes wrought by the political reform movement but also the continuities in development processes between the New Order regime and the era of democratic planning.

In fact, the political revolution did not result in a change of leadership in the capital city. Jakarta's planning and development agenda was administered by the determined and resilient Governor Sutiyoso, who had survived the economic crisis and, in the face of widespread public criticism, was reappointed by President Megawati for a second term in 2003. Sutiyoso took on the governorship in 1997 wedded to the tradition of top-down planning, reflective of New Order government values. Yet unlike his predecessors, his authority was continuously challenged after 1998 by local legislators, civic organizations and competing political parties. As he noted in his second accountability speech at the end of his first term in 2002, there had been '4,538 demonstrations … staged by Jakartans against me…'.[2] He seemed to thrive on opposition.

Sutiyoso, Jakarta's New Activist Governor

Sutiyoso initially embraced what Kusno refers to as 'national urbanism', that is urban development strategies intended to sustain Jakarta as the focus of national identity and as the centre of power and influence. Unlike his predecessors, he did not have either the backing or the directives from a powerful presidency (particularly after the fall of Suharto). Presidents Habibe, Wahid, Megawati and then Yudiyono each confronted almost continuous challenges of their own during relatively brief tenures in office, leaving little time (or inclination) to engage in visioning or planning for the capital city. Instability at the national level provided Sutiyoso with greater latitude to set his own course of action in administering the city.

The governor adopted an activist planning approach remarkably similar in style to that of Ali Sadikin, and commentators frequently made comparisons between these two long-serving governors. Both shared a similar preparation for the powerful Jakarta governorship. Like Sadikin, Sutiyoso assumed the governor's office directly from a prominent position in the military. In Sutiyoso's case, it was as Deputy-Commander in Chief of Kompassus, the army's special forces unit. He was used to decisive actions and not unused to generating controversy by his actions, since his field experiences had been in the two hotly contested and volatile regions of Indonesia, East Timor and Aceh.[3] Sutiyoso also mirrored Sadikin's dogged approach to several of Jakarta's nagging problems. One of these was trying to devise ways to regulate the influx of vast numbers of rural migrants seeking work in the informal sector job market. This was connected to his strong stand on law and order and against vice. Like his predecessors, he also focused on urban beautification projects, on the one hand through improved planning of public spaces but also by the forceful removal of blighted conditions, in particular slum areas that had sprung up along major transport corridors.

Within months of taking office, Sutiyoso was faced with rioting throughout Jakarta triggered by the collapse of the Suharto government and continuing into the early months of the abbreviated presidency of Habibe. In the name of urban beautification, but more importantly to control crowds that gathered daily near the presidential offices alongside Merdeka Square, in 2001 he enclosed the Monas area with a tall fence. This shut out the vendors, the jobless, the homeless, and the political agitators who had turned this national civic area into a staging ground for protests against government actions and inactions. To restore the prestige of this 'historical symbol of Indonesia', as Sutiyoso put it, he 'ordered the paving of the park, the planting of plants, the keeping of deer and the fencing of the whole to "create order and comfort for visitors" as well as to reduce demonstrations and get rid of vendors and the homeless who [had] been occupying the space in the past few years'.[4] He also renovated, at great expense, the fountain within the plaza area across from the Hotel Indonesia. Like the fencing of the Monas, this was designed to make it difficult for demonstrations to take place in this symbolic location since the water now flowed continuously. In both projects, Sutiyoso replicated a pattern of control over the Jakarta environment that borrowed directly from some of his predecessors.

Like Sadikin, Sutiyoso extended his policies and programmes well beyond projects aimed at social control. He tackled several important long-term infrastructure needs, such as the development of an improved transit system and better management of flood conditions during the rainy season. His signature transport project, the busway, was launched in 2004 once it was obvious that the more glamorous (and more expensive) subway system stood little chance of resuscitation in the near future. Sutiyoso latched onto the busway system first employed in Bogota, Columbia, as both a short-term answer to Jakarta's transport ills as well as the first component of an integrated system of mass transit that also included a monorail system, a subway and possibly water-based transport using Jakarta's flood canal system.[5] While Sadikin had focused on the Kampung Improvement Program, roadway construction and government-supported commercial developments to create a modern metropolis out of a collection of villages, Sutiyoso was laying the groundwork for a multi-centred, but integrated megacity. His vision was to transform Jakarta into Asia's 'New York City'. The proposed 12.9 kilometre busway from the Kota area to Blok M in South Jakarta, and the two monorail corridors running east and west (one from Bekasi to Tanggerang, and the other from Casablanca to Roxi) were the first elements of his ambitious infrastructure plan, and the foundations of 'Sutiyoso's Grand Dream'.

The busway buses travel on a physically separated fixed route so as not to compete with other vehicular traffic with limited stops at constructed stations along the route. Passengers access the buses from stations built via overhead walkways to prevent any impediments to other vehicular traffic. The initial line followed the major north-south corridor from the railway station in Kota to the Blok M area in South Jakarta along the Gadjah Mada–Thamrin–Sudirman highway axis. Construction of phase 2 began in 2005 to provide a similar service on an east-west line from East Jakarta to Kilideres in West Jakarta, crossing the

Figure 7.1. Busway vehicle and newly built station along the north-south route between Kota and Blok M. (*Photo*: author)

north-south line in Central Jakarta adjacent to the National Monument. In its first year of operation, the Kota to Blok M fifty-one bus fleet did not achieve the projected daily capacity of 60,000 commuters, but there was evidence that it was luring more of its customers (roughly 14 per cent) from private cars to the system than had been the case in Bogota where only 4.7 per cent of commuters switched to the transit system. From a fiscal standpoint, busways proved less effective. The Rp 238 billion (US$23.8 million) spent on construction of the system generated only Rp 15 billion (US$15 million) in revenues in the first year.[6]

The other component of Sutiyoso's mass transit system was a $650 million monorail system, including a 14.8 kilometre 'green line' to serve the dense business centres of Kuningan, Sudirman and Senayan, with seventeen stations, and a second 12.2 kilometre 'blue line' connecting Kampung Melayu in East Jakarta to the massive mall at Taman Anggrek in West Jakarta, with thirteen stations. The busways, with a one-way fare of Rp 1,500 (US$0.16) were not only an affordable alternative to the car but within the range of a broad segment of Jakarta's working population who could afford neither a car nor a motorcycle. The monorail was intended to serve a different clientele, with anticipated fares ranging from Rp. 3,500 to Rp. 7,500 (US$0.35 to 0.60) for a single journey. The developer of the monorail was a private company, *PT Jakarta Monorail*, with strong international financial support, led initially by the Japanese firm Hitashi.[7] The monorail was anticipated to be completed by 2006/2007 even though realignments of the route, and temporary work stoppages due to disruptions in the flow of funds, halted construction late in 2004 and through mid-2005. The plan called for the completed system to handle 270,000 passengers per day, although some preliminary market surveys along the proposed route indicated that this might be difficult to achieve.[8]

In early 2006, as construction was still underway, the Indonesian Forum for the Environment (WALHI), a long-established environmental organization, called for construction of the monorail to stop since it had been started in 2004 without the required environmental impact analysis being conducted. Sutiyoso's single-minded determination to implement a mass transit system despite the ongoing economic crisis reflected his belief in the importance of preparing for the future by planning Jakarta's development in tandem with modern transit technology. This long-term perspective on Jakarta's development was evident in an interview he granted to a *Tempo* reporter early in 2004:

For 40 years, there have been no substantial changes in our public transport system. We also don't have an integrated system of public transport – from buses, to trains and water transport. If we don't address this problem, by 2014 there will be stagnation that can cause total breakdown.

He had been inspired by the system in Bogota, where upgraded public transport had been 'integrated with good city planning' involving landscaped parks, widened sidewalks to accommodate pedestrians, and good security in a city previously racked by problems of violence and crime.[9] Bogota's system had already made its impact felt; Sutiyoso wanted similar instant results for Jakarta.

It was not just the government sponsored transport projects, but an equally impressive array of new private sector developments, which accounted for the dramatic transformation of Jakarta's landscape after Sutiyoso assumed the governorship in 1997. In support of new private development, the government played a key role in eliminating potential barriers, most notably legal and illegal settlements, and for this the governor earned a reputation as the 'King of Eviction'. But what made urban development policies and projects under Sutiyoso different from previous ones was that all were subjected to closer scrutiny by a newly empowered public and were framed within a more participatory and inclusionary planning process than had existed when Sutiyoso first took office. Kusno notes that the 'rupture' between the policies of the authoritarian national state and the newly emerging democratic society was evident in various initiatives underway in Sutiyoso's Jakarta. While 'liberated from the imposed uniformity of the national framework' of Sukarno and Suharto, there remained a desire, especially among the growing middle class, to find new sources of stability following 'the collapse of the ideology of centralized government' and the seemingly increased lawlessness, violence and conflict that followed in the wake of these changes. A more democratic planning process had emerged as a counterpoint to the centralized model bequeathed by the New Order government, influencing not only Jakarta but all Indonesian cities and districts.[10]

When Sutiyoso took office, the governmental and planning structures in place were those that had been fashioned when the Suharto government consolidated its power in the early 1970s. It was a system where all major policy decisions flowed down to the localities from the central government through the provincial administration. Top regional and local administrators, including the mayor (*walikota*), the district head (*bupati*), the planning director (*kepala Bappeda*) and the governor were only appointed after they had been approved by the national government and Suharto's ruling Golkar party. Under the banner of decentralization, the Indonesian government enacted a new local government statute in 1974 (Law 5/1974) seemingly to shift a greater amount of decision making to lower levels. This law specified the powers and responsibilities of the different levels of local government. One of the unique features of the new system was the creation of central government branch offices in conjunction with all local government agencies to supply guidance to the local offices but also to ensure that national priorities were being addressed at the local level. In essence, this created a duplication of effort, with the local branches of the central government maintaining an advantage because they controlled most of the national government's development funds.[11]

Rather than furthering decentralization, the two decades following enactment of the 1974 law saw a consolidation power in the central government ministries in Jakarta at the expense of local governments. This power was executed through the operations of those offices of central government ministries created at the local level. Local parliaments (at the city, district and provincial levels) merely rubber stamped decisions made by local administrators who were appointed by, and accountable to, central government. Reinforcing the control of central government was a system of public administration whereby all local government officials were employees of a central government agency, namely the Ministry of Home Affairs. Mayors, district heads and their senior staff relied on detailed directives and plans from central government officials in Jakarta, and were neither accountable locally nor made any effort to engage local stakeholders in planning. The same was true for Jakarta the city, as distinguished from Jakarta as the seat of national government. In 1976, a nationwide network of Development Planning Boards (*Bappeda I*) was created in each of the twenty-seven provinces, which included Jakarta, and in 1981 similar institutions (*Bappeda II*) were established to guide planning in districts and cities. These powerful planning bodies coordinated development policies and programmes at the city/district and provincial levels, but directly under the administrative oversight of the Ministry of Home Affairs and the National Development Planning Board (*Badan Perencanaan Pembangunan Nasional*, or BAPPENAS).[12]

In 1995, the New Order government made a tentative step towards real decentralization when it launched a 2-year district autonomy pilot project. This involved transferring select functions from central and provincial levels to local government in twenty-six districts.[13] The pilot project took place, in part, because of continuing pressure from the international donor community to move away from the centralist model to one which demonstrated greater flexibility in meeting objectives, and which was more attuned to local needs. The fundamental limitation of the pilot project was that it did not include complementary transfers of central government funds to support new local functions. All districts and cities (including the twenty-six districts in the pilot programme) continued to rely on grants and loans emanating from and administered by the central government for virtually all local needs.[14] The purse strings held by central government in Jakarta made Indonesia one of the most centrally controlled (non-communist) countries in the world well into the 1990s despite rhetoric of supporting greater decentralization and local participation in planning and policy. When Sutiyoso became governor in 1997, this was the situation and no real changes seemed imminent. The 'crisis' changed that, however.

The Crisis

Between 1997 and 2001, Indonesia was buffeted by a series of crises, economic, political, environmental and social, with Jakarta at the centre of the maelstrom. The fiscal crisis was not the first shock to Indonesia's prosperity. An environmental disaster precipitated by dense smoke and haze from unregulated fires set by large land owners in Sumatra and Kalimantan to clear unwanted growth produced a dense haze that blanketed parts of western Indonesia, Malaysia and Singapore throughout much of 1997. It was so dense and unrelenting that it closed airports in Sumatra and Kalimantan for nearly a month, and disrupted flights and sea traffic throughout the region for several months. As parts of Indonesia were on a slow burn and draped in a cloak of smoke, the broader regional economic crisis picked up its own head of steam. Beginning in mid 1997, a currency crisis took hold of most of East Asia, but hit particularly hard in Indonesia. As explained in earlier chapters, the precipitous drop in the value of the rupiah wiped out banks, halted all government infrastructure projects, and shut down the real estate market in Jakarta. It also chased out most of the foreign investment that had been the basis of Suharto's successful development efforts. A testament to the flight of foreign

Figure 7.2. Partially built Westin Hotel located to the south of the Hotel Indonesia. (*Photo*: author)

investment was the partially built shell of the Westin Hotel on Jalan Sudirman, which remained in this static pose for years, reminding commuters on Jakarta's busiest highway of how the collapse of the capital markets had derailed the city's development momentum.

In Indonesia, bad loans, bad projects, and rampant corruption (which accounted for many of the bad loans and bad projects) were much to blame for the economic crisis. A study by Winarso and Firman notes that, 'it can be concluded that the excessive land development ... by a few developers ... targeted at a small minority of the rich ... caused the housing market collapse and has been part of the trigger of the monetary crisis experienced in the country'.[15] By early 1998, just as President Suharto was beginning his sixth term, the economic crisis intensified, with urban areas like Jakarta hardest hit and protests against ineffective government action taking on a more strident tone. The intervention of the International Monetary Fund to assist Indonesia with its financial challenges exacerbated the unemployment problem, and added to expectations of higher prices on commodities. The capitulation of the Suharto administration to the demands of the IMF to reduce government price supports damaged its already shaken credibility.

Woven into the economic crisis was a political crisis which helped bring about the fall of the Suharto regime in 1998 and generated 4 years of political instability. Political conflict in Indonesia created the image of a country out of control, and consequently unsafe for outsiders.[16] This negative image was made worse by the outbreak of ethnic conflict throughout the country, linked to the economic and political crises but also giving vent to longstanding regional rivalries. The conflict began with attacks on the Chinese community in Jakarta during the final days of Suharto's administration in May 1998 and lasted for several weeks, while the fear of reprisals persisted for months. Ethnic violence hit other parts of Java, including the tourism areas of central Java in Yogjakarta and Solo and Surabaya in East Java (Indonesia's second largest city). These were not so much anti-Chinese demonstrations as demonstrations against all non-Javanese. South and Central Sulawesi, the Malukus, portions of Kalimantan, and Irian Jaya all experienced violent ethnic conflicts for several years, although by far the most volatile areas, Aceh and East Timor, were where the government focused most attention.

President Habibe decided that the nearly three decades of civil war in East Timor, coupled with world opinion opposing Indonesia's continued claims to sovereignty over its poorest province, were not worth sustaining. In a move that won him international acclaim, but intense domestic criticism, Habibe decided to allow the East Timor people to hold a referendum on whether to remain as part of Indonesia or to take the road to independence. Overwhelming popular support for independence plunged this fragile area in Eastern Indonesia into renewed civil war, as an Indonesian military-backed militia laid waste to the region in a last ditch effort to derail the independence movement. Intervention by an international peacekeeping force sustained the process of forming an independent East Timor. But by then Habibe had already lost his bid to remain as president, with the seemingly more democratic and politically independent, Abdurrahman Wahid, becoming president in October 1999.

While Habibe's stance on East Timor plunged the nation into further internal conflict, his other important legacy was to champion a process of government reform that was equally destabilizing, but which also had discernible positive outcomes. His support for the decentralization of power and responsibility from central to local governments further energized the democracy movement. What started out as a policy to facilitate the transition of administration from a centralized structure to one in which planning, policy and implementation was done locally, led within a few years to systemic change whereby all key government administrators and legislators were elected directly by the people.

The change began in June 1999 when the Indonesian national legislature, with Habibe's backing, enacted two decentralization acts (Law 22/99 and Law 25/99). Law 22/99 did away with the New Order's hierarchical system linking local governments to the central government. It granted local governments, both city and district, substantial administrative autonomy and, at least initially, reduced the authority of the governors and provincial government. One key provision was that mayors and district heads were no longer appointed by provincial government. This change was a first important step towards making local government administrators accountable to the local population. According to Ryaas Rasyid, who briefly headed a ministry created specifically to oversee implementation of Law 22, the 'new paradigm' in intergovernmental relations necessitated a fundamental shift from central to local dominance, with districts and municipalities receiving greatly expanded functions.[17] Within a few years this led to the direct election of mayors and district heads by the local electorate, and eventually governors and the nation's president.

Law 22 devolved power to local authorities by specifying the responsibilities of central government, which included foreign policy, defence and security, the judiciary, monetary and fiscal policy, religion, national planning, and natural resource management. All other governmental responsibilities were devolved to the localities, including health, education, urban services, agriculture, the environment, and coastal management, all of which had been under the control of central government ministries in Jakarta. The new law also removed any accountability to provincial officials by stipulating that the decisions of local legislatures and local administrators only needed to be reported to the Ministry of Home Affairs.

While Law 22 failed to specify the role the central government would play in reviewing local decisions, the assumption among local officials was that they now possessed broad discretion as long as their decisions were consistent with national laws. In addition, local government personnel were no longer employees of central government. As a result, central government employees in ministry offices in Jakarta and in the localities were transferred to their local counterparts. At the same time, the demise of what was virtually a 'one-party' system of electing local legislators and the introduction of a multi-party political system at national and local levels strengthened the resolve of locals to press for full decentralization.

The companion act, Law 25, established a new general revenue fund from central government (*Dana Alokosi Umum* or *DAU*) to support decentralization. Specifically it stated localities would retain a substantial share of the proceeds from natural resource extraction in their domain, funds that previously went directly to Jakarta. Many localities suddenly found themselves awash with funds, while an engaged local electorate watched to see how local leaders managed this new wealth.

Evolution of a New Local Planning Paradigm

In direct response to pressures fuelled by the decentralization and democratization movements in Indonesia after 1998, and building on the landmark laws of 1999, a new urban planning approach was introduced. The urban development area programme *(Program Dasar Pembangunan Perkotaan* or *PDPP)* introduced a participatory element into local capital improvements planning that involved local stakeholders in the plan-making process. The locally-focused PDPP process was conceived by international consultants, under a technical assistance project funded by the US Agency for International Development, the Coordinated Local Environmental Action Network in Urban Areas (CLEAN-Urban). The CLEAN-Urban project sought to strengthen the capacity of local governments in Indonesia to finance urban environmental services by: improving administrative and financial management at the local government level; facilitating expanded community participation in local government decision-making; and supporting the development of an enabling legal and regulatory framework. Between 1998 and 2000, CLEAN-Urban worked in 818 individual communities (415 in East Java and 302 in West Java) including 14 cities, to create and use a community participation process; to conduct community needs assessments; to identify opportunities for small-scale infrastructure projects and micro-enterprise projects to create jobs; and to address infrastructure needs. In concert with its East Java local government clients, including the provincial planning agency, CLEAN-Urban created in February 2000 the East Java Coordinating Group (EJCG) to design a process for integrating community development with development planning. The EJCG assistance produced general guidelines for development plans which were later promulgated by the Ministry of Home Affairs to all Indonesian localities that required a participatory process.[18] This became the official sanction for the participatory planning process that was initiated in Jakarta.

The concept of participatory planning found ready acceptance in some of the newly created governments, such as the rapidly urbanizing peripheral area of Jakarta known as Depok. As a newly-designated city in West Java in 1999, Depok had no existing institutions to reform and also no experience in local infrastructure planning to modify. As it had no institutional baggage and was located within the dynamic Jabotabek urban growth corridor, Depok presented a high-profile opportunity to pilot the PDPP participatory planning process. At the time, the Ministry of Home Affairs was still responsible for local government affairs as Law 22/1999 did not become operational until January 2001. Therefore, its approval was necessary to launch the PDPP initiative in Depok. An additional hurdle to overcome was local acceptance of the PDPP model. In February 2000, Depok's Chief of Physical Planning, along with other city and neighbourhood leaders, participated in a 'Town Hall' meeting to discuss local planning under this new decentralized and democratized process, and to consider the PDPP process as a way for the city to plan for urban infrastructure and services. The mayor of Depok issued a letter in March 2000 endorsing the mobilization of technical assistance to launch the PDPP.[19]

Along with the four East Java cities of Kediri, Tulungagung, Pasuruan, and Malang that had first tested the PDPP approach, Depok searched for a vehicle to institutionalize non-government stakeholder involvement. That vehicle was an *ad hoc* group known as the City Forum. The City Forum was a group of local representatives from the business community, universities, religious associations, and other civic groups charged with providing input to local government on city-wide issues, including community development and development planning. Another variation of this was the Stakeholders Forum, a participatory device specifically included as a condition of the World Bank Social Safety Net Adjustment loan that was attempting to address poverty and unemployment generated by the Indonesian economic crisis after 1998. This group was to facilitate transparency and accountability in poverty programme design and implementation by engaging local governments, non-governmental organizations (NGOs), and community groups in planning for labour-intensive projects. Although the objectives of City Forum and Stakeholder Forum extended beyond the PDPP process *per se*, they represented new approaches to assessing local plans and projects prior to review and approval by the local legislature (*Dewan Pemwakilan Rakyat Daerah*, or DPRD) and the mayor (*walikota*). The PDPP initiative in Depok and the eight localities in East Java represented a unique integration of community participation and local government planning.

Under Law 25, the central government shifted financial support to local needs from a system of targeted grants and direct payment of the costs of all government salaries into a single block grant, the DAU. This new fund would cover salaries, development projects and other routine expenditures, with locally generated revenues (*Pendapatan Asli Daerah* or *PAD*) providing additional financing. For most localities, however, PAD represented a small proportion of overall revenues, in most cases less than 30 per cent, although in the case of Jakarta the percentage was appreciably higher because of its large commercial and industrial sectors. Indeed, what many localities discovered under decentralization was that the costs of local employees (including those transferred from the central government offices) exceeded the grant funding coming from local revenues, leaving them with less for non-personnel expenditures than had been the case under the centralized system.[20] There were exceptions, however. For example, resource rich districts, such as Kutai in East Kalimantan (which was later divided into three smaller districts) benefited from redistribution of revenues derived from the extraction of gas, timber and mining. For the great majority of localities which lacked these natural resources, the tendency was to regard the formula for DAU as unfair, and to favour a system where more funds were sent to Jakarta and could be redistributed fairly to resource-poor areas. The real problem they faced was not so much an unfair DAU formula but rather overall declining domestic revenues during the first years of implementation because of the lingering economic crisis, coupled with negligible locally generated revenues that in some cases had fallen in recent years.

As local funding decisions replaced those of central government, there was added pressure to democratize the entire political process. From being in all but name a one-party state Indonesia evolved into a nation where the local legislature, provincial and national legislatures, majors, district heads and governors and then, in 2004, the president and vice president, were elected by popular vote. Between the 1999 legislative reforms and the 2004 election, Indonesia became Southeast Asia's largest democracy.

Under the more democratic presidencies of Wahid, Megawati and the 2004 election of Susilo Bambang Yudiono (or SBY), there was steady recovery from the severe economic conditions of the late 1990s. One impediment to full recovery was a series of tragedies that both challenged the political leadership and diverted the scarce public resources from other necessary improvements. Major bombing incidents connected to the spread of global terrorism rocked Indonesia, the first in Bali in 2002, but several others in Jakarta, such as the Marriott Hotel bombing in the emerging 'Mega Kuningan' commercial hub in August 2003 and another in front of the nearby Australian Embassy 13 months later. These incidents reinforced the impression of instability and lack of security in Jakarta. The wholesale destruction of the city of Banda Aceh when the tsunami struck the northern coast of Sumatra on 26 December 2004 handed the Yudiono government an even greater challenge, and diverted energy from the reform agenda which, a few months earlier, had been so appealing to such a broad segment of the Indonesian electorate.

Planning and Development in the Democratic Megacity

The reform and democracy movements brought to an end the authoritarian traditions of planning that had shaped twentieth-century Jakarta. It was no longer the colonial capital of the Dutch East Indies, nor was it the control centre of the Japanese sphere of influence in Southeast Asia. It had advanced beyond the showplace of Sukarno's strident nationalism and Suharto's centrally planned modernization experiment orchestrated by the development oligarchs. It was now the mega-sized capital city of Southeast Asia's largest democracy. As the economic conditions steadily improved, many of the projects that had been left on the drawing board prior to the crisis or which, like the Westin Hotel, stopped in mid-construction, were back online in rapid order. The atmosphere of intensive new development in 2005/2006 was not unlike the rapid development so distinguishing in the early 1990s, but the circumstances were very different. A fundamental change had taken place in the city's planning and development environment; the projects underway in newly democratized Jakarta did so under the watchful eyes of an empowered civil society and within a more inclusive policy environment. Although democratization, decentralization and improved institutions did not place the general public on a par with the traditionally powerful development lobby, the planning agenda had broadened to incorporate a spectrum of stakeholders.[21] How inclusive, democratic politics had begun to shape the planning approaches to the mega-capital may be clearer if we examine changes in the built environment between my first visit in 1989 and my latest one in mid 2006.

A good place to begin is the route from the Sukarno-Hatta international airport to the city centre. This area formed my first enduring impressions in 1989 as the taxi inched through the narrow, packed streets dominated by the neighbourhood markets and local traffic. It was in every way the densely populated urban village that I had been told was characteristic of the entire metropolis, but the next 17 years saw radical change. The toll road connecting the international airport to all sections of Jakarta looms over what remains of the semi-permanent housing that

Figure 7.3. New inner-city commercial facilities being built in the rejuvenated Hotel Indonesia area. (*Photo*: author)

previously crowded along the adjacent flood canal. Much of the decrepit housing had been obliterated to provide space for the substructure of the highway. On the stretch of the road running along the north coast between the airport and edge of the more densely built areas, sprawling warehouse compounds, apartment complexes, factories, and some more upscale residential areas now filled much of the wetlands and fish farms that previously separated the airport and the city. Although the airport itself is now within the newly created province of Banten (rather than in West Java), it is no longer a satellite development attached to the capital by a limited access highway, but is fully enmeshed within the urban fabric of Jakarta. Located in Jakarta's vast flood plain, planners had tried to exclude development here, but were trumped by developers intent on profit, and with too small a flood canal the area experiences regular flooding.

Further along the toll road towards the centre of Jakarta is a series of high-rise structures, most built in the past decade, including numerous high-rise residential clusters supported by new shopping malls, hotels, hospitals, several private universities, with some older government buildings sprinkled amongst them. These new developments have obliterated many of the *kampungs* which existed in 1989. The traffic moves quickly on a toll road, although the adjacent service roads remain perpetually clogged. There are now more than 2 million vehicles vying for space on Jakarta's streets yet there is just this one route directly from the airport

Figure 7.4. High-rise residential buildings located adjacent to the toll road between the Semanngi interchange and the Soekarno-Hatta International Airport. (*Photo*: author)

to the city centre. At the Semanggi cloverleaf, where the tollroad intersects with Jakarta's major north to south boulevard, the toll road traffic slows appreciably as the exit interacts with the dense traffic on the local streets.

At the Semanggi interchange, the environment is fundamentally different. It is completely modern, first world and intensely commercial. Looking south, north and east from the bridge over Sudirman, there are no telltale signs of the third world metropolis; glittering modern buildings dominate the skyline. To the south is the Jakarta Stock Exchange complex, built during the early 1990s across from the exclusive Hotel Hilton complex. Surrounding the interchange is an assortment of new bank buildings, the renovated campus of Atma Jaya University, and a wall of office buildings and hotels along Jalan Gatot Subroto. To the north is the office tower canyon along Sudirman, erected in the 1990s.

Along the Jalan Thamrin and Jalan Sudirman north-south corridor, the newly installed busway system propels its modest (but growing) volume of passengers at a pace unimaginable for the typical Jakarta bus or automobile commuter. Because the busway still has such limited coverage, it is currently an option only for those who follow the Thamrin-Sudirman route. Despite its less than full capacity use, the system has engendered a groundswell of support for expanded mass transit facilities, including the proposed monorail system to complement the new bus routes. Pillars for the elevated transit system have begun to appear along the designated corridor but funding limitations have impeded progress. Meanwhile, Jakarta's Public Works is planning to build six new toll roads, connecting strategic sections of the inner city to the edge. But not everyone sees these as a solution. According to Bambang Susantoro, Chair of the Indonesian Transportation Society, 'the new roads will only worsen Jakarta's transportation problems'.[22] Critics of the toll road plan contend that the city should focus on mass rail transit, not more highways. But in a response reminiscent of the New Order regime, or perhaps indicative of how traditional planning approaches continue to dominate, the Jakarta Public Works head, Wisno Subagya Yusuf dismissed the protests as irrelevant to the planning process, and publicly stated that they would be built, although he did not know exactly when.

The siting of recent large-scale commercial development in Jakarta has reinforced not only the link between urban development and the highway system, but helps explain the city's polycentric pattern, which in turn makes it even more difficult to forge links to a mass transit system. There are multiple central business districts in Jakarta, and more on their way. The most ambitious of the new centres is the Mega Kuningan area, a massive new commercial conglomeration and the most dramatic transformation of inner Jakarta. Situated behind Jalan Sudirman, it replaced virtually all the neighbourhoods built there between the 1950s and 1970s to accommodate much of Jakarta's swelling population. Unlike the commercial

Figure 7.5. Several of the recently completed residential towers in the Megakuningan area in central Jakarta. (*Photo*: author)

Figure 7.6. A small remaining section of the larger *kampung* area cleared to construct the Megakuningan project. (*Photo*: author)

canyon along Sudirman, Mega Kuningan is a mixed-use area with luxury high-rise residences, office towers, shopping centres and hotels. It is the part of Jakarta which most closely resembles the look and quality of its Southeast Asian rival, Singapore.

The addition of thousands of units of high-rise residential structures not only in Mega Kuningan but throughout central Jakarta is another discernible difference from 1989, when there was almost no housing taller than six storeys. From the top floor of Jakarta's 1980s World Trade Center it once was possible to look down on sprawling *kampungs*, punctuated by clusters of more substantial residences built in earlier decades to house the overflow of the affluent from the adjacent Menteng area. Looking down on that same area 17 years later, all but a few scattered fragments of the once bustling residential areas are gone, replaced by massive modern buildings, transforming Kuningan into an exclusive community as the developers intended.

Where did the displaced *kampung* dwellers go? Some obviously moved into those few areas that escaped the bulldozers. According to Andrea Peresthu, a great many relocated to the urban fringe, drawn there by jobs and housing in the exurban cities of Tanggerang, Bekasi and Bogor. In what Peresthu refers to as 'growth by polarization' over the past 17 years, the megacity took shape on the marginal land between the earlier new town and satellite cities of the 1980s and early 1990s. 'Many empty or unproductive farmlands, which were never considered as valuable and strategic, suddenly were transformed into hospitals, warehouses, universities, and golf courses', as well as settlements to accommodate the outflow of city residents built with government support by the private sector.[23] In addition, suburban 'squatter *kampungs*' sprouted up outside the walls of the affluent new towns. These areas, which have been identified by McGee as 'peri-urban', became even more urbanized as development covered over the rice fields and fruit orchards. Those areas that preserved elements of rural village life within the megacity accommodated many of those displaced from the inner city either because their *kampung* homes had been removed, or because they found it impossible to find an affordable place in urban neighbourhoods. The phenomenon of social spatial segregation and 'growth by polarization' intensified as Jakarta grew from large city to megacity.

There is further evidence that the suburbanization of Jakarta provided a needed check on the historically unmanageable growth in the inner-city population. According to architect and urban analyst Mohammad Dannisworo, the 'self-sustaining cities' along the urban fringe helped to take on the burdens of urban growth previously borne by Jakarta proper. Dannisworo noted that the cities of Bumi Serpong Damai (BSD) and Lippo Karawaci (LK) in Tanggerang, and Jababeka and Lippo Cikarang in Bekasi accounted for as many as 5.5 million of

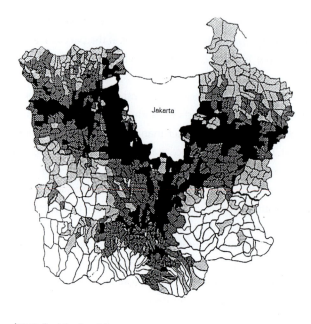

Average Population Growth Rates:

☐ <2% per year   ▨ 3% – 5% per year

☐ 2% – 3% per year   ■ >5% per year

Figure 7.7. Population
distribution within the
Jabotabek megacity area.

the capital city's day time population of 14 million, a phenomenal change from
the early 1990s. These self-sustaining cities provided not only a place to live but
also thousands of jobs both in the formal and informal sectors. He stressed that
one must distinguish between the satellite cities which were made up almost
exclusively of commuters and the self-sustaining cities, which by virtue of their
distance from the centre as well as the planning on which they were created,
were intended to provide a full array of urban functions. Yet as Dannisworo and
others emphasized, the full potential of self-sustaining cities to manage urban
grow has been undermined by the lack of planning for new development in the
areas between these urban nodes. An additional impediment was an inadequate
transit system to connect these areas effectively. The result, they say, is sprawl
and congestion at the urban edges rather than planned growth. Moreover as
the population has grown in the suburban and exurban areas of Jakarta, they
have been confronted with some of the same negative traits previously found
exclusively in the centre city, such as growing unemployment. In September 2002,
Jakarta's economy still felt the after effects of the economic crisis of the late 1990s.
Suburban Tanggerang's Labor Agency reported that an estimated 35,200 of their
residents between the ages of 20 and 39 were jobless. What had hit Tanggerang
so hard that year was a production cut in a local factory under contract with Nike
that had cost 6,800 jobs.[24]

The transformation apparent in the fringe areas of Jakarta has been matched by profound changes in the older inner-city areas, some of a transient nature but others with potentially long-term implications. One of the temporary changes, especially in those areas of inner Jakarta inhabited by Indonesians of Chinese descent, was the creation of new fortified communities in the wake of the May 1998 riots. Since May 1998, and reinforced by the post 9/11 bombings, Jakarta experienced the appearance of what Dutch anthropologist, Peter Nas refers to as the 'architecture of fear'. As he notes, 'after the riots of May 1998, the inhabitants of Jakarta's Chinatown installed barbed wire around their homes'.[25] This protection was augmented by systems of heavy gates and limited access routes to communities, patrolled by neighbourhood residents and hired guards. These architectural amenities are still visible in the Kalapa Gading community in the north-eastern section of Jakarta (near the city's north-east coast), an area of prosperous Chinese Indonesians who have constructed a relatively self-contained city within the inner area of Jakarta. Except for a few places like Kelapa Gading, the prominent displays of barbed and razor wire, supported by armed military vehicles that cordon off the US Embassy from the traffic circling Merdeka Square in central Jakarta, and similar protection near the British Embassy adjacent to the

Figure 7.8. The pervasive neighbourhood protection gates widely employed in many of Jakarta's wealthier areas. (*Photo*: author)

HI plaza, most visible signs of the 'architecture of fear' have disappeared from Jakarta. But what has been left as a permanent feature of the urban landscape is an entrenched system of social spatial segregation that was less evident when the traditional *kampung* structure was the community building block of the city. Gates, traffic barriers, and walls have replaced the human network that previously preserved neighbourhood integrity.

Preservation Amidst Modernization

As a counterpoint to the intensive new development that transformed inner and outer Jakarta, there has also been an effort to safeguard some of the historic symbols of the city as well as to create a more 'green' environment. When Peter Nas visited Jakarta's historic Menteng neighbourhood in 2001, he noted that there seemed to be little interest in protecting it, as evidenced by the advanced deterioration of the Kunstkring ('art centre') on Jalan Teuku Umar, one of the first concrete structures built in the Netherland Indies. For years the Indonesian government had used this architecturally prominent structure as an office building. By 2001, when Nas saw it, the Kunstkring was empty and in 'complete disarray'.[26] By 2006, when I revisited Menteng (where I had worked for three years in the mid-1990s), at least the exterior of the Kunstkring had been thoroughly and tastefully restored and it was now under the control of the Jakarta Cultural and Museum Agency. At the same time, I discovered that the long contemplated plan to restore the historic core of Jakarta, the Kota area, had got a new lease on life. Plans to revitalize the Kota area had been formulated as far back as the 1920s (see Chapter 5), and prior to the economic crisis it had seemed likely that it would happen as part of the grand Waterfront City plan. A recently released 'Old Town Revitalization Plan for 2006–2007' offered a scaled down and more realistic approach to transforming the historic areas around the Fatahillah Square in Kota into an attractive and accessible tourist area. The plan begins where it needs to with a rerouting of vehicular traffic around the area along Kali Besar Barat which runs along the Krukut River and to the east away from the proposed pedestrian plaza in Fatahillah Park. The addition of the busway system, which terminates several blocks to the south in front of the still bustling Kota railway station, has already improved public transport access to this area.

The essence of the plan is to remove the cars, develop several new pedestrian areas among the alleys connecting the park to the river front, eliminate some of the visual debris (such as overhead wires), and so create a cultivated landscape to encourage new tourist businesses to set up in the adjacent seventeenth-century buildings. 'The ultimate goal is to transform Kota into a cultural tourism spot that features heritage values, but still allows room for economic activities', according

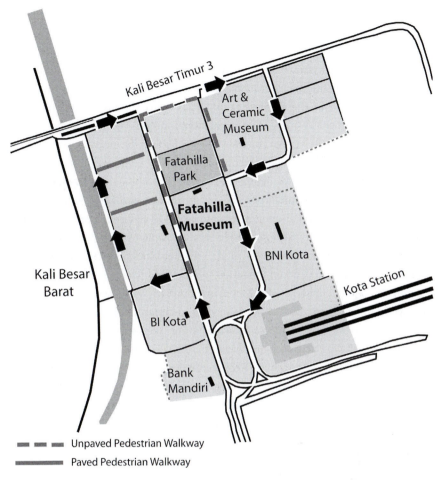

Figure 7.9. Old Town Revitalization Plan, 2006–2007.

to Aurora Tambunan, head of the Jakarta Culture and Museum Agency. Since the early 1990s there has been interest from investors in restoring many of the remaining seventeenth-century structures, but except for renovation of the city hall, the puppet and art and ceramic museums, the popular nightspot, Café Batavia, and some improvements along the Kali Besar (in conjunction with a new hotel), the area had changed very little from the architecturally distinctive but deteriorated, congested, and economically marginal section of old Jakarta I first visited in 1989. With its narrow streets and unrelenting stream of motorcycles, cars and trucks, all trying to find a faster route to the waterfront industrial area, the Fatahillah area could never sustain revitalization without regulation and reduction in the traffic. Whether the 'Old Town Revitalization Plan' can accomplish its goal of changing both the image and reality of this important piece of colonial Jakarta will be a test of the city's capacity to transform visionary plans into reality.[27]

The restoration of the Kota area is likely to be easier now owing to a substantial reinvestment in the commercial area to the south of the historic core, in the predominantly Chinese area of Glodok. In the aftermath of the 1998 riots that destroyed so much of the Chinese commercial district, reinvestment occurred through development of a massive new shopping complex to the east of the older Chinese commercial area, thereby re-establishing the primacy of this area in electronics and textile retailing. Just beyond the new commercial development, which includes some new residential buildings, is the new development on the site of the former Kemayoran airport. Begun during the heyday of Suharto's New Order government, the envisaged international trade centre did not turn out as spatially coherent as had been suggested in the original plans. Nevertheless, its multiple high-rise residential towers, along with new shopping facilities, replaced some of the residential accommodation previously available in the *kampung* settlements. A component of the Kemayoran project was low-cost housing for displaced persons, and these solid, if modest, 4-storey units were built nearby. They serve not only as affordable housing within the inner city but also space for income producing activities that provide both services and jobs for residents. What is remarkable in assessing the Kemayoran project is not just how long it took to implement but how remarkably close to the original concept the final product turned out.

Visions for the Future

Planning has become even more important to twenty-first-century democratic Jakarta than it was in implementing the competing colonial and nationalist visions of the twentieth. This can be seen in the carefully crafted 'strategic plan' now being used to frame development of the capital city. In its discussion of the challenges currently confronting Jakarta, the strategic plan reads much like many of the earlier assessments of urbanization in the capital city, suggesting that perhaps little has changed in the realities of life for many despite the outward appearance of a much larger and more modern city. The social challenges are identified as uncontrolled urbanization which has produced a whole new collection of slum areas, and a higher incidence of crime and social conflict, especially in the aftermath of the economic crisis. Unemployment remains high despite the return of economic growth, income disparity has increased, and there is the general perception that social institutions are not able to suppress 'increasing conflict among social groups'. These inequalities are exacerbated by unequal distribution of the benefits of education and health. Of course, contributing to all of these

Figure 7.10. Jakarta central commercial area in 2006. (*Photo*: author)

problems has been the 'slow economic recovery' since the crisis of 1997. Although by 2000 economic growth had increased to 3.98 per cent and then held at roughly the same level (3.64 per cent) in 2001, unemployment has remained high, causing even more to turn to the informal sector, mainly street vending.

Lingering effects of the economic crisis limited the city's financial capacity to address longstanding infrastructure needs. As expected, the strategic plan underscores the problems of limited water supply, annual flooding, inadequate garbage and sewage management, and the continuing challenge of providing enough decent and affordable housing for low income families. But what is notable about this plan is its emphasis on the environmental deficiencies of the megacity that involve more than just poor infrastructure service. A lack of open space and massive air and water pollution problems topped the list. 'Like problems in most mega cities', the plan observes, 'Jakarta faces a problem of limited open space' largely because it is being crowded out by economic activities. Air and water pollution, including industrial waste, are cited as related environmental deficiencies that helped to give Jakarta the dubious distinction of being 'the third highest polluted city in the world'.[28]

The plan also acknowledges that the low level of trust and acceptance of the government after the reform movement has made it even more difficult to govern

Figure 7.11. Within modern, mega Jakarta there are still strong vestiges of the traditional pre-modern city, including the vast army of street vendors who serve the millions. (*Photo*: author)

and plan effectively. Both the economic crisis and the collapse of the New Order government contributed to a higher level of social disorder and insufficient community participation in governance, despite the changes in the structure of local government. From the standpoint of Jakarta's leadership, decentralization gave new authority to local government officials but did not immediately supply sufficient resources to enable the new responsibilities to be handled effectively. There seemed to be fewer resources to take on more responsibilities, which contributed to the 'low spirit' among government officers now confronted with massive challenges previously taken on in partnership with a powerful central government.

Although the litany of urban ills identified in the plan was essentially the same as those which planners confronted throughout the last half of the century, this new plan is grounded in a fundamentally different notion of the purpose of planning. The vision presented is for the megacity Jakarta to become 'a humane, efficient, and competitive capital supported by a participative, prosperous, well behaved and civilized society in a safe and sustainable environment'. This vision is framed within a series of mission statements that call for an efficient and honest government that will ensure a 'just and sound environmental and community-focused development process' supported by the necessary infrastructure. The plan calls for a phased-in process, beginning with a focus on full economy recovery, improved governance and law enforcement, and some new infrastructure between 2002 and 2004. By 2005, the emphasis would shift from recovery to sustaining the prosperity that had been restored and to ensure that the foundations for social, political and economic development in place would be sustainable.

Throughout the list of specific strategies runs the theme of good planning and management in order to support communities and to minimize social conflicts. It is not just a matter of dealing with the historically big challenges of traffic congestion, flood control, spreading slum areas, and an increasing informal sector in conflict and competition with the formal sector. The sustainable megacity is one that needs to meet the important social needs of its ever changing citizenry, from health care, to education, to supporting community organizations and elevating the moral tone in a capital city traditionally concerned more with generating wealth rather than sharing it. As Jakarta, the megacity, faces the ongoing planning challenges early in the twenty-first century, its leadership now understands more clearly than at any point in the previous century that planning is, in effect, largely a social process even with its obvious physical manifestations. Effective planning for cities are those policies and initiatives that improve the social conditions of the greatest number of its citizens. That had been true during the waning years of the colonial capital in the early twentieth century and it remains ever more true as Jakarta **is** poised to step onto the global stage as a world city in its own right, one in which newly created democratic planning processes might ultimately enable all its citizens to share in the greatness of Southeast Asia's grandest city.

Notes

1.   See Budiman, Hatley and Kingsbury (1999).
2.   Cited in Kusno (2004), p. 2385.
3.   *Ibid.*, pp. 2380–2381.
4.   *Ibid.*, p. 2386.
5.   Endah (2004), pp. 22–24.
6.   *JP*, 27 December, 2004.
7.   *JP*, 3 March, 2004.
8.   *JP*, 28 June and 20 November, 2004; 16 June, 2005.
9.   Endah (2004), pp. 25–27, 31–34.
10. Kusno (2004) *op. cit.*
11. Walker (1991), pp. 94–102.
12. See McAndrews (1986).
13. Beier and Farrazzi (1997).
14. Devas (1998).
15. Winarso and Firman (2002), p. 503.
16. Maher (2000).
17. Alm and Bahl (1999).

18. Indonesia, Walikota Depok, Pembentukan Tim Teknis Program Dasar Pembangunan Perkotaan (PDPP) Kota Depok Tahun Anggaran 2000.
19. Silver (2000).
20. See Usman (2002); Silver, Azis and Schroeder (2001), pp. 345–362.
21. See Rosser, Roesad and Edwin (2005); Robison and Hadiz (1999), pp. 171–191.
22. *JP*, 26 May, 2005.
23. Peresthus (2005), p. 53.
24. *JP*, 4 July and 8 August, 2005.
25. Nas and Pratiwo (2003), p. 289. See also Kusno (2003), pp. 149–177.
26. Nas and Pratiwo (2003), p. 274.
27. *JP*, 6 June, 2006.
28. Jakarta, DKI (2002).

Bibliography

Interviews

Bowo, Fauzi, Vice Governor, DKI Jakarta, 7 January, 2005.

Chajaridipura, Ery, Former Head of BAPPEDA, DKI Jakarta, 5 January, 2005.

Damais, Adjit, Former Director of Jakarta City Museum and Special Assistant to Vice Governor, DKI Jakarta, 7 January, 2005.

Pasaribu, Maurits, Former Director of Urban and Regional Development, Ministry of Public Works, Jakarta, 4 January, 2005.

Rais, T. M., Former Head of BAPPEDA and Vice Governor, DKI Jakarta, 12 January, 2005.

Sadikin, Ali, Former Governor, DKI Jakarta, 4 January, 2005.

Sari, Vera Revina, BAPPEDA, DKI Jakarta, Infrastructure and Environment, 3 January, 2005.

Tisnawinata, Kandar, Former Head of BAPPEDA, DKI Jakarta, 5 January, 2005.

Yudha, Chair of Jakarta Chapter of Indonesian Association of Architects, 6 January, 2005.

Zhang, Wastu Pragantha, Former Special Assistant to Governor Ali Sadikin, 14 January, 2005.

Books, Articles, Documents

Abeyasekere, S. (1989) *Jakarta: A History*, revised ed. Singapore: Oxford University Press.

Abrams, C. (1964) *Housing in the Modern World: Man's Struggle for Shelter in an Urbanizing World*. Cambridge, MA: MIT Press.

Adams, C. (1965) *Sukarno: An Autobiography as told to Cindy Adams*. New York: Bobbs-Merrill Company.

Akilhary, H. (1988) *Architectuur & Stedebouw in Indonesie, 1870–1970*. Zutphen: De Walburg Pers.

Akihary, H. (1996) *Ir. F.J.L. Ghijsels: Architect in Indonesia, 1910–1929*, translated by T. Burrett. Utrecht: Seram Press.

Alm, J. and Bahl, R. (1999) Decentralization in Indonesia: Prospects and Problems. USAID Working Paper, Jakarta, June.

Anderson, B.R.O'G. (1983) Old state, new society: Indonesia's new order in comparative historical perspective. *Journal of Asian Studies*, **42**(3), pp. 477–496.

Archer, R.W. (1994) Urban land consolidation for Metropolitan Jakarta expansion 1990–2010. *Habitat International*, **18**(4), pp. 37–52.

Argo, T.A. (1999) Thirsty Downstream: The Provision of Clean Water in Jakarta, Indonesia. PhD dissertation, University of British Columbia, Vancouver.

Arctander, P.A. (1961) Urban Mass Housing for the People of Djakarta. Unpublished study, Djakarta, 4 October.

Arndt, H.W. (1972) Australian aid, in *Australia and Asia: Economic Essays*. Canberra: Australian National University Press, pp. 54–61.

Atman, R. (1975) Kampong improvements in Indonesia. *Ekistics*, **40**(238), pp. 216–220.

Batavia, Municipality of (1948) *Batavia in Post War Days*. Batavia: John Kappee.

Beier, C. and Farrazzi, G. (1997) The District Autonomy Pilot Program: A New Approach to Decentralization in Indonesia. Policy Paper, Indonesian-German Technical Cooperation Project, GTZ, Jakarta, April.

Bellen, M. (1995) Cultural institutions in Batavia, 1900–1942, in Nas, Peter J.M. (ed.) *Issues in Urban Development: Case Studies from Indonesia*. Leiden: Leiden University, pp. 98–114.

Benjamin, S. and Arifin, M.A. (1985) The housing costs of low-income *kampung* dwellers. *Habitat International*, **9**(1), pp. 91–110.

Berlage, H.P. (1931) *Mijn Indische Reis*, Rotterdam: Gedachten over Culture in Kunst.

Bidani, N.D. (1985) Demographic characteristics of the urban population in Southeast Asia, in Krausse, G.H. (ed.) *Urban Society in Southeast Asia*. Volume 1. *Social and Economic Issues*. Hong Kong: Asian Research Service, pp. 15–42.

Boddy, T. (1983) The political uses of urban design, in Webster, D. (ed.) *The Southeast Asian Environment*. Ottawa: University of Ottawa Press.

Boedhisantoso, S. (1967) Djagakarsa: a fruit-producing village near Jakarta, in *Koentjaraningrat: Villages in Indonesian*. Ithaca, NY: Cornell University Press.

Bogarers, E. and Ruijter, P. de (1986) Ir Thomas Karsten and Indonesian town planning, 1915–1940, in Nas, P.J.M. (ed.) *The Indonesian City: Studies in Urban Development and Planning*. Dordrecht: Foris Publications, pp. 71–88.

Breuning, H.A. (1936) Nat Zal er van Oud-Batavia worden. *Heemsdaut*, **13**(3), pp. 18–23.

Bruening, H.A. (1954) *Het Voormalig Batavia*. Amsterdam.

Broeze, F. (ed.) (1989) *Bridges of the Sea: Port Cities of Asia from the 16th–20th Centuries*. Kensington, NSW: New South Wales University Press.

Browder, J.O., Bohland, J.R. and Scarpaci, J.L. (1995) Patterns of development on the metropolitan fringe: urban fringe expansion in Bangkok, Jakarta, and Santiago. *Journal of the American Planning Association*, **61**, pp. 310–326.

Brown, C. (2003) *A Short History of Indonesia: The Unlikely Nation*. Crown Nest, NSW: Allen and Unwin.

Brownell, B.A. (1975) The commercial-civic elite and city planning in Atlanta, Memphis and New Orleans in the 1920s. *Journal of Southern History*, **41**, pp. 339–367.

Brunn, S.D., Williams, J.F., and Zeigler, D.J. (2003) *Cities of the World: World Regional Urban Development*. Lanham, MD: Rowman & Littlefield.

Brunner, E.M. (1961) Urbanization and ethnic identity in North Sumatra. *American Anthropologist*, **63**(3), pp. 508–521.

Budihardjo, E. (1987) The Indonesian experience in the Kampong Improvement Program. *Indonesian Journal of Geography*, **17**(53), pp. 55–61.

Budiman, A., Hatley, B., and Kingsbury, D. (eds.) (1999) *Reformasi: Crisis and Change in Indonesia*. Clayton, Victoria: Monash University.

Cangi, E.C. (1993) Civilizing the people of Southeast Asia: Sir Stamford Raffles' town plan for Singapore, 1819–23. *Planning Perspectives*, **8**, pp. 166–187.

Caring for our heritage (1995) Editorial. *Jakarta Post*, June 17.

Castles, L. (1967) The ethnic profile of Djakarta. *Indonesia*, **1**(April), pp. 153–204.

Castles, L. (1991) Jakarta: the growing centre, in Hill, H. (ed.) *Unity and Diversity: Regional Economic Development in Indonesia since 1970.* New York: Oxford University Press.

Central Bureau of Statistics, Indonesia (1969) *1968–1969 Jakarta Survey.* Jakarta: Biro Pusat Statistik.

Cobban, J.L. (1970) The City in Java: An Essay in Historical Geography. PhD dissertation, University of California, Berkeley.

Cobban, J.L. (1976) Geographical notes on the first two centuries of Djakarta, in Yeung, Y.M. and Lo, C.P. (eds.) *Changing South-East Asian Cities.* Singapore: Oxford University Press, pp. 45–49.

Cobban, J.L. (1985) The ephemeral historic district in Jakarta. *Geographical Review,* **75**(3), pp. 330–318.

Cobban, J.L. (1992) Exporting planning: the work of Thomas Karsten in colonial Indonesia. *Planning Perspectives,* **7**, pp. 329–344

Cobban, J.L. (1993) Public housing in colonial Indonesia, 1900–1940. *Modern Asian Studies,* **27**(4), pp. 871–896.

Cote, J. (2002) Towards an architecture of association: H.F. Tillema, Semarang and the construction of colonial modernity, in Nas, P.J.M. (ed.) *The Indonesian Town Revisited.* Singapore: Institute of Southeast Asian Studies, pp. 319–347.

Council Wants Quick Relocation of Warehouses (1995) *Jakarta Post,* 21 July.

Cowherd, R. (2002) Cultural Construction of Jakarta: Design, Planning and Development in Jabotabek, 1980–1997. PhD dissertation, Massachusetts Institute of Technology.

Cribb, R. (ed.) (1994) *The Late Colonial State in Indonesia: Political and Economic Foundations of the Netherlands Indies 1880–1942.* Leiden: KITLV Press.

Day, C. (1904) *The Policy and Administration of the Dutch in Java.* New York: Macmillan (reprinted by Oxford University Press, KL, 1966).

Devas, N. (1986) *Indonesia's Kampung Improvement Programme: An Evaluation Case Study.* Birmingham: University of Birmingham Institute of Local Government Studies.

Devas, N. and Rakodi, C. (1993) *Managing Fast Growing Cities: New Approaches to Urban Planning and Management in the Developing World.* Harlow: Longman.

Devas, N. (1998) The Subsidi Daerah Otonom: A Review of the Issues. Unpublished paper, School of Public Policy, University of Birmingham..

Dick, H. (1981*a*) Urban public transport, Part I. *Bulletin of Indonesian Economic Studies,* **17**(1), pp. 66–82.

Dick, H. (1981*b*) Urban public transport, Part II. *Bulletin of Indonesian Economic Studies,* **17**(2), pp. 72–88.

Dick, H. (2002) Formation of the nation-state, 1930s–1966, in Dick, H., Houben, V.J.H., Lindblad, J.T. and Wie, T.K. (eds.) *The Emergence of a National Economy: An Economic History of Indonesia, 1800–2000.* Crows Nest, NSW: Allen and Unwin, pp. 157–158.

Dimitriou, H.T. (1991) An integrated approach to urban infrastructure development: a review of the Indonesia experience. *Cities,* August, pp. 193–208.

Dipokusumo, S. (1961) The Housing Problem in Djakarta. Unpublished typescript, 6 June. Jakarta.

Doebele, Mary R. (1959) The Krekot Dalam Housing Project. A Social Survey. Djakarta, June 1959.

Dogan, M. and Kasarda, J.D. (eds.) (1988) *The Metropolis Era.* Volume 1. *A World of Giant Cities.* Newbury Park, CA: Sage.

Doorn, J. van (1982) *The Engineers and the Colonial System: Technocratic Tendencies in the*

Dutch East Indies. Comparative Asian Studies Programme, Vol. 6. Rotterdam: Erasmus University.

Doorn, J. van (1983) *A Divided Society: Segmentation and Mediation in Late-Colonial Indonesia*. Comparative Asian Studies Programme, Vol. 7. Rotterdam: Erasmus University.

Dorléans, B. (1976) *Etude géographique de trois 'kampong' à Djakarta*. Paris: Département de Géographie de l'Université de Paris-Sorbonne.

Dorléans, B.(1994) *L'économie de l'Indonesie*. Paris: PUF.

Douglass, M. (1989) The environmental sustainability of development: coordination, incentives and political will in land use planning for the Jakarta Metropolis. *Third World Planning Review*, **11**(2), pp. 211–238.

Endah, W.S. (2004) Beautiful dusk in Bogota. *Tempo*, 6–12 January, pp. 25–27.

Evans, J. (1984) The growth of urban centres in Java since 1961. *Bulletin of Indonesian Economic Studies*, **20**(1), pp. 44–57.

Evers, H.D. and Korff, R. (2000) *Southeast Asian Urbanism: The Meaning and Power of Social Space*. New York: St. Martin's Press.

Fasseur, C. (1994) Cornerstone and stumbling block: racial classification and the late colonial state in Indonesia, in Cribb, R. (ed.) *The Late Colonial State in Indonesia: Political and Economic Foundation of the Netherland Indies*. Leiden: KITLV, pp. 31–56.

Feith, H. (1962) *The Decline of Constitutional Democracy in Indonesia*. Ithaca, NY: Cornell University Press.

Firman, T. (1992) The spatial pattern of urban population growth in Java, 1980–1990. *Bulletin of Indonesian Economic Studies*, **28**(2), pp. 95–109.

Firman, T. (1996) Patterns and trends of urbanization: a reflection of regional disparity, in Jones, G.W. and Hull, T.H. (eds.) *Indonesia Assessment: Population and Human Resources*. Canberra: Research School of Pacific and Asian Studies, Australian National University, pp. 101–117.

Firman, T. (1997*a*) Urban Land Development Issues in Indonesia. Unpublished manuscript (in possession of the author).

Firman, T. (1997*b*) Land conversion and urban development in the northern region of West Java, Indonesia. *Urban Studies*, **34**(7), pp. 1027–1046.

Firman, T. (1999) 'From global city to city of crisis': Jakarta metropolitan region under economic turmoil. *Habitat International*, **23**(4), pp. 447–466.

Firman, T. (2004) New town development in Jakarta metropolitan region: a perspective of spatial segregation. *Habitat International*, **28**(3), pp. 349–368.

Firman, T. and Dharmapatni, I.A.I. (1994) The challenges to sustainable development in the Jakarta metropolitan region. *Habitat International*, **18**(3), pp. 79–94.

Firman, T. and Dharmapatni, I.A.I. (1995) Problems and challenges of mega-urban regions in Indonesia: the Case of Jabotabek and the Bandung metropolitan area, in McGee, T.G. and Robinson, I.M. (eds.) *The Mega-Urban Regions of Southeast Asia*. Vancouver: University of British Columbia Press, pp. 296–314.

Fishermen fall victim to waterfront project (1995) *Jakarta Post*, April 27.

Flieringa, G. (1930) De Zorg Voor de Volkshuisvesting in de Stadsgemeenten in Nederlandsch Oost Indie, in *Het bijzonder in Semarang*. s-Gravenhage: Nijhoff.

Forbes, D. (1990) Jakarta towards 2005: planning mechanism and issues. *Bulletin of Indonesian Economic Studies*, **26**(3), pp. 111–120.

Forbes, D. (1996) *Asian Metropolis: Urbanization and the Southeast Asian City*. Melbourne: Oxford University Press.

Ford, L. (1993) A model of Indonesian city structure. *Geographical Review*, **83**, pp. 374–396.

Forrester, G. and May, R.J. (eds.) (1999) *The Fall of Suharto.* Singapore: Select Books.

Franklin, G.H. (1961) The Planning Aspects of the Provision of Prefab, Multi-Storied Mass Housing for the People of Djakarta. Typed memo, Djakarta, 17 September.

Franklin, G. H. (1964) Assignment in Djakarta – a personal view of planning in Indonesia. *Royal Australian Planning Institute Journal*, **2**, pp. 229–231.

Frederick, W. H. (1983) Hidden change in late colonial urban society in Indonesia. *Journal of Southeast Asian Studies*, **14**(2), pp. 345–371.

Frederick, W. H. (1989) *Visions and Heat: The Making of the Indonesian Revolution.* Athens, OH: Ohio University Press.

Friedmann, J. (2005) *China's Urban Transition.* Minneapolis: University of Minnesota Press.

Friend, T. (2003) *Indonesian Destinies.* Cambridge, MA: Harvard University Press.

Fryer, D.W. (1953) The million city in Southeast Asia. *Geographical Review*, **43**(4), pp. 474–494.

Furnivall, J.S. (1939, 1967) *Netherlands India: A Study of Plural Economy.* Cambridge: Cambridge University Press.

Future city development in Indonesia (1995) *Indonesia Property Report*, Vol 1 (Third Quarter), pp. 16–19.

Geertz, H. (1963) Indonesian cultures and communities, in McVey, R.T. (ed.) *Indonesia, Southeast Asia Studies.* New Haven, CT: Yale University and H.R.A.F. Press, pp. 24–96.

Giebels, L.J. (1986) JABOTABEK: an Indonesian-Dutch concept on metropolitan planning of the Jakarta-Region, in Nas, P.J.M. (ed.) *The Indonesian City: Studies in Urban Development and Planning.* Dordrecht: Foris Publications, pp. 101–115.

Gilbert, A. (ed.) (1996) *The Mega-city in Latin America.* Tokyo: The United Nations Press.

Gill, R. (1995) Jakarta's urban heritage: restoration of the urban memory of Kota, in Nas, P.J.M. (ed.) *Issues in Urban Development: Case Studies from Indonesia.* Leiden: Research School CNWS, pp. 65–97.

Ginsburg, N.S. (1955) The great city in Southeast Asia. *American Journal of Sociology*, **60**, pp. 438–445.

Ginsburg, N., Koppel, B., and McGee, T.G. (eds.) (1991) *The Extended Metropolis: Settlement Transition in Asia.* Honolulu: University of Hawaii Press.

Gooszen, H. (1999) *A Demographic History of the Indonesian Archipelago, 1880–1942.* Leiden: KITLV Press.

Gouda, F. (1995) *Dutch Culture Overseas: Colonial Practice in the Netherland Indies, 1900–1942.* Amsterdam: Amsterdam University Press.

Government urged to preserve old buildings (1995) *Jakarta Post*, 1 June.

Haan, F. de (1935) *Oud Batavia.* Bandoeng.

Hadinoto, K. (1961) Housing in the Sphere of Socialism of Indonesia. Unpublished manuscript.

Hammer, A.M., Steer, A.D., and Williams, D.G. (1986) *Indonesia: The Challenge of Urbanization.* Working Paper No. 787. Washington, DC: World Bank.

Harjati and Gajus Siagian (1962) *Djakarta Guide: A Year-Round Vacation City.* Djakarta: PT Gunung Agung.

Harsono, G. (1977) *Reflections of an Indonesian Diplomat in the Sukarno Era.* St. Lucia, Qld: Queensland University Press.

Hauser, P.M. (ed.) (1957) *Urbanization in Asia and the Far East.* Calcutta: UNESCO.

Heeren, H.J. (1955) The urbanisation of Djakarta. *Ekonomi dan Keuangan Indonesia*, **8**(11), pp. 349–368.

Heiden, C.N. van der (1990) Town planning in the Dutch Indies. *Planning Perspectives*, **5**, pp. 63–84.

Henderson, J.V., Kuncoro, A. and Nasution, D. (1996) The dynamics of Jabotabek development. *Bulletin of Indonesian Economic Studies*, **32**(1), pp. 71–95.

Herbowo, *et al.* (1961) *Pulo Mas: Project for a Low-Cost Housing District for the Djakarta Municipality Prepared Under the United Nations Technical Assistant Programme.* Copenhagen: self published, October.

Herbowo, Tisnawinata, K., Moochtar, R. and Simonsen, O.C. (1962) Compilation of Data on Indonesia: Presented as a Collection of Tools for Future Planning. Unpublished typed manuscript in possession of Kanar Tisnawinata.

Heuken, A. (1982, 1989) *Historical Sights of Jakarta.* Singapore: Times Books.

Heuken, A. and Pamungkas, G. (2001) *Menteng: Kota Taman Pertama di Indonesia.* Jakarta: Yayasan Cipta Loka Caraka.

Hoff, R. van der and Steinberg, F. (1992) *Innovative Approaches to Urban Management.* Aldershot: Avebury.

Hoffman, M.L., Walker, C., Struyk, R.J., and Nelson, K. (1991) Rental housing in urban Indonesia. *Habitat International*, **15**, pp. 181–206.

Houben, V.J.H. (2002) Java in the 19th century: consolidation of a territorial state, in Dick, H., Houben, V.J.H., Lindblad, J.T. and Wie, T.K. (eds.) *The Emergence of a National Economy: An Economic History of Indonesia, 1800–2000.* Crows Nest, NSW: Allen and Unwin, pp. 56–81.

Hughes, J. (1968) *The End of Sukarno: A Coup That Misfired; a Purge that Ran Wild.* London: Angus and Robertson.

Hugo, G. (1980) *Population Movements in Indonesia During the Colonial Period.* Canberra: Australian National University, Research School of Pacific and Asian Studies.

Hugo, G., Hull, T., Hull, Valerie, and Jones, G. (1987) *The Demographic Dimension in Indonesian Development.* Singapore: Oxford University Press.

Jakarta, DKI (1961) *Djakarta: Its Rehabilitation and Development.* Jakarta: DKI Jakarta.

Jakarta, DKI (1966) *Master Plan, 1965–1985.* Jakarta: DKI Jakarta.

Jakarta, DKI (1972) *Jakarta Metropolitan Area Transportation Study, 1972–1974.* Jakarta: DKI Jakarta.

Jakarta, DKI (1992) *Jakarta Retraced.* Jakarta: Department of City Planning.

Jakarta, DKI (1994) *Jakarta: A Dynamic World City at the Threshold of the 21st Century.* Jakarta: City Planning Department.

Jakarta, DKI (1995a) *Jakarta Water Front Development: Toward the 21st Century.* Jakarta: Department of City Planning.

Jakarta, DKI (1995b) *Sunda Kelapa: A New Vision for a Historic City.* Jakarta: Jakarta Metropolitan Government.

Jakarta, DKI (1999) *Jakarta 2010: Rencana Tata Ruang Wilayah (RTRW) DKI Jakarta* (DKI Jakarta Provincial Spatial Plan, RTRW). Jakarta: DKI Jakarta.

Jakarta, DKI (2002) *Rencana Strategis Daerah Propinsi: DKI Jakarta Tahun 2002–2007* (Strategic Plan of Jakarta Province). Jakarta: Jakarta Metropolitan Government

Jakarta, DKI (2004) *Rencana Pembangunan MRT/Sub Way dan Pembangunan Rumah Susun di DKI Jakarta* (Plan for Development of Metropolitan Rapid Transit/Subway and Development of Modest Houses in DKI Jakarta). Jakarta: Pemerintah Propinsi DKI Jakarta.

Jakarta, DKI (2005) *Development of Multistory Housing in DKI Jakarta Province.* Jakarta: City Planning Department.

Jakarta, DKI (nda) *Jakarta: City of History.* Jakarta: DKI Jakarta.

Jakarta, DKI (ndb) *Jakarta: City in Development.* Jakarta: DKI Jakarta.

Jakarta, DKI, Dinas Tata Kota (1967) *The Master Plan of Djakarta, 1965–1985* (translated from Rentjana Induk Djakarta, 1965–1985). Djakarta: Dinas Tata Kota.

Jakarta Waterfront Implementation Board (1997) *Jakarta Waterfront Development Program*. Jakarta: DKI Jakarta.

Jamieson, N. (1991) The dispersed metropolis in Asia: attitudes and trends in Java, Ginsburg, N., Koppel, B., and McGee, T.G. (eds.) *The Extended Metropolis: Settlement Transition in Asia*. Honolulu: University of Hawaii Press, pp. 275–297.

Jellinek, L. (1991) *The Wheel of Fortune: The History of a Poor Community in Jakarta*. London: Allen and Unwin.

Jellinek, L., Manning, C. and Jones, G. (1977) *The Life of the Poor in Indonesian Cities*. Melbourne: Center for Southeast Asian Studies.

Jessup, H. (1989) Netherlands Architecture in Indonesia, 1900–1942. PhD dissertation, Courtald Institute of Art, University of London.

JMCG (Jakarta Metropolitan City Government) (1996) *Jakarta: 50 Tahun Dalam Pengembangan dan Penataan Kota*. Jakarta.

Jones, G. (2002) Southeast Asian urbanization and the growth of mega-urban regions. *Journal of Population Research*, **19**(2), pp. 119–136.

Jones, G. and Mamas, Si Gde Made (1996) The changing employment structure of the Jakarta metropolitan region. *Bulletin of Indonesian Economic Studies*, **32**(1), pp. 51–70.

JRDPB (Jakarta Regional Development Planning Board) (1985) *DKI Jakarta Structural Plan, 1985–2005*. Jakarta: Bappeda.

Karamoy, A. and Dias, G. (1980) Delivery of urban services in kampungs in Jakarta and Ujung Pandang, in Yeung, Y.M and McGee, T.G. (eds.) *Community Participation in Delivering Urban Services in Asia*. Ottawa: International Development Research Centre.

Karsten, T. (1930) Stedebouw, in Kerschman, F.W.H. (ed.) *25 Jaren decentralisatie in Nederlandsch-Indie, 1905–1930*. Semarang: Vereeniging voor Locale Belangen, pp. 137–144.

Karsten, T. (1930) Volkshuisvesting, in Kerschman, F.W.H. (ed.) *25 Jaren decentralisatie in Nederlandsch-Indie, 1905–1930*. Semarang: Vereeniging voor Locale Belangen, pp. 159–60.

Karsten, T. (1937) Het Konigsplein plan. *Locale Techniek*, **7**.

Keyfitz, N. (1961) The ecology of Indonesian cities. *American Journal of Sociology*, **66**(4), pp. 348–354.

Kerschman, F.W.H. (ed.) (1930) *25 Jaren decentralisatie in Nederlandsch-Indie, 1905–1930*. Semarang: Vereeniging voor Locale Belangen.

Kim, T.J., Aziz, I. and Knaap, G. (eds.) (1992) *Spatial Development in Indonesia*. Aldershot: Avebury.

Koentjaraningrat, R.M. (1977) The system and spirit of 'Gotong Royong'. *Prisma*, **6**, pp. 20–27.

Kota warehouses will undergo transformation (1995) *Jakarta Post*, 5 June.

Krausse, G.H. (1975) *The Kampungs of Jakarta, Indonesia: A Study of Spatial Patterns in Urban Poverty*. Pittsburgh: University of Pittsburgh.

Krausse, G.H. (ed.) (1985) *Urban Society in Southeast Asia*. Volume 1. *Social and Economic Issues*. Hong Kong: Asian Research Service.

Krausse, G.H. (1988) From Sunda Kelapa to Jabotabek: a socio-cultural profile of Indonesia's capital city, in Krausse, G.H. (ed.) *Urban Society in Southeast Asia*. Volume 2. *Political and Cultural Issues*. Hong Kong: Asian Research Service.

Kroef, J.M. van der (1958) *Indonesian Social Evolution*. Amsterdam: C.P.J. van der Peet.

Kusno, A. (2000) *Behind the Postcolonial: Architecture, Urban Space and Political Cultures in Indonesia*. New York: Routledge.

Kusno, Abidin (2004) Whither national urbanism? Public life in Governor Sutiyoso's Jakarta. *Urban Studies*, **41**(12), pp. 2377–2394.

Leaf, M. (1991) Land Regulation and Housing Development in Jakarta, Indonesia: from the 'Big Village' to the 'Modern City'. PhD dissertation, University of California, Berkeley.

Leaf, M. (1994) The suburbanization of Jakarta: a concurrence of economics and ideology. *Third World Planning Review*, **16**(4), pp. 341–56.

Leaf, M. (1996) Building the road for the BMW: culture, vision, and the extended metropolitan region of Jakarta. *Environment and Planning A*, **28**(9), pp. 1617–1635.

LeClerc, J. (1993) Mirrors and the lighthouse: a search for meaning in the monuments and great works of Sukarno's Jakarta, 1960–1966, in Nas, P.J.M. (ed.) *Urban Symbolism*. Leiden: Brill, pp. 38–58.

Lee, M. (1996) The evolution of housing finance in Indonesia: innovative responses to opportunities. *Habitat International* **20**(4), pp. 583–594.

Legge, J.D. (1961) *Central Authority and Regional Autonomy in Indonesia: A Study in Local Administration, 1950–1960*. Ithaca, NY: Cornell University Press.

Leich, H. (2000) Structures and functions of private new towns in Jabotabek, in Grijns, K. and Nas, P.J.M. (eds.) *Jakarta-Batavia: Socio-Cultural Essays*. Leiden: KITLV Press, pp. 89–100.

Liddle, R.W. (1996) *Leadership and Culture in Indonesian Politics*. Sydney: Allen and Unwin.

Lindblad, J. T. (2002) The Late Colonial State and Economic Expansion, 1900-1930s, in Dick, H., Houben, V.J.H., Lindblad, J.T. and Wie, T.K. (eds.) *The Emergence of a National Economy: An Economic History of Indonesia, 1800–2000*. Crows Nest, NSW: Allen and Unwin, pp. 111–152.

Leur, J.C. van (1955) *Indonesian Trade and Society*. The Hague: W. van Hoeve.

Logan, W.S. (2000) *Hanoi: Biography of a City*. Seattle, WA: University of Washington Press.

Logsdon, M.G. (1979a) Neighborhood organization in Jakarta. *Indonesia*, **18**, pp. 53–70.

Logsdon, M.G. (1979b) Leaders and Followers in Urban Neighborhoods: An Exploratory Study of Djakarta, Indonesia. PhD dissertation, Yale University.

Lohanda, M. (1994) *The Kapitan Cina of Batavia, 1837–1942: A History of Chinese Establishment in Colonial Society*. Leiden: KITLV.

Lohanda, M. (2002) *Growing Pains: The Chinese and the Dutch in Colonial Java, 1890–1942*. Jakarta: Yayasan Cipta Loka Caraka.

Maher, M. (2000) *Indonesia: An Eyewitness Account*. New York: Viking.

Malo, M. and Nas, P.J.M. (1996) Queen city of the East and symbol of the nation: the administration and management of Jakarta, in Ruland, J (ed.) *The Dynamics of Metropolitan Management in Southeast Asia*. Singapore: Institute of Southeast Asian Studies.

Marcussen, L. (1990) *Third World History in Social and Spatial Development: The Case of Jakarta*. Aldershot: Avebury.

McAndrews, C. (1986) The structure of government in Indonesia, in McAndrews, C. (ed.) *Central Government and Local Development in Indonesia*. New York: Oxford University Press.

McCloud, D.G. (1995) *Southeast Asia: Tradition and Modernity in the Contemporary World*. Boulder, CO: Westview Press.

MacDonald, G. (1995) Indonesia's Medan Merdeka: national identity and the built environment. *Antipode*, **27**(3), pp. 270–293.

McGee, T.G. (1967) *The Southeast Asian City: A Social Geography of the Primate Cities of Southeast Asia*. New York: Frederick A. Praeger.

McGee, T.G. (1991) The emergence of Desakota regions in Asia: an expanding hypothesis, in Ginsburg, N., Koppel, B. and McGee, T.G. (eds.) *The Extended Metropolis: Settlement Transition in Asia*. Honolulu: University of Hawaii Press.

McGee, T. (1994) The future of urbanization in development countries: the case of Indonesia. *Third World Review*, **16**, pp. iii–xiii.

McGee, T.G. (1997) *Five Decades of Urbanization in Southeast Asia: A Personal Encounter*. Hong Kong: Hong Kong Institute of Asia-Pacific Studies.

McGee, T.G. and Robinson, I.M. (eds.) (1995) *The Mega-Urban Regions of Southeast Asia*. Vancouver: University of British Columbia Press.

McTaggert, W.D. and Stormont, D. (1975) Urbanization concepts in the restructuring of Indonesia. *Journal of Tropical Geography*, **41**, pp. 34–44.

Merrillees, S. (2002) *Batavia in Nineteenth Century Photographs*. Richmond, Surrey: Curzon Press.

Milone, P.D. (1966) *Urban Areas in Indonesia: Administrative and Census*. Concepts, Research Report no. 10. Berkeley: Institute of International Studies, University of California.

Murphey, R. (1957) New capitals of Asia. *Economic Development and Cultural Change*, **5**(3), pp. 216–243.

Nas, P.J.M. (ed.) (1986) *The Indonesian City: Studies in Urban Development and Planning*. Dordrecht: Foris Publications.

Nas, P.J.M. (1990) The origin and development of the urban municipality in Indonesia. *Sojourn*, **5**, pp. 86–112.

Nas, P.J.M. (ed.) (1993) *Urban Symbolism*. Leiden: Brill.

Nas, P.J.M. (ed.) (1995) *Issues in Urban Development: Case Studies from Indonesia*. Leiden: Leiden University.

Nas, P.J.M. (ed.) (2002) *The Indonesian Town Revisited*. Singapore: Institute of Southeast Asian Studies.

Nas, P.J.M. (ed.) (2005) *Directors of Urban Change in Asia*. London: Routledge.

Nas, P.J.M., Boon, L., Hladka, I., Sudarmoko, K., and Tampubolen, N.C.A. (2005) The kampong. Unpublished article in possession of author.

Nas, P.J.M. and Malo, M. (2000) View from the top: accounts of mayors and governors of Jakarta, in Grijns, K. and Nas, P.J.M. (eds.) *Jakarta-Batavia: Socio-Cultural Essays*. Leiden: KITLV Press, pp. 229–244.

Nas, P.J. M. and Pratiwo (2003) The streets of Jakarta: fear, trust and amnesia in urban development, in Nas, P.J.M., Persoon, G.A. and Jaffe, R. (eds.) *Framing Indonesian Realities: Essay in Symbolic Anthropology in Honour of Reimar Schefold*. Leiden: KITLV Press, pp. 275–294.

Needham, B. (1988) Housing, town planning and land: the Dutch trinity, in Hallet, G. (ed.) *Land and Housing in Europe and North America*. London: Croom Helm.

New towns and satellite cities: problems and prospects. (1995) *Indonesia Property Report*, **1**(Third Quarter), pp. 10–16.

Nicoletta, J. (2005) The New York World's Fair of 1964–65: Globalization and Postcolonial. Paper presented at the 11th Biennial Conference of the Society of American City and Regional Planning History, Coral Gables, FL.

Niessen, N. (1995) Indonesian municipalities under Japanese rules, in Nas, P.J.M. (ed.) *Issues in Urban Development: Case Studies from Indonesia*. Leiden: Leiden University, pp. 115–131.

Nitisastro, W. (1970) *Population Trends in Indonesia*. Ithaca, NY: Cornell University Press.

Noormohamed, S. (1980) Housing the poor in Jakarta, in Garnaut, R.G. and McCawley, P.T. (eds.) *Indonesia: Dualism, Growth and Poverty*. Canberra: Research School of Pacific Studies, Australia National University, pp. 501–514.

O'Connor, R.A. (1995) Indigenous Urbanism: Class and Society in Southeast Asia. *Journal of Southeast Asian Studies*, **26**(1), pp. 30–45.

Osborne, M. (2002) *Exploring Southeast Asia: A Traveler's History of the Region*. Crows Nest, NSW: Allen and Unwin.

Papanek, G.F. (1975) The poor of Jakarta. *Economic Development and Cultural Change*, **24**(1), pp. 1–28.

Patton, C.V. and Subanu, L.P. (1988) Meeting shelter needs in Indonesia, in Patton, C.V. (ed.) *Spontaneous Shelter: International Perspectives and Prospects*. Philadelphia: Temple University Press, pp. 168–190.

Payne, G. (ed.) (1984) *Low-Income Housing in the Developing World: The Role of Sites and Services and Settlement Upgrading*. New York: Wiley.

PDKIJ (Pemerintah Daerah Khussus Ibukota Jakarta) (1977) *Karya Jaya, Kenang-Kenangan Lima Kepala Daerah Jakarta, 1945–1966*. Jakarta.

Peresthus, A. (2005) Jakarta's exurbia kampongs. *Urban Perspectives*, No. 1, www.etsav.upc.es/urbpersp, pp. 49–58.

Planning Group (1963) *Pulo Mas: Project for a Low-Cost Housing District for the Djakarta Municipality Prepared Under the United Nations Technical Assistance Programme By a Group of Indonesian and Danish Architects, Planners and Civil Engineers As a Model Project for the Growing Towns of Indonesia and Other Countries: Development Plan*. Copenhagen: Royal Danish Academy of Fine Arts, October.

Polano, S. (ed.) (1988) *Hendrik Petrus Berlage: Complete Works*. New York: Rizzoli.

Political will vital in preservation of city museums (1995) *Jakarta Post*, 17 June.

Polle, V.F.L. and Hofstee, P. (1986) Urban kampung improvement and the use of aerial photography for data collection, in Nas, P.J.M. (ed.) *The Indonesian City: Studies in Urban Development and Planning*. Dordrecht: Foris Publications, pp. 116–135.

Rachman, E. (1996) *Jakarta: 50 Tahun Dalam Pemgembangan dan Penataan Kota 1995*. Jakarta: Jakarta Metropolitan Government.

Raffles, T.S. (1817) *The History of Java*, 1st ed. London.

Rakodi, C. (1997) *The Urban Challenge of Africa: Growth and Management of Large Cities*. Tokyo: United Nations University Press.

Reid, A. (1980) The structure of cities in Southeast Asia, fifteenth to seventeenth centuries. *Journal of Southeast Asian Studies*, **9**(2), pp. 235–250.

Reinink, A.W. (1970) American Influences on Late Nineteenth Century Architecture in the Netherlands. *Journal of the Society of Architectural Historians*, **29**, pp. 163–174.

ROI (Republic of Indonesia) (1956) *5-Year Development Plan of Indonesia, 1956–1960*. Djakarta: Biro Perantjang Negara.

ROI (Republic of Indonesia) (1962) *Indonesia 1962*. Jakarta: Department of Foreign Affairs.

ROI, DOI (Republic of Indonesia, Department of Information) (1989/90) *Indonesia 1990*. Jakarta: Indonesia Department of Information.

ROI, MFA (Republic of Indonesia, Ministry of Foreign Affairs) (1962) *Djakarta Guide*. Jakarta: Ministry of Foreign Affairs.

ROI, MPPW (Republic of Indonesia, Menteri Permukiman dan Prasarana Wilayah) (2003) *Beberapa Ungkapan: Sejarah Penataan Ruang Indonesia, 1948–2000*. Jakarta: Direktorat Jenderal Penataan Ruang.

ROI, MPWP (Republic of Indonesia, Ministry of Public Works and Power) (1953) *Pembangunan Kota Baru Kebajoran*. Jakarta: Ministry of Public Works and Power.

ROI, MPWP (Republic of Indonesia, Ministry of Public Works and Power, Directorate General of Housing, Building Planning and Urban Development (1973) *Jabotabek: A Planning Approach of Its Absorption Capacity for New Settlements Within the Jakarta Metropolitan Region in Cooperation with Netherlands Directorate for International Technical Assistance.* Jakarta: Directorate General of Housing, Building Planning and Urban Development, April.

ROI, MPWP (Republic of Indonesia, Ministry of Public Works and Power), Directorate General of Housing, Building, Planning and Urban Development (1980) *Jabotabek Metropolitan Development Plan: Proposed Guided Land Development Programme for Greater Jakarta.* Technical Report No. T/29. Jakarta: Cipta Karya, December.

Richardson, H.W. (1989) The big, bad city: megacity myth. *Third World Planning Review*, **11**(4), pp. 355–372.

Rijnaarts, P.J. (1978) Jakarta-Amsterdam Cooperation Program 1977. Project City Planning, Final Report, June 12–July 14. Typescript in Library, Royal Tropical Institute, Amsterdam.

Robison, R. and V. Hadiz, V. (1999) Surviving the meltdown: liberal reform and political oligarchy in Indonesia, in Robison, R. *et al.* (eds.) *Politics and Markets in the Wake of the Asian Crisis.* London: Routledge, pp. 171–191.

Rossem, V. van (1988) Berlage and the Culture of City Planning, in Plano, S. (ed.) *Hendrik Petrus Berlage: Complete Works.* New York: Rizzoli.

Rosser, C. (1983) The evolving role of a national agency for housing and urban development in Indonesia. *Habitat International*, **7**(5/6), pp. 137–149.

Rosser, A., Roesad, K. and Edwin, D. (2005) Indonesia: the politics of inclusion. *Journal of Contemporary Asia*, **35**(1), pp. 53–77.

Ruland, J. (ed.) (1996) *The Dynamics of Metropolitan Management in Southeast Asia.* Singapore: Institute of Southeast Asian Studies.

Rutz, W. (1987) *Cities and Towns in Indonesia: Their Development, Current Positions and Functions With Regard to Administration and Regional Economy.* Berlin: Gebruder Borntraeger.

Sari, Y.N. (1995) Independent body will manage waterfront city. *Jakarta Post*, 3 May.

Schagen, F. van (ed.) (1967) *Essays in Honour of Professor Jac. P. Thijsse.* The Hague: Mouton.

Schmautzer, E.J.M. (1977) *Dutch Colonial Policy and the Search for Identity in Indonesia, 1920–1931.* Leiden: Brill.

Schwartz, Adam (1999) *A Nation in Waiting: Indonesia's Search for Stability*, 2nd ed. Boulder, CO: Westview Press.

Sendut, H. (ed.) (1995) Urban Development in Southeast Asia. Bound typescript. University of Malaya, in the Institute of Southeast Asian Studies Library, National University of Singapore, Singapore.

Setiono, D. (1991) Bandar Kamayoran: New Town in Town: An Evaluation of the Effect of the Development of Bandar Kemayoran On the Urban Problems of Jakarta. MA thesis, Flinders University of South Australia.

Silas, J. (1984) The Kampung Improvement Programme of Indonesia: a comparative case study of Jakarta and Surabaya, in Payne, G.K. (ed.) *Low Income Housing in the Developing World.* New York: Wiley, pp. 69–84.

Silver, Christopher (1984) *Twentieth Century Richmond: Planning, Politics and Race.* Knoxville, TN: University of Tennessee Press.

Silver, C. (2000) *Urban Development Framework Program: Innovation in Capital Investment Planning and Progamming in Depok, Indonesia.* Report prepared the US Agency for International Development, Jakarta, Indonesia.

Silver, C., Azis, I.J., and Schroeder, L. (2001) Intergovernmental transfers and decentralization in Indonesia. Bulletin of Indonesian Economic Studies, **37**(3), pp. 345–362.

Silver, C. and Sofhani, T. F. (2006) Toward an Empowered Participatory: Evolving Participatory Planning In Indonesia's Development Policy. Paper presented at the 2nd World Congress of Schools of Planning, Mexico City, Mexico.

Singapore National Heritage Board (1998) *Singapore: Journey into Nationhood*. Singapore: Landmark Books.

Singelenberg, P. (1972) *H.P. Berlage: Idea and Style: The Quest for Modern Architecture*. Utrecht: Haentjens Dekker & Gurnbert.

Soegijoko, B.T.S. (1986) The *becaks* of Java. *Habitat International*, **10**(1/2), pp. 155–164.

Soegijoko, B.T.S. (1996) Jabotabek and globalization, in Lo, F. and Yeung, Y. (eds.) *Emerging World Cities in Pacific Asia*. Tokyo: United Nations University Press, pp. 377–414.

Soegijoko, B.T.S. (1999) National urban development strategy in Indonesia – case study: Jabotabek, in Brotchie, J., Newton, P., Hall, P. and Dickey, J. (eds.) *East West Perspectives on 21st Century Urban Development: Sustainable Eastern and Western Cities in the New Millennium*. Brookfield, VT: Ashgate, pp. 125–144.

Soesilo (1936) Socio-technical and town architectural studies on the regencies. LocaleTeknik 3 (May) translated from the original Dutch by B. M. K. Jakti (February 1963), typescript in Library Institute of Southeast Asian Studies, Singapore.

Sostroatmodjo, S. (1977) Mengabdi Dalam Keadaan Yang Sukar: Pengalaman Menjadi Kepala Pemerintahan di Jakarta pada Masa Perjuangan Mengembalikan Irian Barat dan Confrontasi, in *Karya Jaya: Kenang Kenangan Lim Kepala Daerah Jakarta, 1935–1966*. Jakarta: Permerintah Daerah Khussus Ibukota Jakarta.

Sternstein, L. (1984) The growth of the population of the world's pre-eminent 'primate city': Bangkok at its bicentenary. *Journal of Southeast Asian Studies*, **15**(1), pp. 43–68.

Steinberg, F. (1991) Urban infrastructure development in Indonesia. *Habitat International*, **15**(4), pp. 3–26.

Steinberg, F. (1992) People's participation and self-help in the Indonesian kampung, in Mathey, K. (ed.) *Beyond Self-Help Housing*. London: Mansell, pp. 353–376.

Stolte, W. (1995) From Jabotabek to Pantura, in Nas, P.J.M. (ed.) *Issues in Urban Development: Case Studies from Indonesia*. Leiden: Leiden University, pp. 228–245.

Sujarto, D. (1997) Toward the Metropolitan New Towns in Indonesia: The Case of Jakarta Metropolitan Area. Paper presented at the Association of Schools of Asia Conference, Bandung.

Sujarto, D. (2002) Towards the development of metropolitan new towns in Indonesia, in Nas, P.J.M. (ed.) *The Indonesian Town Revisited*. Singapore: Institute of Southeast Asian Studies.

Surjomihardjo, A. (1977) *The Growth of Jakarta*. Jakarta: Penerbit Djambatan.

Suselo, H., Taylor, J.L., and Wegelin, E.A. (eds.) (1995) *Indonesia's Urban Development Infrastructure Development Experience: Critical Lessons of Good Practice*. Tokyo: United Nations Center for Human Settlements.

Sutiyoso's Grand Dreams (2004) *Tempo*, 6–12 January, p. 22–24.

Tadie, J. (2002) The Hidden Territories of Jakarta, in Nas, P.J.M. (ed.) *The Indonesian Town Revisited*. Singapore: Institute of Southeast Asian Studies, pp. 402–423.

Taylor, J.L, and Williams, D.G. (eds.) (1982) *Urban Planning Practice in Developing Countries*. New York: Pergamon Press.

Taylor, J.L. (1982) Upgrading of low-income residential areas in Jakarta and Manila, in Taylor, J.L, and Williams, D.G. (eds.) *Urban Planning Practice in Developing Countries*. New York: Pergamon Press, pp. 239–258

Taylor, J.L. (1983) An Evaluation of Selected Impacts of Jakarta's Kampung Improvement Program. PhD dissertation, University of California, Los Angeles.

Tesch, J.W. (1948) *The Hygiene Study Ward Centre at Batavia: Planning and Preliminary Results, 1937–1941*. Leiden: University of Leiden.

Than, M. and Rajah, A. (1996) Urban management in Myanmar: Yangon, in Ruland, J. (ed.) *The Dynamics of Metropolitan Management in Southeast Asia*. Singapore: Institute of Southeast Asian Studies, pp. 225–252.

Thahir, A.R. (1982) *Low Income Settlement within the Jakarta Region*. Copenhagen: Royal Danish Academy of Art.

Thijsse, J.P. (1947) Stadsplannen voor Indonesia. *Tijdschrift voor Economische Geographie*, **38**(9), pp. 217–228.

Thijsse, J.P. (1950) Low cost housing in tropical areas: new materials and methods of construction, in *Housing and Town and Country Planning, Bulletin no. 3*. New York: United Nations, pp. 31–37.

Tillema, H.F. (1915–1922) *Kromoblanda: Over't vraagstuk van het wonen in Kromo's groote land*. The Hague: Wassenaar, 5 volumes.

Tjahjono, G. (1997) New town: urban future for expanded metropolis in Indonesia. *Journal of Southeast Asian Architecture*, **1**(November).

Toelichting (1938) *Toelichting Op de Stadsvormingsordonnantie stadagemeenten Java*. Batavia: Landsdrukkerij.

Tyner, J. (2003) Cities of Southeast Asia, in Brunn, S.D., Williams, J.F., and Zeigler, D.J. (eds.) *Cities of the World: World Regional Urban Development*. Lanham, MD: Rowman & Littlefield, pp. 372–411.

Usman, S. (2002) *Regional Autonomy in Indonesia: Field Experiences and Emerging Challenges*. Jakarta: SMERU Research Institute.

Van der Hoff, R. and Steinberg, F. (eds.) (1992) *Innovative Approaches to Urban Management: The Integrated Urban Infrastructure Development Programme in Indonesia*. Aldershot: Avebury.

Vos, J. (1887) *Batavia and Environs, 1885*. Batavia.

Walker, M. (1991) Decentralized planning for sustainable development: the case of Indonesia. *Review of Urban and Regional Development Studies*, **3**, pp. 94–102.

Watts, K. (1957) *Outline Plan Djakarta-Raya*. Djakarta: Djawatan Pekerdjaan Umum.

Watts, K. (1960) The planning of Greater Djakarta: a case study of regional planning. *Ekistics*, **10**, pp. 401–405.

Watts, K. (1961) A planning study of the metropolitan region of Djakarta (Division of Regional and City Planning, Bandung Institute of Technology, February), in Sendut, H. (ed.) (1995) *Urban Development in Southeast Asia*. Bound typescript in the Institute of Southeast Asian Studies Library, National University of Singapore, Singapore, pp. 750–793.

Watts, K. (1992) Urban planning and development 1948–1989: a personal memoir. *Habitat International*, **16**(2), pp. 13–35.

Watts, K., Danunagoro, R.S. and O'Brien, L. (1957) *Rentjana Pendahuluan/Outline Plan Djakarta Raya*. Djakarta: Kotapradja Djakarta Raya.

Wertheim, W.F. (1958) *The Indonesian Town: Studies in Urban Sociology*. The Hague and Bandung: W. van Hoeve.

Wertheim, W.F (1964) Urban characteristics in Indonesia, in Wertheim, W.F. (ed.) *East-West Parallels: Sociological Approaches to Modern Asia*. The Hague: W. van Hoeve, pp. 165–181.

White, R. and Whitney, J. (1989) Cities in the environment: an overview, in Stren, R., White, R. and Whitney, J. (eds.) *Sustainable Cities: Urbanization and the Environment in International Perspective*. Boulder, CO: Westview Press, pp. 8–51.

Wijanarka (2003) Tat Ruang Kota Di Kaliantan Tengah Dan Palangkaraya, in Indonesia, Republic of, Menteri Permukiman dan Prasarana Wilayah. *Berberapa Ungkapan Sejarah Penataan Ruang Indonesia, 1945–2000*. Jakarta: Direktorat Jenderal Penataan Ruang.

Winarso, H. and Kombiatan, B. (1997) Land-use Dynamics in Jabotabek Region: Issues Related to Land Use Changes and their Magnitude in the Development of a Mega Urban Region. Unpublished paper, Asian Planning Schools Association Papers, Yuan, L.L. (ed.), National University of Singapore.

Winarso, H. (1999) Private residential developers and the spatial structure of Jabotabek, in Chapman, G.P. *et al.* (eds.) *Urban Growth and Development in Asia.* Volume 1. *Making the Cities.* Aldershot: Ashgate.

Winarso, H. and Firman, T. (2002) Residential land development in Jabotabek, Indonesia: triggering economic crisis? *Habitat International*, **26**, pp. 487–506.

Wirosardjono, S. (1974) Conditions Leading to Rapid Urbanization in Jakarta and Its Policy Implications. Paper presented at a United Nations Conference, Nagoya, Japan, 28 October to 8 November.

Wood, M. (2005) *Official History in Modern Indonesia: New Order Perceptions and Counterviews.* Leiden: Brill.

World Bank (1969) *Kampung Improvement Programme Jakarta, Indonesia Ongoing Since 1960.* Washington: World Bank.

World Bank (1971) *Greater Djakarta, The Capital City of Indonesia.* Economic Staff Working Paper, No. 105, prepared by R.W. Oliver. Washington, DC: IBRD.

World Bank (1995) *Enhancing the Quality of Life in Urban Indonesia: The Legacy of Kampung Improvement Program.* Report No. 14747-IND. Washington, DC: World Bank.

World Bank (1997) *World Bank Development Report 1997.* Washington DC: The World Bank.

Yeung, Y. (1985) The housing problem in urbanizing Southeast Asia, in Krausse, G.H. (ed.) *Urban Society in Southeast Asia.* Volume 1. *Social and Economic Issues.* Hong Kong: Asian Research Service, pp. 43–66.

Zwier, J. (1950–51) Do Opzet van het Bestuur van de Satellietstad Kebayoran nabij Djakarta (1948–1950). *Indonesie*, No. 4, pp. 419–441.

Index

Note: Figures and Tables are indicated by
italic page numbers, notes by suffix 'n[ ]'

Abrams, Charles 129
Aceh (North Sumatra) 24, 40
adat law 45, 46, 52
administrative leadership 92–96
administrative units, Jakarta (5 'cities')
   93–94
'affordable' housing 106, 113, 147
   diminishing supply 148
agricultural land, conversion to urban use
   23, 120, 159
airports 4
   see also Halim Airport; Kemayoran Airport;
      Soekarno–Hatta International Airport
Ancol Amusement Complex (North Jakarta)
   116, 200
Aquifer Recharge Zone 120, 206
   developments threatening 160, 173
'architecture of fear' 10, 233
Art Center (*Gedung Kunstkring*, Menteng
   district) 58, 59, 234
Asian Games (1962) 5, 95

bajaj (three-wheeled vehicle) 11, *156*, 157,
   191
Bakrie, Aburizal 193, 195
Bambang Trihatmodjo (Suharto's son) 173,
   186, 194
Bandung (capital of West Java province) 4,
   19, 20
   population growth *91*
   proposed move of capital city to 84, 97
Bangkok (Thailand) 19, 20, 27, 30
   commercial and market areas 31
Banten (northwest Java) 24–25
Banten province 228
Banteng Square 90
Batavia (colonial name for Jakarta) 1, 2,
   36–80
   Berlage's (1923) redevelopment plan 73,
      74, 176

expansion southwards 41–45
local governance system 47–48
Municipal/Public Works Department
   48, *49*, 50
planning, early 20th C. 48–53
population 1, 25, 37, 82
   ethnic composition 25, 38
   growth 14, 27, 28
   racial identity in 45–46
bazaar economy, compared with firm-
   centred economy 30
becaks (three-wheeled pedicabs) 156, *181*
   arguments for and against 157
   banned from city 140–141, *181*, 191
   drivers 141, 157
Becht, C. (planner) 143
Bekasi
   built-up areas *165*
   as growth centre 15, 110, 113, 117, 154,
      159
bemo (three-wheeled vehicle) 157, 191
Bendungan Hilir housing development 204
Berlage, Henrik Petru 73, *74*, 80n[89], 176
Bimantara Group 186, 193
Bina Graha (President's operational office) 8
Bintaro Jaya 169
Blankenberg, J.K.L. 59
Blok M (market) area 11
Bogor
   agricultural land lost 23
   built-up areas *165*
   as growth centre 15, 110, 113, 154, 159
   Jonggol project 173
   population growth 159
Bogotá (Colombia, South America), busway
   system 216, 218
Borneo (*now* Kalimantan), proposed move
   of capital city to 97–99
Bugis fishing village, restoration of 180
built-up areas, growth in *165*
Bumi Serpong Damai (BSD) new town 159,
   168, 169–172, 200, 231
   compared with LK new town 172–173
   house prices 171

transport links 172
'bundled deconcentration' approach 119, 123, 154
Burgemeester Bischopsplein *50, 51*, 59
  see also Taman Suropati
buses
  numbers 135, 155, 157, 162
  trams replaced by 95, 155
'busway' scheme 163, 192, 216–217, 229

capital city district 4
capital city (of Indonesia)
  confirmation of Jakarta as 94
  proposed move(s) 84, 94, 97–99, 173
car ownership 158, 161
Cempaka Putih housing project 95, 115
Cengkerang housing development 105
central business district (CBD) 6, 7, 31, *237*
central government control
  in 1950s–1960s 93, 94, 95, 97, 100–101, 122
  consolidation in 1970s–1990s 219–220
Central Planning Bureau (CPB) 84
Chinese community 9–10, 32, 53–56
  attacks against 9, 10, 210, 222
  gated neighbourhoods 10, 233
  Karsten's views 69
  and racial classification system 45, 53
  see also Glodok area
Chinese Council 55
Cibinong, as growth centre 117
Cikarang new town 159
Cipanang Galur housing development 105
Cipete Cilandak housing development 105
Ciputra (architect/developer) 134, 152n[17], 169, 170, 193
Ciputra City 168, 199
Citra Lamtoro Gung Group 186, 193, 195
City Forum (under PDPP approach) 225
City Hall (*now* City Museum) 9, 73, *74*, 174–175, 176, 178, *178*
civil servants/bureaucrats 96, 202
CLEAN-Urban project 224
'closed city', attempt to declare Jakarta as 140, 198
coastal land reclamation (North Jakarta) 16, 149, 180–182, 199–200
colonial city
  types 26
  see also Batavia
colonial influences 2, 25–29
commercial areas, post-colonial cities 31, 32
commercial centre, expansion in 1990s 187–190
Community Infrastructure Program 143
concept plans

1952 plan 88, *89*
1957 (Watts) plan 88–90, 94–95, 106
  Karsten's ideas (1930s) 67
conservation projects 15, 174–184, 234–236
corruption (in 1990s)
  economic crisis affected by 221
  exposure of 213
cross-subsidy law ('1-3-6' law) 148–149, 168–169
currency crisis (1997–98) 209, 213, 220
  see also fiscal crisis

Daendels, Herman Willem (Governor General, Batavia, 1808–1811) 39, 41
Dana Alokosi Umum (DAU) local grant/fund 223, 225
  limitations 225–226
decentralization of decision-making
  and central government control 219–220
  in colonial period 14, 63, 66
  lack of resources to deal with at local level 238
  national laws (1999) 222–223
deconcentration approach 119, 121, 151, 154
democratization 226
  of planning process (1999/2000 onwards) 214, 222–223
Depok
  as growth centre 117, 119–120
  housing project 145
  participatory planning process piloted in 224–225
desakota ('city villages') 19
Design Development Group 170
Djakarta Raya (Great Jakarta) project 87, 88
dollar/rupiah exchange rates 152n[30]
Doxiadis Associates 170
Dutch colonial policies 38–41
  Agrarian Law (1870) 40, 54
  Agrarian Law (1960) 134
  Cultivation System (1830) 39, 40
  Decentralization Law (1903) 38–39, 47
  Ethical Policy (1901) 38–39, 46–47
  racial classification system 45–46, 53
Dutch colonial rule 2, 36–81
Dutch East India Company 2, 36

East Timor
  independence referendum 222
  military action in 215, 222
economic collapse/crisis (1997–98)
  effects on urban development 22, 148, 160, 220–221, 237
  recovery after 214, 226–227, 237
education level 40

environmental issues about new projects 160, 173, 208, 218, 224
ethnic conflict 9, 10, 210, 222
ethnic enclaves 9–10, 32
European enclave 44–45
'extended metropolitan region' 19–20, 20–21
    Jakarta as 20, 21

family planning programme 197–198
Fatahillah Square
    City Hall (*now* City Museum) 9, 73, *74*
    restoration projects 176, 178, *178*, 234, *235*
firm-centred economy, compared with
    bazaar economy 30
fiscal crisis (1997–98), effects 148, 160, 205,
    209, 213, 220–221
flood-control plans 112, 208, 228
forest fires (1997), smoke haze from 220
'fortified communities' 233

garden city model 58, 85, 88
gated communities/enclaves 10, 196, 233
Gedung Kunstkring (Art Center, Menteng
    district) 58, 59, 234
geographical situation of city 1
Ghijsels, Frans Johan 48, 49, *49*, 50, 59, 73, *75*
Giebels, Lambert 88, 97, 117, 118, 119, 154
Glodok area (Chinese district) 9, 10, 42, 54
    restoration of 176, 179, 236
'Golden Triangle' (commercial/financial
    area) 6, 164, 167, 189
    land prices 164
Golkar Party 209
Gondangdia housing development 50, 52
gotong royong (mutual cooperation) 142
growth centres 30
    in Jabotabek project 110, 119
'growth by polarization' 231
Guided Democracy programme (Sukarno
    government) 93

Habibie (President, 1998–99) 210, 222
Halim Airport 4
Hanoi (Vietnam) 19, 26
Harmonie Club (in Konigsplein/Merdeka
    Square) 42, 177
Heeren, H.J., population growth study 91, 92
Henk Ngantung (governor of Jakarta,
    1964–65) 96
Herbowo (planner) 106
'Heritage Park' project 180
high-rise housing 147, 150, 208, 228, 231
highway development programmes 5,
    12, 113, 116, 121, 123–124, 134, 154–155,
    157–163

Hilton Hotel 6, 187, 229
historic district, preservation and restoration
    of 174–184
Ho Chi Minh City (Vietnam) 19
Hotel Indonesia 93, 94, 98, 100, 114, *115*,
    188–189, *188*, *227*
Hotel Indonesia roundabout 188, *188*
    fountain(s) at *188*, 216
Hotomo Mandala ('Tommy') Putra
    (Suharto's son) 186
housing prices 146, 147, 171, 202–204
housing programmes 15, 33–34, 85–88, 93,
    105, 106–111, 143–151
    see also Kampung Improvement Program
    (KIP)
Husan, Bob (Suharto's business friend) 209

immigration control (into Jakarta) 198, 215
income
    poor people 147, 201
    World Bank forecast 186
indigenous urban elite 29
    residences 11, 60
Indisch style architecture 60, 86
infrastructure provision/renewal
    programmes 12–13, 52
Inpres Desa Tertinggal ('Very Poor Village
    Improvement') programme 12, 200–201
institutional changes 29–34
Integrated Urban Infrastructure
    Development Program 143
International Monetary Fund, effects of
    intervention 221

Jabotabek Metropolitan Development Plan
    121
Jabotabek project (Greater Jakarta area) 15,
    88, 117–121, 123
    built-up area percentages *165*
    population growth rates *232*
    transport links 158, 160
Jagorawi highway/toll road 121, 123, 157,
    158, 160
Jakarta Waterfront Implementation Board
    (JWIB) 181–182
Jalan Gatot Subroto (road) 164, 189, 190, 229
Jalan Rasuna Said (road) 164, 189, 190
Jalan Sudirman (road) 6, 164, *166*, 189, 190
    intersection with Jalan Thamrin 7, 188,
    188
    roof gardens 199
Jalan Thamrin (road) 7, 114, *114*, 134, *162*,
    190
    intersection with Jalan Sudirman 7, 188,
    188

Japan International Cooperation Agency
    solid waste disposal study 208
    transport study 191–192
Japanese occupation 78, 133
Jaya Karta (old name for Jakarta) 2, 25
Jonggol project 173, 200

Kajuh Naga new town 168
Kali Besar (river/canal), restoration of 175,
    176, 179, 235
Kamal Muara fishing village (North Jakarta)
    201
Kampung Improvement Program (KIP) 12,
    15, 118–119, 128, 129, 132, 136–139
    beneficiaries 140
    funding 136–137, 137, 150
    infrastructure improvements done 137, 150
    participation by residents 137, 142
    standardized development objectives 138
    summary of achievements and costs 137,
        137, 150
    winding down of 150, 201
kampung improvement programmes (1920s/
    1930s) 14, 52, 56, 64–65, 128, 132
kampung settlements 6, 37, 60–62, 118
    assessment of (1969) conditions 136
    displacement of
        for 'affordable' housing (1980s)
            145–148
        for commercial developments (1960s
            and 1980s/1990s) 93, 147, 150, 167,
            189, 200, 228, 230
        for European residential expansion
            (1920s) 61
    incorporated into urban areas 61,
        131–132
    jurisdiction in 52
    Karsten's (1930s) views 68
    locations 141
    Marcussen's study 61, 138, 139
    meaning of term 61, 130
    origin in pre-colonial times 131
    population densities 72, 137
    property rights for inhabitants 147, 150
    public health study 70–73
    relocation of inhabitants 231
    rural–urban continuum 131, 132
    studies 139
    and urban reform 62–65
kapitan cina (major Chinese officials) 53, 54
Kapuk Naga housing project 168, 200
Karsten, Thomas 48, 50, 56–57, 63, 65–69
    plan for Konigsplein 74–75, 76
Kebayoran Baru (South Jakarta) 11, 85–88,
    122, 126

Kebayoran Lama 87, 193
Kebun Kacang kampung 61–62, 132–134
    clearance (1950s) for Hotel Indonesia
        development 93
    demolition (1980s) for new housing
        145–147
    during Japanese occupation 133
    prosperity during 1960s 134
    rural origins 133
Kelapa Gading, 'fortified community' 233
Kemayoran airport 4
    international trade centre project 167,
        202, 236
    residential redevelopment 167–168, 197,
        236
Klender housing project (East Jakarta) 129,
    144–145
Konigsplein (now Lapangan Merdeka/
    'Freedom' Square) 42, 74–76, 88
    fair-buildings (Pasar Gambir) 77, 197
    Karsten's plan 74–75, 76
Kota ('city') district 9, 41, 135
    restoration projects 174–175, 179, 234–236
Kuala Lumpur (Malaysia) 19, 20
Kubatz, F.J. 51, 59

land development, 1970s–1990s 163–168
land planning and development 113, 123
land prices
    in central Jakarta 160, 164
    effect on low-cost housing 15, 22, 33, 147,
        165, 202
    effect on middle-class housing patterns
        205
land speculation 33
Lippo Cikarang new town 168, 231
Lippo Group 172, 193
Lippo Karwaci (LK) new town 168, 169,
    172–173, 231
    compared with BSD new town 172–173
local governance system
    in colonial city 47–48
    factors affecting lack 147–150
low-cost housing 106, 113, 202–204
    non-affordability for low-income
        residents 147, 202
Luar Benteg kampung 180

makeshift/temporary housing 5, 131, 136
    clearance of 5, 202
Manggarai transport project 193, 194
Manila (Philippines) 19, 20, 27, 30
maps 3, 37, 51, 87, 141
    1960/65 master plan 104, 112
    transport systems 158, 192

Marcussen, Lars, *kampung* study 61, 138, 139
market areas, post-colonial cities 31
mass transit systems 16, 112, 155–157, 190,
    191–196
    Governor Sutiyoso's proposals 161, 202,
        216–218
master planning, post-Independence 14–15
master plans
    1918 (Kubatz) plan 51, 59, 82
    1960/65 plan 15, 96, 103–105, 123
    1985 plan 121, 200, 205
    '2010 plan' 16, 200, 206–208
Medan (capital of North Sumatra province)
    20, 29
    population growth *91*
Meester Cornelis district (*now* Jatinagara)
    41–42, 51, 82
megacity
    advantages 20
    examples in Southeast Asia 19
    Jakarta as 19
    meaning of term 19, 20
    spatial configuration 20
Megakuningan mixed-use (commercial/
    residential/retail) development 229–231
Megawati Soekarnoputri (President, 2001–
    04) 161, 214
Menteng suburb 10–11, 44, 51, 56–60
    conservation of 176, 183, 234
Merdeka ('Freedom') Palace 8
Merdeka ('Freedom') Square 7–8, 8–9, *8*,
    76, 97
    restoration of 183
'metropole' concept 30
middle-class housing 203, 204
    colonial period 10–11, 44, 51, 56–60
middle-income neighbourhoods 11–12
minibuses/minivans 156, 157, 163
mission statements 238–239
Mohammed Husni Thamrin Project 128, 138
    see also Kampung Improvement Program
    (KIP)
monorail system 217–218, 229
Monument Ordinance (1931) 73, 176
Moochtar, Radinal 106, 109–110, 117
Mooijen, P.A.J. 57–58, 58–59
Municipal Council 47, 64, 77, 102

National Development Planning Board
    (*Bappenas*) 10, 220
    and Jabotabek project 123
    offices *50*, 59, 183
national housing agencies, Southeast Asia 33
National Housing Authority 144
National Land Agency permits 164, 174

National Monument (Monas) 7, *8*, 94, 183
National Mosque (in Merdeka Square) *8*,
    94, 183
    enclosure of (in 2001) 215–216
nationalism, growth of 76–78
neighbourhood security 12
Netherland Indies, colonial capital (Batavia)
    1, 36
'New Order' (Suharto) government 10, 128,
    129, 174, 187, 213
    decentralization pilot project 220
    demise of 214
new towns 85–88, 106–111, 159, 168–174
New York World's Fair (1964), Indonesian
    Pavilion 101–102
North Jakarta Area Revitalization and
    Waterfront Reclamation Project 180–181

Old Town Revitalization Plan (2006–2007)
    234–236, *235*
one-party state, Indonesia as (virtually) 186
    introduction of multi-party system 223,
        226
open spaces 42, 44, 51
    expansion plans 206, 207
    loss of 198–199
Outline Plan, 1957 (Watts) plan 88–90,
    94–95, 106, 120, 122

Pademangan *kampung* 138–139
    clearance and rebuilding 204
Palangkaraya (Borneo, *now* Kalimantan),
    proposed move of capital city to 97–99
Papanek, Gustav F., poverty study by
    140–142
parks 10, 197, 198
participatory planning (PDPP) process 224
    piloted (1999) in Depok new city 224–225
Parung Panjang housing complex 202
Pasar Gambir (fairgrounds in Konigsplein/
    Merdeka Square) *77*, 197
Pasar Ikan (Fish Market) 176, 179
Pasar Minggu housing development 87, 105
peripheral urbanization 4, 23–25
PERUMNAS 143, 144, 151
    housing projects 129, 144–145, 146, *149*
Phnom-Phen (Cambodia) 28
planning
    Batavia (colonial city) 48–53, 65–69
    change in focus 214
    decentralization/democratization of 219,
        223–226
    Karsten's role 65–69
    President Sukarno's interventions 94, 95,
        97, 100–101, 122

planning system, uncertain lines of
    authority in 13
Plaza Indonesia shopping centre 188
Pluit shopping mall (North Jakarta) 196–197
political revolution 16, 214
pollution problems 237
polycentric metropolitan restructuring
    21–22, 117–121, 182, 229
Pondok Indah 169
population
    Batavia (colonial Jakarta) 1, 25, 37
    Jakarta 1, 4, 18, 19, *91*, 92
    various megacities 19
population density 4, 23, 167
    in *kampungs* 72, 137
population growth
    Bekasi, Bogor and Tanggerang 159
    forecasts in master plans 121, 205
    Indonesia 198
    Jakarta 90, 91–92, 165–166, *167*, 197, 198,
        205
    various Indonesian cities *91*
Portman Associates 170, 171
poverty alleviation programmes 12, 142,
    200–201
poverty-level income 201
preservation projects 15, 174–184, 234–236
primate cities, meaning of term 18
prostitution 140
province status (of Jakarta) 102
PT Pembangunan Jaya (development
    company) 96, 114, 116, 134, 169, 193
PT Pembangunan Sarana Jaya 148, 177
PT Permuka (railway company) 95, 193
public health programme 70–73
public hearings, absence 173–174
public markets 31
public transport projects 121
Pulo Gading housing project 87, 109
Pulo Mas housing project 95, 105, 106–111,
    115
    changes to original design 109
    data sources for 106
    infrastructure 108

racial classification system 45–46, 53
Raffles, Sir Thomas Stamford 25–26, 37, 39,
    42, 45
railway system 121, 157, 191
Rangoon (Burma) 27, 29, 30, 34
    see also Yangon (Myanmar)
reconstruction, postwar 84–85
regional planning 116–121
rental housing 150–151
    cost per month 145, 168

residency permits 140
revitalization of old Jakarta 15, 174–184
Riady, James (head of Lippo Group) 172
rich–poor income gap, factors affecting 197,
    199
ring road system 5, 107, 121, 127, 157, 158,
    160, 189, 190–191
rioting (1998) 10, 210, 215
river clean-up programmes 179, 199, 206,
    207–208
road development programmes 5, 12, 113,
    116, 121, 123–124, 134, 154–155, 157–163
    and conservation planning 177
rural–urban migration 28–29, 91
    cultural effect 29
rural 'villages' within city 19, 32

Sadikin, Ali (governor, Jakarta, 1966–1977)
    15, 96, 109, 110–111, 127–129, 132, 134–136
    and 1960/65master plan 111–116
    kampung improvement programme 119,
        128, 129, 132, 137
    leadership style 129
    World Bank award 127–128
Saigon (Vietnam) 27, 30
    see also Ho Chi Minh City
Salim Group 169, 200
satellite cities 11, 85–88, 106, 110, 122, 145
self-sufficient satellite cities 169–172, 173,
    231–232
Semanggi road interchange 6, 7, 160, 187,
    229
    'massacre' 7, 187, 209–210
Semarang 50, 62
    population growth *91*
Senayan sports complex 95
    road to airport 5
Senen Triangle market area 30–31, *103*, 177
shopping centres/malls 188, 196–197
Sigit Hardjojudanto (Suharto's son) 186
Singapore 19, 20, 27, 30, 34
    Raffles's plan (1822) 25–26
Siti Hardijanti Rukmana ('Tutut' – Suharto's
    daughter) 161, 186, 192, 193, 209
Siti Hedijati Herijadi (Suharto's daughter)
    186
Siti Hutami Endang Adiningsih (Suharto's
    daughter) 186, 200
Sjamsuridjal (mayor of Jakarta, 1951-53) 93
slum clearance 33, 105, 149, 202
Soegijoko, B.T.S., on 1990s transport policy
    194–195
Soegoto, Duddy (PERUMNAS project
    manager) 146
Soekarno–Hatta International Aiport 4

road into city centre 2, 5, 227–228

Soemarno (governor of Jakarta, 1960–64, 1965–66) 95–96, 113

Soewirjo (mayor of Jakarta, 1945, 1950-51) 93

solid waste, collection and disposal plans 112, 208

Sorenson, Abel 101

Southeast Asia, urbanization in 13–14

spatial planning law (1992) 205

Special Territory status (of Jakarta) 4, 102

Stakeholders Forum (under PDPP approach) 225

Stasium Kota (main railway station) 73, *75*

Stock Exchange complex 119, 187, 229

strategic plan, 21st-century city 236–239

street vendors *238*

student protests (1998) 7, 187, 209–210

Study Ward project (Tanah Tinggi area) 70–73

'suburban cities' within Jakarta megacity 4

suburban new towns 168–174

suburbanization 15, 151

subway projects 161–162, 181, 191, 192–193, *192*, 194, 195

Sudarsono, R.M. 101

Sudiro (governor of Jakarta, 1953–60) 93–95

Sudwikatmono (Suharto's cousin) 170

Suharto, T.N.J. (President, 1966–1998)
   companies owned by family members 161, 186
   cronyism 200, 209
   elections 186, 209
   family 170, 186
   Jabotabek project instruction 120, 154
   military support for 187
   nepotism 209
   'New Order' government 10, 128, 129, 174, 187, 213
   resignation 7, 16, 187, 210
   rise to power 4–5

Sukarno, Ahmed (President, 1945–1966)
   Guided Democracy programme 93
   highway developments 5, 12, 154
   intervention in planning decisions 94, 95, 97, 100–101, 122
   proposal to relocate capital city 97–99
   removal from office 10
   vision for national capital 87, 88, 96–103, 111
   see also Soekarno

Sunda Kelapa (Jakarta's traditional harbour) 2, *3*, 25
   restoration of 176, 179, 182

Suparno Wiryosoebroto (Speaker of City Council) 198

Surabaya (capital of East Java province) 19, 20, 24, 41
   population growth 27, 28, 39, *91*

Surjadi Soedirdja (governor of Jakarta, 1992–97) 194, 198, 200

Susilo (planner) 67, 85

Sutiyoso (governor of Jakarta, 1997–2007) 16, 149, 161, 196, 201–202, 211, 214–220
   compared with Governor Sadikin 215, 216
   military background 215
   transport projects 161, 196, 202, 216–218

Taman Anggrek mixed-use (retail/ residential) development 196

Taman Suropati (Suropati Park) 10

Tanah Abang housing project 145, 146

Tanah Tinggi study 65, 70–73

Tanggerang
   built-up areas *165*
   as growth centre 15, 110, 113, 117, 154, 159
   new towns 169–173, 231
   population growth 159
   unemployment 232
   see also Bumi Serpong Damai; Cikarang; Lippo Karwaci; Tigoraksa

Tanjung Priok (Jakarta's deep-water harbour) 38, 43

taxi cabs 157, 163, 190

Thamrin, Mohammed Husni 76, 114, 128, 132

theme parks 172, 180

Thijsse, Jacques P. (planner) 67, 84, 85

'three-in-one' (three persons per vehicle) policy 190

three-tier mass transit system (project) 193, 194, 195–196

Tigaraksa new town 22, 159, 168

Tillema, Henry Freek 62–63

Tisnawinata, Kandar 106, 109

toll roads 5, 12, 15, 123, 157–158, *158*, 160, 190–191, 228, 229
   'freezing' and resumption of programme 160, 161

tourism 175

town planning, Karsten's views 67

tram system 12, 43
   replacement by buses 95, 155

transport problems/crisis 12, 112, 162, 190

transport schemes
   megacity 190–197
   see also busway...; ring roads; subway...; toll roads

tsunami disaster (2004) 226

unemployment 232, 237
urban decentralization model
   in 1960 master plan 104
   'bundled' deconcentration approach 119,
      121, 151, 154
urban development area programme
   (PDPP) 224–225
urban poverty study 140–142
urban 'sprawl', factors affecting 164, 232
urbanization
   Indonesia (forecast) 186
   Southeast Asia compared with other
      regions 18

van Gorkem, W.J, mortality rate study 70
van Romondt, V.R., Kebayoran Baru plan 85

Wahid, Abdurrahman (President, 1999–
   2001) 161, 176, 210, 222, 226
ward master system (in colonial period) 55
waste collection and disposal 112, 208
water supply systems 52, 86
'waterfront city' (North Jakarta) 16, 149,
   180–182, 199–200, 208
Waterlooplein (now Lapangan Banteng) 42
   see also Banteng Square
Watts, Kenneth A. (planner) 88, 89, 90, 105

Welcome Statue (at Hotel Indonesia
   roundabout) 114, 188, 188
Weltevreden (southern suburbs of colonial
   city) 41–45, 61
West Java province 4
Westin Hotel 189, 221, 221, 226
Wisma Nusantara office building 114, 115
Wiyogo Atmodarminto (governor of
   Jakarta, 1987–92) 177, 191
World Bank
   award to Governor Sadikin 127–128
   funding
      for Kampung Improvement Program
         136–137
      for solid waste disposal facility 208
   report (1997) on Indonesia 186
   Social Safety Net Adjustment loan 225
'world city' vision 13, 15–16, 187
World Trade Center (North Jakarta) 166, 231
World War II, effects 14

Yangon (Myanmar) 19
   see also Ragoon (Burma)
Yogjakarta 39, 97
Yudiono, Susilo Bambang (President, 2004
   onwards) 226